Sword & Salve

NEW MILLENNIUM BOOKS
IN INTERNATIONAL STUDIES

Series Editors

Deborah J. Gerner, University of Kansas

Eric Selbin, Southwestern University

NEW MILLENNIUM BOOKS issue out of the unique position of the global system at the beginning of a new millennium in which our understandings about war, peace, terrorism, identity, sovereignty, security, and sustainability—whether economic, environmental, or ethical—are likely to be challenged. In the new millennium of international relations, new theories, new actors, and new policies and processes are all bound to be engaged. Books in the series are of three types: compact core texts, supplementary texts, and readers.

Editorial Board

Titles in the Series

Military-Civilian Interactions, Second Edition
Thomas G. Weiss

Negotiating a Complex World, Second Edition
Brigid Starkey, Mark A. Boyer, and Jonathan Wilkenfeld

Global Politics as if People Mattered
Mary Ann Tétreault and Ronnie D. Lipschutz

International Law in the 21st Century
Christopher C. Joyner

Globalization and Belonging
Sheila Croucher

The Global New Deal
William F. Felice

The New Foreign Policy
Laura Neack

Global Backlash
Edited by Robin Broad

Sword & Salve
Peter J. Hoffman and Thomas G. Weiss

Forthcoming in the Series

Liberals and Criminals
H. Richard Friman

Law in International Politics
B. Welling Hall

The Information Revolution and World Politics
Elizabeth C. Hanson

The Peace Puzzle
George A. Lopez

Elusive Security
Laura Neack

Political Violence
Philip A. Schrodt

Sword & Salve

Confronting New Wars and Humanitarian Crises

Peter J. Hoffman and Thomas G. Weiss

ROWMAN & LITTLEFIELD PUBLISHERS, INC.
Lanham • Boulder • New York • Toronto • Oxford

ROWMAN & LITTLEFIELD PUBLISHERS, INC.

Published in the United States of America
by Rowman & Littlefield Publishers, Inc.
A wholly owned subsidiary of The Rowman & Littlefield Publishing Group, Inc.
4501 Forbes Boulevard, Suite 200, Lanham, Maryland 20706
www.rowmanlittlefield.com

P.O. Box 317, Oxford OX2 9RU, UK

British Library Cataloguing in Publication Information Available

Library of Congress Cataloging-in-Publication Data

Hoffman, Peter J.
 Sword & salve : confronting new wars and humanitarian crises /
Peter J. Hoffman and Thomas G. Weiss.
  p. cm. — (New millennium books in international studies)
 Includes bibliographical references and index.
 ISBN-13: 978-0-7425-3977-8 (cloth : alk. paper)
 ISBN-10: 0-7425-3977-6 (cloth : alk. paper)
 ISBN-13: 978-0-7425-3978-5 (pbk. : alk. paper)
 ISBN-10: 0-7425-3978-4 (pbk. : alk. paper)
 1. Humanitarianism—Political aspects. 2. War and society. I. Title: Sword and
salve. II. Weiss, Thomas George. III. Title. IV. Series.
 HV553.H66 2006
 363.34'988—dc22

                                                              2005024515

Printed in the United States of America

∞™ The paper used in this publication meets the minimum requirements of
American National Standard for Information Sciences—Permanence of Paper
for Printed Library Materials, ANSI/NISO Z39.48-1992.

Contents

Illustrations

FIGURES

TABLES

MAPS

PHOTOS

Abbreviations

ALNAP	Active Learning Network for Accountability and Performance in Humanitarian Action
CAP	Consolidated Appeals Process
CARE	Cooperative for Assistance and Relief Everywhere
CPA	Coalition Provisional Authority
DAC	Development Assistance Committee
DHA	Department of Humanitarian Affairs
DRC	Democratic Republic of the Congo
EO	Executive Outcomes
FAO	Food and Agriculture Organization of the United Nations
ICISS	International Commission on Intervention and State Sovereignty
ICRC	International Committee of the Red Cross
IDP	internally displaced person
IED	improvised explosive device
IFRC	International Federation of Red Cross and Red Crescent Societies
IGO	intergovernmental organization
IHL	international humanitarian law
IRC	International Rescue Committee
MSF	Médecins Sans Frontières (Doctors Without Borders)
NATO	North Atlantic Treaty Organization
NGO	nongovernmental organization
NSA	nonstate actor
OCHA	Office for the Coordination of Humanitarian Affairs (United Nations)
ODA	overseas development assistance
OECD	Organisation for Economic Co-operation and Development
PMC	private military company

POW	prisoner of war
PRT	provincial reconstruction team
RMA	revolution in military affairs
UN	United Nations
UNDP	UN Development Programme
UNDRO	UN Disaster Relief Organization
UNHCR	UN High Commissioner for Refugees
UNICEF	UN Children's Fund
UNRRA	UN Relief and Rehabilitation Agency
UNRWA	UN Relief and Works Agency (for Palestinian refugees)
USAID	U.S. Agency for International Development
WFP	World Food Programme (United Nations)
WMD	weapons of mass destruction

Foreword

An outsider eavesdropping on conversations taking place among those in the humanitarian sector might be surprised to hear such a distressed take that differs from popular perceptions. Surface appearances suggest that humanitarianism is very much alive and well: it is firmly entrenched on the global agenda. Actors in international politics are gradually accepting the legitimacy of humanitarian intervention. Many states now have humanitarian units within their foreign and defense ministries. Funding levels for humanitarianism tripled between 1990 and 2000. Nongovernmental organizations that once had limited capacities now have global reach and have become household names. Humanitarianism is no longer reserved for the provision of independent and impartial relief to victims of conflict. It now includes attempts to advance human rights, increase access to medicines, further development, promote democracy, and build responsible states. The devastating tsunami in late December 2004 provided a showcase for humanitarianism in action, with a record amount of funds flowing to agencies to help those across the Indian Ocean. Aid workers are glorified as modern-day heroes in documentaries and newscasts and are even portrayed in major motion pictures. Humanitarianism appears to be thriving.

Yet the conversation in the humanitarian sector hardly overflows with self-congratulatory, triumphalist rhetoric. There has been no humanitarian version of the staged landing on the USS *Abraham Lincoln* or the vitriolic claim of "mission accomplished"—indeed, just the opposite. Increasingly over the last decade those in the sector speak of "humanitarianism in crisis," because recent relief operations have led to a set of problems, dilemmas, and disappointments that have caused retrospective self-doubts and prospective fears about the future.

Peter J. Hoffman and Thomas G. Weiss's *Sword & Salve* is an indispensable contribution to the debate on the current circumstances and possible future of humanitarian action. That *Sword & Salve* succeeds is hardly surprising. After all, the authors have impeccable credentials. Since the early 1990s, Tom Weiss has been one of the unauthorized biographers of the humanitarian sector. Beginning with his contributions to the Humanitarianism and War Project and continuing through his many essays and books, Weiss has ranked among the shrewdest observers of the fast life and changing times of humanitarian action. Yet he has not been content to simply sit on the sidelines and chronicle the changes. Instead, he has consistently provided clearheaded analyses of the causes behind the changes, as well as sharp policy recommendations for meeting the challenges provoked by these changes. In *Sword & Salve* he once again delivers astute analysis and practical prescriptions, though this time with his latest collaborator, Peter Hoffman, who has worked on various research endeavors over the last five years, including the International Commission on Intervention and State Sovereignty and the Inter-University Consortium on Security and Humanitarian Action. Weiss and Hoffman make a formidable team.

The two authors offer a seemingly straightforward but essential observation—changing times call for new thinking. A stark prediction follows: if humanitarian organizations continue to operate in a business-as-usual manner, they risk failure. What has changed? Virtually everything, from the distribution of funding to the growing role of militaries and commercial firms in the delivery of relief to questions about the very legitimacy and effectiveness of humanitarian action. Although Hoffman and Weiss recognize the importance of these and other developments, they rightly concentrate on the impact of the "new wars." Although the "new wars" are not a post–Cold War invention, they have certainly thrived. In chapter 3, Hoffman and Weiss ably distinguish between the "old" and "new" wars, but two features are worth highlighting. One is that the new wars are populated by a motley assortment of militaries, paramilitaries, mercenaries, militias, bandits, and rogue elements—actors who have ugly motives and operate in informal and shadow networks. The other is that these actors frequently adopt various tactics, including forcible expulsion, mass killings, and deportations, which are intended to demoralize the population so that citizens submit or flee. The victims of war are now the actors' intended targets.

Humanitarian organizations are limited in what they can accomplish under these circumstances. Getting access to the populations in need frequently requires agencies to negotiate with the people who are directly responsible for the emergency. Not only do such negotiations put money, food, and medicine in the hands of the very combatants who have caused such misery, but these resources can fuel wars. Humanitarian organizations, frustrated at their inability to effectively channel relief to where it is needed and at their own feelings of helplessness in the face of such tragedy, frequently lobby external actors, including the United Nations and powerful states, to intervene and provide armed protection for aid workers and vulnerable populations. Sometimes states oblige. Yet this development creates its own complications for humanitarian organizations: to associate themselves too closely with militaries can compromise agencies' impartiality, independence, and neutrality. The new wars challenge humanitarian organizations from below and above, creating the wellspring for the new humanitarianisms.

Humanitarian organizations have reacted to the new wars but have not adapted. Ideally, they would identify their objectives, the constraints on their objectives, and the different strategies and tactics available and then select the most efficient response that gives them the highest chance of success. Aid agencies have generally ducked such strategic exercises, arguing that the heat of battle does not permit such reflection. In other words, agencies prefer to provide relief first and ask questions later. To be sure, the sector now routinely undertakes evaluation exercises that are designed to identify lessons learned and best practices; however, as Hoffman and Weiss convincingly argue, such exercises do not go far enough, because they do not recognize the necessity of undertaking an effective and meaningful strategic analysis.

At one level this demand is a technical one, expecting organizations to acquire the intellectual infrastructure and mental technologies to transform raw information into usable knowledge. Yet at another level, this demand involves a political move. Any reconsideration of the means, strategies, and goals involves a discussion about politics. We have heard before about the laws of war, but Hoffman and Weiss introduce us to the seeming "laws of humanitarian action." Humanitarian agencies are debating the core principles of humanitarianism, questioning whether laws that functioned for the old wars are equally functional for the new wars. For some aid agencies, providing aid directly to—or receiving assistance from—any combatants would represent unthinkable breaches of principles. But are there extenuating circumstances that might make such assistance permissible? A changing environment requires reconsideration of not only strategies but also the desired goals. Is relief enough, or should agencies be prepared to engage in reconstruction—that is, enter the world of politics?

Peter Hoffman and Tom Weiss insist that humanitarian organizations must recognize that they live in a political world. As their activities have political consequences, humanitarian organizations must weigh the impacts of their efforts as they reimagine best means for achieving their goals. Humanitarian organizations must be prepared to change with the changing times. Although not every reader will agree with Hoffman and Weiss's recommendations, their positions nonetheless evolve from an undeniable premise: humanitarian agencies must define their future for themselves before others define it for them.

Michael Barnett
September 2005

Preface

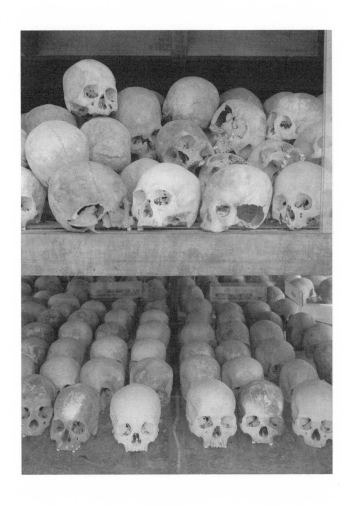

Confusion can inspire clarity. The painful glut of facts and figures chronicling the horrors of war is always emotionally overwhelming, but it can also be intellectually baffling. Disorienting, disturbing events shatter formulaic models and unnerve even the most steely-eyed observers. Certainly this became evident on the clear, blue-skied autumn morning of September 11, 2001.

At that time we were engaged in the final preparations for releasing the report of the International Commission on Intervention and State Sovereignty (ICISS) entitled *The Responsibility to Protect* and its accompanying research volume.[1] Our focus on intervention for the purposes of human protection was no surprise; consolidating norms for situations in which a state violates the rights of populations within its borders seemed a logical evolution in the international humanitarian system.

In retrospect, we were on the wrong page—politically and historically. Make no mistake: *The Responsibility to Protect* is a vital contribution, the cornerstone of an invaluable normative framework to save the innocent. As the most comprehensive statement to date on humanitarian intervention, it will undoubtedly frame future policy debates and actions. A host of largely positive academic reviews have already appeared.[2] Former *New York Times* columnist Anthony Lewis went so far as to describe the report as capturing "the international state of mind,"[3] and even one of the concept's harshest opponents, Mohammed Ayoob, admits its "considerable moral force."[4] As a result, Thomas G. Weiss wrote a second edition of the first book published for this Millennium Book series and retitled it *Military-Civilian Interactions: Humanitarian Crises and the Responsibility to Protect* (2005).

Nonetheless, we began to reflect on what we were witnessing. The churning violence of the persistent civil war in Afghanistan was taken to a new level by U.S. forces working with local warlords to end the Taliban's harsh political domination. Women and girls were liberated from the yoke of Islamic mullahs, and hopes arose that international attention would hasten aid to a country that had rarely experienced investment and development. Yet, strange and dangerous paradoxes were at hand: for a time, both cluster bombs and emergency relief rained from the sky in a color and a form that were indistinguishable.

As humanitarians worked in the confusion on the front lines in the so-called war on terrorism, Washington and London's misadventure in Iraq began in March 2003 without Security Council approval and was accompanied by a powerful chorus of international dissent. Almost as soon as President George W. Bush landed on the aircraft carrier USS *Abraham Lincoln* in May and declared "victory," Secretary of State Colin Powell began to describe the influence of humanitarians as "force multipliers" for U.S. interests. The presumption that humanitarians were intended as supplements to, if not entirely products of, U.S. forces interjected an unwelcome dose of politics.

We ruminated not just about what humanitarians should be doing with respect to Afghanistan and the wars on terrorism and Iraq but also about how we came to this "new" historical epoch: Did humanitarians see it coming? How do they understand changes in war? How have agencies reacted—and how should they react—to new challenges? And, ultimately, are there historical patterns in the relationship between war and humanitarianism?

In short, we returned both to our analytical drawing boards and to a longer historical perspective in examining, in the words of our friend Larry Minear, where the "humanitarian enterprise" has been and where it is currently going.[5] Fortunately, other projects permitted us to review cases of humanitarian action and contemporary armed conflicts. Time and again parallels and significant disconnects with the past percolated to the surface. In addition to the confidence and generosity extended to us as individuals by Foreign Affairs Canada (including Lloyd Axworthy, Jill St. Clair, Patrick Wittmann, Heidi Hulan, and Don Hubert) and as the Research Directorate for ICISS by the Ralph Bunche Institute for International Studies, we are grateful for the opportunity to have worked together on four other projects whose deliberations find their way in various forms in the present book.

Beginning in 2003, with funding from the Andrew W. Mellon Foundation, we began administering the Inter-University Consortium on Security and Humanitarian Action. This undertaking provides support to graduate students doing field research. As part of the process, we encountered new and refreshing work from the next generation, which emanated from research in such places as the Congo, Croatia, Chechnya, Turkey, Israel, Kosovo, Gaza, Sierra Leone, Afghanistan, and Iraq.[6] This project also permitted Peter J. Hoffman to undertake some of the research necessary for this volume. We are grateful to Carolyn Makinson, a program officer at Mellon at the time and now the executive director of the Women's Commission on Refugee Women and Children, for having had the vision to devote foundation resources to this arena.

Over almost two years (2001–2003) we benefited from the opportunity provided by the Stanley Foundation to discuss with some fifty practitioners and analysts the challenges faced in contemporary complex emergencies. We are grateful to David Shorr for the confidence extended to us to act as chair and rapporteur for the group UN on the Ground.[7] One of the most insightful of our colleagues in that adventure was the late Arthur Helton, who was killed in the tragic attack on UN headquarters in Baghdad in August 2003, a week after one of our sessions. Arthur's last book, as well as his life, decried "the price of indifference."[8] Our book is an effort to extend his commitment "to help us to avoid paying the high human, economic, political, and security costs" of knowing too little.

In the academic year 2004–2005, we had the pleasure to participate in a set of discussions entitled "The Transformation of Humanitarian Action," organized by the Social Science Research Council. Led by Michael Barnett and Craig Calhoun, these wide-ranging conversations honed our thinking and coincided with the drafting of this manuscript.

In the midst of these projects, we began an especially fruitful investigation for our chapter "Making Humanitarianism Work" for *Making States Work: State Failure and the Crisis of Governance*, edited by Simon Chesterman, Michael Ignatieff, and Ramesh Thakur.[9] We are grateful to the editors for their thoughtful comments and rigorous demands, which forced us to push our thinking and fully flesh out our argument for their volume, which is embroidered here in chapter 4. After we completed a first draft, we initially thought that we would do a short companion piece about the "real" nature of "new wars," which had been a brief background component of the chapter but ended up on the editing floor. But once we began assembling a coherent draft, it became clear that we needed more room to do justice to the complexities and connections of war and humanitarianism. Hence, this book appropriately finds its way into the New Millennium Books on International Studies series. Jennifer Knerr, at the time the senior editor at Rowman & Littlefield, was most encouraging and professional—just what authors need from a publisher (and we hope to do that shorter article soon!).

We wish to express our gratitude to five colleagues who agreed to be exploited and who read an earlier draft: Michael Barnett (University of Minnesota), David Forsythe (University of Nebraska), Edward Newman (UN University), Hugo Slim (Centre for Humanitarian Dialogue), and Roy Williams (Center for Humanitarian Cooperation). Zeynep Turan tidied up early drafts and helped select photos. Danielle Zach helped massage the drafts and check facts; her careful attention to details substantially improved the quality of the presentation. We are grateful to everyone, but responsibility for remaining errors of fact or interpretation is ours.

We apologize in advance for the use of social-science alphabet soup. The discourse of soldiers and humanitarians, like that of UN and nongovernmental organization (NGO) officials, is plagued by the use of abbreviations and acronyms, and the readability of our text would not have improved had we completely spelled out institutions.

In the years since the ashes of the World Trade Center have given way to a cornerstone for the Freedom Tower, the world has tread a tear-stained, blood-soaked road. It is the narcissism of our own time to forever proclaim beginnings and endings, magnifying the extreme and unique and dubbing that which is not readily familiar and digestible as "new."

From a historical perspective, politics, war, and humanitarianism do not always or conveniently conform to categories or easily divide into periods. We approached the daunting task of synthesis for this book not by presuming that we were going to split the proverbial atom but by discerning basic properties and analyzing interactive dynamics.

This short volume is an initial foray into understanding contemporary wars and humanitarianisms. The plural forms and aggregation of elements and processes into one analytic framework signify multiple interactions of multiple realities. We hope that we have taken a step toward building historical perspectives on current phenomena and processes, as well as framing ongoing and future challenges for agencies and academics. It is always presumptuous to make such a claim, and so we wish to make crystal clear at the outset that this book is our first but certainly not our final word.

Finally, we acknowledge that our efforts are informed by and respond to a tradition of social scientific scholarship dedicated to asking meaningful questions with important practical applications. Indeed the title *Sword & Salve* harkens back to classics such as Inis Claude Jr.'s seminal study of international organizations, *Swords into Plowshares*. Claude's poetic title— taken from Isaiah's invocation to soldiers to become farmers—succinctly conveys that the search for peace requires redressing the means of war and material sustenance.[10] With this book we take a somewhat similar tack: we examine and emphasize a relationship between two "tools." While we share Claude's concern with "swords" (war), we mostly set aside his "plowshares" (issues of collective security and economic development) to concentrate on "salves" (humanitarianism). Our subtitle further spells out our commitment to applying this approach to contemporary conditions and cases to derive policy-relevant analysis.

The history of war is replete with lessons written in blood, and these traumas have often embedded themselves into the psyche of humanitarians. When a jarring personal crisis has confronted them, innovations have followed. In the nineteenth century, Henri Dunant was inspired at the Battle of Solferino to form a standing agency specifically to attend to wounded soldiers. In the early twentieth century, pogroms and population displacements in Eastern Europe highlighted the plight of refugees and resulted in new mechanisms to provide relief and resettlement. Raphael Lemkin was so stunned at the extent to which minorities were being killed by Nazi Germany that he created a new term to characterize it, *genocide*. In the 1970s, the terror of mass executions was revisited in the "killing fields" of Cambodia, and the severity of this trauma led humanitarians to designate Vietnamese military action to overthrow the Khmer Rouge regime a "humanitarian intervention." Since the end of the Cold War, humanitarians have again struggled to grasp and cope with the nature of disasters—for example, "ethnic cleansing" in the Balkans. Once more, trauma was the harbinger of criticism and reflection as that typified by the pain felt by General Roméo Dallaire as the Rwandan genocide unfolded. The 2003 bombings of UN and Red Cross compounds in Baghdad and a spate of kidnapped and killed aid workers are recent shocks to the humanitarian consciousness.

Although our focus is on war-related humanitarianism, the challenges created by natural disasters often stimulate similar imperatives to make humanitarian action more effective. For instance, following its bungled responses to the destruction caused by back-to-back hurricanes along the Gulf Coast in August and September 2005, the U.S. Federal Emergency Management Agency faced severe criticisms of its poor performance. Subsequently, Congress held hearings to assess the agency and evaluate emergency response plans.

While humanitarianism has reacted, whether it has responded effectively is not always clear, as we are reminded today by the atrocities in Darfur or by the torching of aid offices in Afghanistan. From a historical point of view, our efforts to distill the lessons of war and humanitarianism are hardly unique. But the nature of our time inspires us to review the past to understand the present and glimpse the future. We take courage from the words of Ralph Waldo Emerson, who wrote at the beginning of the nineteenth century, "Each age, it is found, must write its own books; or rather, each generation for the next succeeding. The books of an older period will not fit this."[11] We hope that this book helps readers to understand the ways of war so that when future crises erupt, the health and the hope of humanitarianism remain vital.

Peter J. Hoffman and Thomas G. Weiss
New York, September 2005

Introduction

The history of armed conflict and its victim-strewn battlefields has usually been told as two distinct stories: one about the means and methods of war, the "sword," and the other about the succor and security supplied by humanitarians, the "salve." But as humanitarians instantly recall, the historical narratives and potent processes of both overlap and interweave. Starting with the onslaught of what are often dubbed the "new wars"—armed conflicts that seem incongruent with the largest wars of the twentieth century—international humanitarian mechanisms, those largely established since World War II, have misinterpreted elements of these violent conflicts and as a result have misdirected their relief and protection efforts. The least that one could say is that these elements represent "challenges" to humanitarians.

War and humanitarianism continue to influence each other, but many observers now question whether humanitarianism is keeping pace with changes in warfare. If the grisly images and stories of violence that dominate headlines and newscasts are any indication, the sword seems ascendant. By creating more victims and more dire circumstances in which emergency assistance is rendered, swords are shaping salves to a greater extent than seen in the past. Moreover, the constant struggle in shielding and sustaining war victims suggests that salves are not so much constraining swords as they are barely coping with the gory consequences.

Long before the United States launched attacks in Afghanistan and Iraq as part of the apparently never-ending war against terrorism, the accumulated human costs of recent wars were visible everywhere. By the turn of the twenty-first century, at least fifteen million were refugees and approximately twenty-five million to thirty million more were internally displaced persons (IDPs).[1] As if the spread and severity of humanitarian crises were not enough, these horrors were accompanied by a deep sense of angst among humanitarians—one that threatens the mantle, impact, and viability of the enterprise.

In the process of helping, aid agencies have earned a variety of criticisms—being judged insufficient, inefficient, ineffective, imperialistic, parasitic, politicized—but their altruistic bottom line remains that of saving lives. To fully appreciate the persistence of challenges and to gauge the veracity of current criticisms, we require a historical analysis of war and humanitarian action—defined as delivering lifesaving aid, providing physical protection from violence, and safeguarding the basic rights of noncombatants caught in armed conflicts. The distinctions between the military and legal aspects of protection are hard to sustain: physical safety is a necessary, if insufficient, part of protection; the supervision of basic rights guaranteed by international conventions is a necessary complement. The how and why of today's crises and challenges necessitate our understanding yesterday's interrelationship between the nature of war in the interstate system and the early foundations of the international humanitarian system. We then can apply insights to contemporary configurations in order to discern lessons for the aid agencies working in today's zones of armed conflict.

War and humanitarianism—in particular, the networks of actors that embody and propel their processes—are conventionally understood as discrete systems, suggesting that warriors and humanitarians have little or nothing in common. Although we do not claim to speak for either party, our careful look suggests that aid agencies can benefit from emulating the learning culture exhibited by the best armed forces. The lessons for agencies, we contend, are twofold. The first is to recognize how war and humanitarianism are interrelated and, thus, that changes in warfare have implications for humanitarian programming. The second is to emulate the success of the time-tested approach of militaries by analyzing and adapting their strategies and tactics to ever-changing environments.

The quip that generals always fight the last war can be a cheap shot from antimilitarists that hides a crucial reality. Although often accused of rigidity that stifles creativity, preeminent military forces prioritize allocating resources to enable optimal adaptation. Militaries have a structure and tradition that foster institutional memory to inform continued learning, adapting, and strengthening of capabilities. Knowledge and its application are never perfect, and wishful political thinking can color the harshest realities rosy in military analyses, as in other analyses—to wit, Custer's posture at Little Bighorn, British blunders exposed by Isandhlawana, France's faith in the Maginot Line, and U.S. policymakers' boasts that Iraq would be a "cakewalk." Nevertheless, military and defense establishments are justified in investing in analytic capacities: reflections on detailed analyses of the past are a necessary prerequisite, although not an absolute guarantee, of foresight and adaptation in the future.

An unsettling and diverse range of actors capable of wielding organized violence are now omnipresent in war zones—from motley assemblages of foot soldiers of back-alley thugs to highly trained, organized, and resourced graduates of top military academies such as Westpoint and Sandhurst—and all of them recognize the extent to which war has undergone a profound change. New elements, or those thought extinct, have come to the fore along with a host of traditional actors.

What about humanitarians? Reflection, with few exceptions, is not part of career development and may even be viewed as an occupational hazard. Long-standing skepticism about examining, instead of attacking, problems—and even fear of "paralysis by analysis"—is exacerbated by the need for priority setting and triage. Humanitarians are reluctant to engage in systematic contemplation, documentation, and promulgation of shared learning and challenges to conventional wisdom. They often view such endeavors as luxuries because scarce resources for research and analysis are directly deducted from funds to providing relief, logistics, facilities, and staff. Indeed, it is difficult to understand why humanitarians are so far behind other norm-based actors trying to do good.

Nevertheless as a result of wars beginning in the 1990s, much anxiety has arisen in humanitarian circles and in a veritable library of soul-searching publications.[2] The UN's Office for the Coordination of Humanitarian Affairs (OCHA) commissioned a special report entitled *The Humanitarian Decade*, whose subtitle in many ways summarizes the task of this volume—*Challenges for Humanitarian Assistance in the Last Decade and into the Future*.[3] Even the subtitles from two books commissioned by the two private agencies that have won Nobel Peace Prizes for their humanitarian work in war zones—the International Committee of the Red Cross (ICRC) and Médecins sans Frontières (MSF; Doctors Without Borders)—demonstrate a clear recognition of the new era: *Moral Dilemmas in Humanitarian Intervention* and *Violence, Politics, and Humanitarian Action*.[4] Yet, among the casualties of the "new wars" has been creative thinking.

The dominant chorus within agencies is to retain the traditional operating principles of independence, impartiality, and neutrality. Even such a strident critic as David Rieff has come full circle and recommends a return to the "good old days," when the standard operating procedures of all humanitarians were the minimalist principles of the ICRC and its offshoot MSF (also called the Doctors Without Borders movement). He now favors impartiality and neutrality and attacks by name Michael Ignatieff and other activists who preach "a revolution of moral concern" because they have not "actually kept a single jackboot out of a single human face."[5]

Didier J. Cherpiel, the secretary-general of the International Federation of Red Cross and Red Crescent Societies (IFRC), is quite aware that "there are no simple answers" in light of the complexity of today's war zones, "calling for sound humanitarian judgment."[6] Nonetheless, he and far too many humanitarians clutch to the familiar past in spite of systemwide efforts such as ALNAP—the Active Learning Network for Accountability and Performance in Humanitarian Action—and intense in-house looks such as Avenir at the ICRC.[7] Hoping that the guidelines of another time will suffice in the new era is radically different from what militaries do to enhance their means to overwhelm enemies. Rather than "muddling through," to use Ernst B. Haas's language,[8] humanitarians must develop "learning institutions" and mimic the approach by the armed forces who customarily devote substantial human and financial resources to examining lessons from past and ongoing operations.

The tasks of humanitarians have never been easy. Hugo Slim provides a bit of historical context by denying "that things used to be much better. Even a brief glance at humanitarian history shows this to be a rather eccentric view."[9] And nothing that we write here should be interpreted as suggesting otherwise.

Indeed, the massive human suffering and logistic challenges from recent natural disasters—as typified by the devastating December 2004 tsunami in the Indian Ocean or the August 2005 hurricane that laid New Orleans to waste—may open the door for malicious actors to pursue exploitative strategies and push aid agencies to the limits. But this book is about contemporary "man-made disasters": armed conflicts.[10] Here the challenges of suffering and logistics also confront lethal hazards born of armed belligerents—as Henri Dunant recognized when founding the ICRC in the nineteenth century or as the late Fred Cuny, who was executed in Chechnya in the mid-1990s, would attest.

Our underlying proposition is that as warfare changes, so too must the humanitarian enterprise. That a huge proportion of humanitarians wish to stick to their guns, figuratively speaking, and respect the operating principles that have guided their endeavors suggests a steep learning curve ahead. "When the data are uncertain, humanitarians are guided by hunches, inferences, past experience, and conceptions of past experience," David Kennedy observes. "A pragmatism of consequences runs into difficulty when expertise of this type substitutes for careful analysis of long- and short-term consequences."[11]

This book is about continuity and change in the art of war and humanitarianism. Our objective is to explore the terrain that humanitarians occupy and, more specifically, the challenges that they face in contemporary war zones. We present multiple perspectives on events, processes, and trends so that we may improve our understanding and examine the disparity between the respective methodologies and means for institutional learning as normally practiced by soldiers and humanitarians. This volume is not one of case studies but one of systems and structures, although we refer to concrete examples throughout in order to locate the position of humanitarian agencies and ground deductions. We have also structured into this argument the periodization of war and humanitarianism to identify aspects of continuity and change.

In chapter 1, "Concepts and Connections of War and Humanitarianism," we begin with an overview of the complex historical relationship that frames this book. We start with a brief discussion of key terms and then focus on broad outlines of theoretical connections. Our synopsis lays the conceptual groundwork for subsequent discussions and hints at the final analysis and major argument of the book. What constitutes change and what constitutes continuity loom large in this discussion and fore-shadow analytical struggles to accurately depict indications of both in subsequent chapters. This chapter is geared more to advanced social scientists; the less theoretically inclined can read it mainly for definitions and concepts and avoid getting bogged down in the abstract framework.

Chapter 2, "Foundations," examines the international humanitarian system in interstate warfare. States and wars between them precede the creation of a recognizable international humanitarian system by centuries, but the roots of a global order that made humanitarianism possible are part of the story of early state formation. After reviewing interstate war, this chapter examines the establishment and growth of the international humanitarian system, from its inception in the late nineteenth century through its reinforcement after World War II. Included are the signing of international agreements and the establishment of the United Nations, as well as efforts to respond to human needs during the early stages of the Cold War.

In chapter 3, "'New Wars,'" we dissect the dynamics of the "new wars" of the 1980s and especially those of the 1990s. Their origins are ostensibly buried in the decolonization and revolutionary struggles of the Cold War period, though their distinctive elements have become armed conflict mainstays over the past fifteen years. Although not everything about the "new wars" is new, recent wars have unusual elements that make them particularly dangerous and challenging for the inhabitants of afflicted areas, as well as for outsiders who come to the rescue. Among the elements we discuss are the fragmentation of authority, the growth of nonstate actors (NSAs), war economies, civilian victims, technological advances, and the media. We use scare quotes around "new wars" here to indicate our analytical perspective that, depending on the context and the eyes of the beholder, not everything that is dubbed "new" actually is. Moreover, the "s" is also critical to indicate the multiplicity of realities, even within a single armed conflict, because of the differences in violence, political interests, and economic activity that vary by region and over time.

In chapter 4, "'New Humanitarianisms,'" we scrutinize the multiple developments in the international humanitarian system along similar analytical dimensions to determine the extent and range of the nascent "new humanitarianisms"—a phrase coined by Mark Duffield to describe the species "claiming to correct the wrongs of the past."[12] We discuss normative and operational aspects to crystallize challenges—space and access creation, engagement dilemmas, economic dimensions, victim and aid-worker protection, military technology, and media attention. The humanitarian enterprise has been far more adept at addressing the challenges of traditional wars than those of contemporary wars. Just as armed conflicts vary from arena to arena and from era to era, the "s" on "new humanitarianisms" is designed to indicate the importance of multiple, often simultaneous, approaches to rescue. One size, whether one of weapon or humanitarian action, does not fit all armed conflicts.

In chapter 5, "Humanitarianism and Collective Action," we address the implications of numerous agencies with their own operational philosophies acting in shared theaters and drawing on a common pool of donors—a burgeoning atomization within a burgeoning international humanitarian marketplace. Agencies do not speak or act in unison. Segmented efforts exacerbate long-standing collective action problems within particular crises as well as between crises and undermine the overall coherence of the system. Chapter 5, along with chapter 4, explores both the changes in the system connected to "new wars" and the stresses emanating from within. New humanitarianisms mostly underpin, but sometimes overcome, endemic collective action problems.

Chapter 6, "Making Sense of Afghanistan and Iraq," extrapolates our analysis of the "new wars." We take the pulse of the humanitarian system in the wake of September 11, 2001, to identify elements of continuity and change in the two theaters that are the current obsessions of the United States and the UN, of soldiers and civilian humanitarians. The uncomfortable disconnects between traditional principles and the difficult challenges of the "new wars" are even more glaring in the humanitarian landscapes of Afghanistan and Iraq. Although the job description of social scientists is not supposed to contain forecasting, the contemporary configurations in Afghanistan and Iraq substantiate the existence of three noteworthy trends that were less apparent in other recent wars. First, politicization holds the prospect that agencies are used and viewed increasingly as political tools. Second, the greater and more frequent use of militarized forces by agencies and their partners breaks down the boundaries between warriors and humanitarians. Third, the mounting impact of neoliberalism has pushed both marketization (with aid agencies behaving as commercial ventures) and privatization (with humanitarian tasks being contracted to for-profit companies as well as not-for-profit aid agencies).

Chapter 7, "Humanitarian Strategic Thinking . . . and Doing," is our prescription and prognosis for some of what ails the humanitarian enterprise. The "new wars"—especially the "newest," in Afghanistan and Iraq—require critical reflection and strategic action in order to tune agencies to the frequencies of contemporary challenges and shrink the gap between intentions and outcomes. Despite a handful of recent efforts by aid agencies to assess the past and adapt, the requisite changes are fundamentally in orientation—that is, to think and act more strategically. It is critical that agencies dedicate resources to prevent or at least limit abuse. One strategic element involves humanitarian practitioners developing partnerships with scholars to help bring to bear the kind of specialized knowledge that exists in the academy but is in short supply in agencies.

Humanitarianism is often dismissed as being naïve, particularly when its results appear self-defeating or counterproductive. Our findings highlight the adage that the road to hell is often paved with the best of intentions, but we firmly contend that good intentions and good outcomes are not necessarily antithetical. Ignorance and ideology exacerbate shortcomings in current approaches to humanitarian action. While military academies and war colleges strive to make sense of the seeming nonsense of today's armed conflicts, humanitarians too often blindly grope through operations and cling to what worked in the past. We have written this volume to build bridges between the wisdom of warriors and the hearts of humanitarians because the current array of salves treats too few of the wounds from contemporary swords.

1

Concepts and Connections of War and Humanitarianism

War and humanitarianism may have distinct logics and values, but historically they are intimately linked. Swords trigger humanitarian crises and responses; violent conflicts cause casualties and displace people, which require salves. Humanitarian action—including documentation of, legal protections for, and material assistance to victims, from prisoners of war (POWs) to civilians—alters how wars are fought and affects their outcomes. It is impossible to draw exact, let alone measure, causal relations between war and humanitarianism, but each has clear consequences for the other.

An overview of concepts and connections between war and humanitarianism would be useful. This brief discussion foreshadows the overall argument of the volume: many shortcomings in the performance of aid agencies reflect dated structures and cultural impediments in the international humanitarian system as well as challenges resulting from changes in warfare. Strategic frameworks and capabilities, akin to modus operandi of militaries, are crucial to sustaining the humanitarian enterprise.

The argument here is that new thinking is, alas, in short supply but essential if we are to foster what David Kennedy aptly calls "a pragmatic renewal of humanitarian activism and policy making." Rather than examine the new landscape and adapt, the customary reaction is to become accustomed to the "dark side" of humanitarianism and look for scapegoats: "When things do go wrong, rather than facing the consequences of humanitarian work, we too often redouble our efforts and intensify our condemnation of whatever other forces we can find to hold responsible."[1] While humanitarian solutions by themselves cannot solve humanitarian problems—military and political forces often determine outcomes—it is essential to be cognizant of rehabilitative as well as debilitative impacts of humanitarian action.

THE LEXICON

Several terms are integral to our undertaking, and so we begin with a few definitions. *War* is the organized use of force to achieve essential objectives—usually political, often economic. The production of violence serves three purposes: to coerce (intimidate enemies), to control (conquer or manipulate; impose will on enemies), and to destroy (physical diminution of enemies). Frequently, war is the lever or product of change in the distribution of power.

When violent armed conflict erupts between two or more parties, there are two possible explanations: either a unit is attempting to reconfigure relations among units, or relations have already been reconfigured because of distribution of power between units.[2] Exemplifying change through war that results in a shift in the relative power of states is the case of Germany's mounting strength in the 1930s and how it foreshadowed a meaningful struggle over global order in World War II. By comparison, the Spanish-American War demonstrates that power may already have effectively shifted prior to the outbreak of war and that the armed conflict represents the outcome of earlier changes.

Military as an adjective pertains to the use of force. To perpetrate violence on a grand scale requires organization and an institution to be the focal point—the *military*. But as shown in later chapters, the military do not always exclusively control the production of violence. In other words, nonmilitary actors can become *militarized*. Both professional militaries and militarized actors stand in contrast to civilian actors, who have no direct connection to the production of violence. Those who make the organized use of force their profession have theoretical frameworks, *military science*. The application of principles in the context of armed conflicts renders *strategies* for militaries to fight war, to determine what military objectives win wars. Strategies diffuse down through the structure of organized militaries, who apply *tactics* to achieve strategic ends. Military leaders and analysts evaluate the success and failures at both tactical and strategic levels; command structures promulgate information, and *military academies* pass on this knowledge to officers.

Humanitarianism refers to improving the welfare of the human beings. Those who find this definition weak and circular are not alone. In fact, this nonideal wording dates back to 1986 in a case brought by Nicaragua against the United States, where the International Court of Justice failed to come up with a sharper definition. Rather than provide any more specificity, the judges basically referred to the ICRC's principles and work.[3] Although the term can be applied to various forms of assistance granted to people, our focus is on emergency aid to locally affected civilian populations in exceptional distress as the result of war, as opposed to natural disasters. War-related *humanitarian action* ranges from ensuring physical well-being to affording legal protection—that is, efforts to save lives by providing food and medical assistance to surviving victims and mitigating other suffering, such as by protecting human rights. The *international humanitarian system* is inspired by *humanitarian ethics* and is composed of an assortment of institutions—some legal (*international humanitarian law*) and some operational (*humanitarian agencies*). The *humanitarian enterprise* embodies both the values of humanitarianism and the institutions of the international system.

In turning to connections between war and humanitarianism, at the most rudimentary level normative and material dimensions meet. At the center of both war and humanitarianism is order, a configuration of ideas and power at the international, state, and intrastate levels. The interface is order, not in the form of a particular world organization or hegemonic political entity but as governance—how the totality of actors' capabilities and structural constraints determine action. Although there is no central authority behind global order, there are patterns that connect war and humanitarianism. For instance, as the next chapter explores, the way that war is fought—the who, how, and why of each armed conflict—denotes where power resides and how humanitarian action develops. The next two sections outline theoretical bonds between war and humanitarianism.

WAR'S IMPACT ON HUMANITARIANISM: TRIGGERING CRISES AND ELICITING RESPONSES

War's impact on humanitarianism occurs in two steps: violence triggers humanitarian crises, and victims stimulate humanitarians to respond. War has material consequences—fatalities, wounds, famine, disease, and displacement. For civilian victims in particular, war often generates a new set of immediate needs—medical attention, psychological treatment, food, and shelter—after traditional coping mechanisms have been overwhelmed. Furthermore, the nature and scope of violence are indicative of the type and breadth of challenges that humanitarians face—if war is rampant throughout a country, humanitarian needs will be greater than if violence is concentrated in a smaller area.

Although military forces and humanitarians may sometimes share goals in general terms of wanting to spare human lives, their respective priorities, means, and ends often vary dramatically. In armed conflict, the military views the application of tactical military force as being necessary to meet strategic goals, but humanitarians interpret the material and normative implications differently. To humanitarians, the message of war concerns the treatment and welfare of populations caught in the switches of violence: they concentrate on victims and are moved to relieve their suffering. In summary, one of war's material effects (victims) stimulates the humanitarian impulse, which may or may not result in humanitarian action, depending on the availability of economic resources, political will, and security.

HUMANITARIANISM'S INFLUENCE ON WAR: INSPIRING NORMS AND ALTERING OUTCOMES

Humanitarianism influences war on both normative and material levels. Humanitarian ethics dictate that the costs of war, measured in suffering, should be avoided or minimized. To that end, humanitarians have worked vigorously to stem the harm inflicted by armed violence by shaping ideas about war and its outcomes. Fundamental to this approach is the "just war" tradition, which covers justifications for going to war (*jus ad bellum*) and for conduct in it (*jus in bello*).[4] The most concrete manifestation of normative influences is international law—the legal demarcation of acceptable behavior. There are practical implications to this ideological point of departure. For example, with the world aghast at the use of chemical weapons during World War I, humanitarians developed and massaged international agreements to prohibit their use in subsequent armed conflicts.

In recognition of how powerfully humanitarian concerns have infused the norms of organized armed conflicts, the "laws of war" (*jus in bello*) are also referred to as "international humanitarian law" (IHL). While perhaps surprising to newcomers, the vocabulary explicitly acknowledges that warriors and humanitarians peer through different lenses at a common reality.

The positive impact of IHL is behind the widespread support for the 1949 Geneva Conventions and Additional Protocols of 1977.[5] What may be viewed as the law for human rights in armed conflict, both international and civil, has the support of states, as indicated by the number that has ratified them.[6] And the status of these treaties is such that they are so respected that even states that have not signed and ratified parts of them often willingly abide by them. This is not to imply that humanitarian principles and the letter of the law have not been routinely violated but rather to point out that an overwhelming number of important military and militarized actors have acknowledged if not respected the laws of war.

In addition to the humane values behind them, governments and their military establishments have an evident self-interest in backing IHL. While some belligerents have suggested that the exigencies of war and survival permit deviating from international humanitarian commitments, for the most part soldiers appreciate the legally defined status of "combatant" and its commensurate protections provided by the Geneva Conventions. For instance, the conventions improve the morale of soldiers, who fight harder knowing that they have access to medical care and decent treatment if captured and that their families will be notified in case of death. Although humanitarian norms do not uniformly inspire all those in uniform, a remarkable record of resonance exists within the ranks. A recent illustration of the tension between the military's recognition of the importance of IHL and the existence of more pressing considerations arose in the United States in early 2005. When President George W. Bush nominated Alberto Gonzales to be U.S. attorney general, several retired generals publicly opposed the move as being shortsighted because of his earlier memos as White House legal counsel that characterized IHL as "outmoded" and "quaint" in light of the war on terrorism.

At the same time, humanitarianism can materially alter the course of war by changing the behavior of soldiers. An obvious illustration is that the military at times carries out operations that have come to be conventionally recognized as the domain of humanitarians, such as the delivery of emergency assistance. In many cases after the course of a war has been determined but its bloody aftermath lingers, members of the armed forces have distributed relief supplies. Thus, one material outcome from humanitarian norms is to influence the use of military forces for humanitarian purposes.

Redirecting resources to populations in war-torn areas also has material consequences within the crisis zone. The provision of assistance and protection interjects resources into poverty-stricken contexts, changing the arrangements of power. During and after wars, aid is of paramount importance, and those with access to it are positioned to benefit in terms of addressing their own needs and being able to help others. In war, armed forces strip resources from their enemies either to coax them to surrender or to annihilate their ability to resist. However, humanitarian assistance brings resources to these same populations, thereby potentially altering the outcome intended by military forces. In a bizarre and what some might call perverse twist of logic, defeated parties can use aid resources to regroup and relaunch their struggle. Furthermore, the manipulation of aid—using it to curry political favor or for economic gain—may help solidify the status quo. Although saving lives in the course of and following war is humanitarianism at its finest, for military forces it can work against desired outcomes. To soldiers, the opposition's ability to attract help to heal its fighters is the functional equivalent of decreasing the former's power to inflict harm and is therefore a concern in achieving overall strategic goals. Thus, the influence of humanitarianism extends further into the military and political realms. In short, the arrival of the "Good Samaritan" may not be universally welcomed.

The possibility that humanitarianism can perpetuate armed conflict has provoked some pacifist and humanitarian quarters. Past scrutiny of the ICRC, the gold standard of humanitarianism, has centered on the possibility that "charity" makes war more likely and harder to halt. John Hutchinson, for one, points to the irony encapsulated by Evelyn Waugh in his 1961 novel *Unconditional Surrender* when a memorable brigadier quips, "There's nothing wrong with war, except the fighting." Hutchinson goes on to note that instead of contributing to conflict resolution as the founders had hoped, the ICRC "found itself acting principally as a service agency for the conscript armies of the belligerents."[7]

In later chapters we discuss more specifically how the infusion of humanitarian resources, mixed with political agendas and exploitative economics, may play a role in fueling conflict. As can be seen from the aforementioned thumbnail sketches of relationships between sword and salve, the central dynamic of the latter is usually propelled by conscience; however, the results can also be haphazard or even counterproductive and make the impact of the sword cut deeper. Table 1.1 sequentially models

**Table 1.1.   Connecting War and Humanitarianism:
The Dynamic in Five Stages**

Influence	*Implications*
1. *Jus ad bellum**	Belligerents weigh waging war*
2. War, violence, humanitarian crises	Victims
3. Victims	Humanitarian impulse*
4. Humanitarian impulse*	Humanitarian action by agencies International humanitarian law / *jus in bello**
5. Humanitarian action by agencies International humanitarian law / *jus in bello**	Save lives

NOTE: Asterisks (*) indicate normative dimensions; no asterisks denote material facets.

the dynamics that connect war and humanitarianism in the buildup to armed conflict and after violence has broken out. Asterisks indicate normative dimensions; no asterisks suggest material facets.

In the first stage, actors weigh norms guiding *jus ad bellum*. In the second stage, the decision to go to war has material consequences leading to violence and victims. At the third stage, the humanitarian impulse is aroused. In the fourth stage, the impulse propels *jus in bello* concerns by the military and action by humanitarian agencies. Last, in the fifth stage, assistance is furnished and lives are saved. But armed conflicts may recur, and what may seem as a final stage may actually prime the pump for future violence.

A final thought about dynamics comes from Michael Walzer, one of the world's most eminent philosophers on ethics and war. In light of the nation-building activities of the last decade, he notes that, in addition to *jus ad bellum* and *jus in bello*, "we have to add to those two an account of *jus post bellum* (justice after the war)."[8] There is thus on the horizon the possible expansion of the laws of war or IHL, not only to cover better the peculiar violence of civil wars, but also to expand to the practice of peacemaking, occupation, and political reconstruction. Again, the crucial reality is that war and humanitarian action are intimately intertwined.

CHANGE AND CONTINUITY IN WAR AND HUMANITARIANISM

As the goal of this book is to attempt to understand the current performance and future prospects of humanitarianism, the extent to which agencies and their actions are suited to today's wars is our primary focus. Patterns of change and continuity are important indicators of how the term "new" has been used with reference to war and humanitarianism, a point that is analyzed extensively in chapters 3 and 4. Before dissecting specific conflicts and terminology of the 1980s and 1990s, we find it is useful to situate the dynamics and debates of the "new wars" and "new humanitarianisms" with reference to broader notions of historical change.

Fundamentally, a strong strand of continuity exists between war and humanitarianism, as earlier discussions illustrate. Chapter 2 fleshes out historical bonds between the institutions and processes that circumscribe warfare and humanitarian action. In subsequent chapters, although we are on the lookout for change, the relationship between war and humanitarianism remains a constant, defining characteristic of our analytical approach. That is to say, we show where change has taken place at three levels: *elemental*, the respective nature of war and humanitarianism and how changes in their configurations are codetermined; *unit*, the practices and power of humanitarian agencies; and *systemic*, the network of humanitarian agencies and its relationship to external influences, which shape the authority and capacity of the enterprise.

Changes in war are probed as reference points for our main focus, material and normative changes in humanitarianism. Material changes considered here include the conditions under which agencies operate in the field (the scale and nature of humanitarian needs in war zones) and in agencies (which create and implement policy, including the size and diversity of agencies). Normative changes refer to how the traditional body of principles that constituted the core of humanitarian identity and practice has shifted for some actors in the international humanitarian system.

"Change" can be a problematic concept, but an analysis of the nature and evolution of war and of humanitarianism in different historical periods is crucial to understanding and determining the current ability of the system to deliver emergency assistance. Looking to identify momentous change through a crisis-by-crisis approach is misleading to the story that we are trying to tell. In fact, a large part of our tale is that of uneven change within the international humanitarian system with reference to substantial alterations in the nature of warfare. Thus, on our scorecard of change, we evaluate quantitative data to appreciate when an indicator ratchets up or surges—for example, refugee flows, budgets of agencies, or attacks against aid workers. However, we are also concerned with what the numbers say or suggest about that which cannot necessarily be quantified.

Kal Holsti has written *Taming the Sovereigns*, probing the concept of change and ways of measuring it. He points out that change is quite different for someone playing today's stock market and for those of us trying to understand it in international relations, where recent events are not of interest unless they have a demonstrable effect on how diplomatic, military, or humanitarian work is actually done. He notes, "This is the

Hegelian and Marxist problem: at what point does quantitative change lead to qualitative consequences?"[9] In other words, we can also characterize as "new" a tipping point where quantitative change is so substantial that it constitutes something qualitatively "new."

In the end, we do not expect to settle grand debates about change versus continuity. Our underlying proposition is that there is continuity in the interrelationship of war and humanitarianism, and at the same time change has occurred in both the nature of warfare and the material and normative dimensions of humanitarianism. To guide our efforts at measuring what has really changed in the international humanitarian system, we analyze different periods at three levels: *elements, units,* and *system.* By examining each we are better able to depict and gauge the drama and the subtleties in change and continuity in humanitarianism. Table 1.2 provides an overview and summarizes what each offers in terms of explanatory power. These categories organize information at each level of analysis of change. The relationship between these levels of analysis is modeled in figure 1.1. We further detail each level in the following section. This discussion is intended for social scientists interested in theory. Those who are eager to move to the empirical chapters without getting bogged down in the theoretical framework would still benefit from familiarizing themselves with the key terms in italics, which are subsequently unpacked.

Table 1.2. Lenses on Change: Categories and Explanatory Power of Levels of Analysis

	Levels of Analysis		
	Elements	*Agencies*	*Systemic*
Explanatory power	Predominant forms of period, "new," or seemingly novel phenomena	Behavior and tendencies of humanitarian agencies (especially dysfunction)	Processes and trends in the international humanitarian system
Types	War and humanitarianism • Locus • Agents • Economies • Targets and victims • Technologies • Media	Policy and operational environs • Transagency • Interagency • Intra-agency	Ideological, security, and economic • Expansion • Integration • Politicization • Bureaucratization • Professionalization • Marketization • Internationalization • Privatization • Militarization

Figure 1.1.   Model of Relations between Levels of Analysis

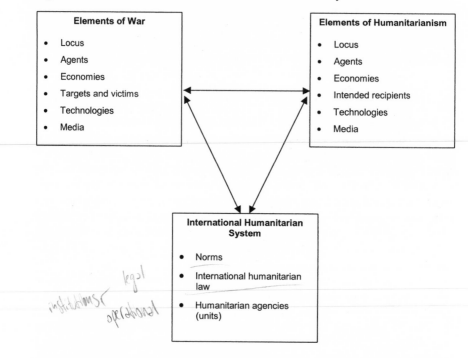

Elements of War and Humanitarianism

Elements refer to the predominant forms of war and humanitarianism. This approach parses armed conflicts and international humanitarian responses by looking at six aspects—locus (where action occurs), agents (who are actors), economies (role of economic power), targets and victims (who suffers or receives assistance), and media (role of media power). We indicate what is "new" or at least seemingly so and also explain why. This same structure is followed in chapter 2 (on the founding period), chapter 3 (on the "new wars"), chapter 4 (on the "new humanitarianisms"), and chapter 6 (on Afghanistan and Iraq).

Units of Humanitarianism

The units of analysis of most direct interest are individual agencies. Unit-level analysis considers the operational (in the field) and policymaking environments to understand three types of relations: that between humanitarian agencies and other sorts of actors (transagency), such as military forces or donors; that between humanitarian agencies (interagency); and that within an agency (intra-agency), such as between the field and headquarters. Furthermore, concentrating on individual agencies provides a look into the cultural and economic aspects of institutions, which may reveal any pathological or dysfunctional behaviors. Throughout the historical narrative (chapters 2, 3, 4, 6) we provide examples of agencies and their behavior, but a more thorough unit-level depiction is in chapter 7.

International Humanitarian System

Some may find a systemwide level of analysis too broad and abstract, but it is telling in identifying the most outstanding features of the enterprise as a whole. Here we are concerned with processes that affect most agencies. This analytic parsing allows us to draw connections among processes, relate them to issues of change versus continuity (their "newness"), examine how widespread trends are, and finally spotlight aspects that may imperil today's enterprise. Four major themes recur throughout this book, even if the extent to which each influences the system fluctuates in different historical periods. We note changes in the pervasiveness or intensity of each when and where pertinent.

Bureaucratization and *coordination* refer to the creation of organizational structures to administer assistance that alters the institutional dynamics of humanitarian action. Developing and improving procedures to make the delivery of humanitarian relief more effective and credible is an essential development in the history of the international humanitarian system. Agencies have become bureaucracies, and this dynamic influences the execution of humanitarian action. This development is not bad or dangerous, although, as we shall see, some humanitarians are uneasy with the move away from voluntarism and informality, which they see as strengths. In fact, a closer examination of this theme suggests many desirable outcomes. The most common improvement associated with bureaucratization is professionalization, or putting knowledgeable, capable staff in positions to effectively implement policies. In humanitarian circles, professionalization has established specialized technical skills and divisions of labor—from those who raise funds to logisticians and on-the-ground aid workers.

Bureaucratization also relates to the mechanics of how agencies work together or fail to work together. Rooted in collective action problems within the enterprise, this theme refers to the integration of humanitarian action into other international responses, such as postconflict peacebuilding and economic development. The maturation of the international humanitarian system has increased the number of moving parts, and bureaucratization has evolved from questions regarding the staffing and backgrounds of humanitarian personnel to the host of issues surrounding coordination within and among agencies as well to other international efforts to address armed conflicts. Accordingly, our analysis of bureaucratization moves beyond the understanding of humanitarianism

as a value-based philosophy to explore these organizations as institutions and management structures. Bureaucratization appears mainly in
the discussion of the founding of the system (chapter 2), the coordination
problems raised by the response of "new humanitarianisms" to "new
wars" (chapter 5), and especially in Afghanistan and Iraq (chapter 6).

Politicization is a second theme that considers the interests of agencies
and the political undertones of their actions. Politics is ubiquitous in
humanitarian action—in its implications if not intentions. Specifically,
we note that politicization operates at two levels: one referring to the
assumptions of the international humanitarian system, the other targeting the particular behavior of the units in specific crises. The politics or
power structures at the global level that are reflected in humanitarian
organizations denote systemic politicization. The system has largely
been designed to address interstate war, and as a result it conforms to
the interests of states. In many ways, applying the label of "neutral" to
humanitarians—deeming them nonbelligerents in wars—is an expression of the political interests of states.

A second strain of politicization is more overt and manifest in the
behavior of aid agencies. When the drivers (e.g., donors) of humanitarian
action are primarily political, we emphasize swells of politicization. Neutral and impartial practices of agencies are an attempt to avoid politics but
are in fact political statements in their own right. Although one level is
often emphasized without reference to the other, our analysis connects
them. For example, political constraints that preclude working with NSAs
suggest the orientation of the system but also signal how agencies are
likely to behave in providing relief in crises.

Militarization has long played a role in humanitarian affairs beyond
being the cause of crises, but the exact relation is often hazy. Three the-
matic offspring are evident. First, militarization as securitization entails
viewing humanitarian crises as potential security challenges. As such,
humanitarian disasters may be accompanied by large-scale population
displacements, which in turn may be viewed as posing yet other military,
political, or economic threats. Second, militarization also represents the
penetration of the military into humanitarian roles. The military was the
first institution to engage in what could be classified as humanitarian
action—the delivery of relief to those ravaged by war. The international
humanitarian system was developed as an entity distinct from armed
forces. Hence, the return of the military into the humanitarian sector—
which, within military circles, is often considered a form of "mission
creep"—by performing tasks conventionally associated with humanitarian agencies may marginalize aid agencies. Third, militarization also
involves the utilization of military resources by humanitarians. The community of aid agencies may see this scenario as being antithetical to its
values and as a form of "mission creep": to capitalize on the bundle of

logistical or security capabilities possessed by armed forces in achieving the goals of agencies is the inverse of military penetration. The use of force in these cases is subject to unfamiliar criteria for militaries; in fact, most instances of military utilization are predicated on rules of engagement that are based primarily on self-defense—protection of an area is a more likely posture than aggressive operations.

Although humanitarian action has some unusual aspects—for instance, values factor in heavily—it nonetheless resembles other commodities, which thus explains the fourth theme, *marketization* and *privatization*. That humanitarians are not motivated by profits does not mean that they are immune to market forces—in particular, to pursuing their agenda that excludes or overshadows other agencies. Marketization occurs especially when humanitarian action is reduced to a "deliverable."

Furthermore, the transformation of humanitarian action largely into a market product attracts other private service providers that seek profits. Humanitarian agencies' implementing policies or initiating action, both intergovernmental and private, may require subcontracting or utilizing the capacities of a host of other actors. Historically, humanitarian agencies draw their legitimacy from being value based and receive a form of international authorization for their efforts (sanctioned under IHL). However, with the development of logistical capacities in the private sector, aid agencies have come to use and in some cases rely on private contractors. The analysis of privatization investigates how subcontracting tasks to private actors—both not-for-profit and for-profit companies—has become integral to operations. As the phenomenon of for-profit contractors has come to play an especially key role in recent years, the bulk of our analysis of privatization trends is found in the treatment of Afghanistan and Iraq.

System-level analysis thus captures key themes that shape immediate and long-term prospects for saving lives, and it helps us to understand interactions among them and how they come together or diverge during particular historical periods. We historically situate the four themes—bureaucratization, politicization, militarization, marketization—at the end of chapters 2, 3, and 4. Chapter 5 then takes a detailed look at an especially important systemic thread of the past fifteen years—that of coordination. Chapter 6 focuses on the particularly traumatic situations in Afghanistan and Iraq and what they portend for the future. Chapter 7 draws on the themes to assess the current status of the enterprise.

PUTTING THE LENSES TOGETHER

Looking across the battlefield, we see so much: belligerents winning and losing, soldiers fighting and fleeing, and victims bleeding and dying.

However, what is clearly in focus in the foreground is often explained by the role and the spectacles worn by a viewer. Whether the varying ego-centric inclinations of human nature or institutional blinders are at fault, we tend to shape our understanding of the world by what we deem most important and valuable, and we downplay, dismiss, or even deride concerns that are not priorities.

Ultimately, we seek to appreciate how changes in the elements of war and humanitarianism have had an impact on the international system. The changes charted by this study of the elements of war and humanitarianism, aid agencies, and the international humanitarian system allow us to see not only patterns underscoring continuity in the dynamic between war and humanitarianism (mutually codetermining normative and material dimensions) but, more important, the nature of genuine contemporary challenges to humanitarianism. Many of the challenges of the last fifteen years are original—not only do they call out for a creative humanitarian response, but their nature threatens to alter and possibly erode the humanitarian enterprise. The establishment of the modern international humanitarian system from almost a century and a half ago has evolved from a handful of small, private, voluntary charitable organizations operating at the margins of interstate war to what Ian Smillie and Larry Minear characterize in truly capitalist terms: "Since the fall of the Berlin Wall and the winding down of the Cold War, humanitarianism has become a big business, now involving some $10 billion annually."[10]

We take a broad historical approach to understand this transformation. Where we see change in the international humanitarian system—in operational contexts (elements), in agencies (units), and in the enterprise writ large (system)—we identify it, trace its origins, and plot its implications. This analysis of the international humanitarian system seeks to tabulate the elements in each period, explain the behavior of aid agencies, and deduce systemic processes—all of which serve as focal points for apprehending change.

Therefore, our analysis is not predicated on one perspective—such as that of one agency or the examination of a single variable—but is composed of synthesized analyses at multiple levels. We consciously try to peer through both microscopes and telescopes in order to gauge the trajectories and impacts of systemwide variables. We put the lenses together to measure and evaluate today's trends and to interpret debates raging in humanitarian circles over change versus continuity. Is the enterprise in crisis? For those who cannot wait until chapter 7, the answer is yes.

There are significant differences between war and humanitarianism and, indeed, between warriors and humanitarians, but it is a mistake to segregate their study. Military science tries to understand the mêlée, and military strategists study how blood is shed in order to spare their fellow soldiers and, most of all, to win battles and campaigns in pursuit of objectives set by government authorities. Humanitarians too are preoccupied with bloodshed but in a specific way—traditionally asking only, what are the material needs of victims? Their concentration on the shedding of blood is praiseworthy and understandable, but it is insufficient. Good intentions are hardly a guarantee of success. What is necessary is a science of humanitarian action, which systematically analyzes and processes the challenges in humanitarian efforts and which considers the precise mechanics and relationships of violence as well as the impulse to help victims.

This point is not to suggest that such a pursuit could be entirely rational and scientific—any less than the fighting of war is an art—relying as much on instinct as on experience. However, humanitarian action does contain scientific features—many aspects can be measured, and many responses can be gauged as a result—that would support and strengthen the application of the humanitarian arts. David Kennedy concludes his powerful reassessment of international humanitarianism by stating that "renewal has meant setting aside dogmatism about humanitarian values and learning the governance vocabularies of political science, economics, or military science in order to enter the practical world of statesmen. The best modern humanitarian professionals combine fidelity to humanitarian ends with pragmatism about means."[11]

In short, knowledge that blood has been shed must be complemented with information on who shed it, why they shed it, and how they shed it. It is important to recognize the flow of influences and measure how action produces reactions. Even this initial sketch of relations between war and humanitarianism suggests the urgent need for aid agencies to be diligent in adapting to changing circumstances within particular operational theaters and across the international humanitarian landscape.

To better understand these connections and specifically their consequences for aid and protection personnel, one needs to examine the respective and joint histories of sword and salve. The next chapter begins this task by analyzing the foundations of the humanitarian phenomenon within the context of interstate armed conflict.

2

Foundations

A look at the foundations of interstate war and the international humanitarian system indicates parallel and interactive dynamics between their processes and institutions. This chapter begins by tracing the history of interstate war and then turns to the roots and establishment of the international humanitarian system. Understanding both provides the necessary moorings for our inquiry in the turbulent waters of today's wars and humanitarian responses.

THE RISE OF INTERSTATE WAR

The nature of war has fascinated strategists, tacticians, politicians, and scholars from time immemorial. Early attempts to apprehend war and its consequences span Western and Eastern traditions. Thucydides chronicled the struggle between Athens and Sparta in the Peloponnese, and his commentary develops a theory of war, specifically wedding it to political ends. In the Melian dialogues, he points to the dominant role of force in the relations of political protagonists and posits the prevalence of power politics—"the strong do as they have the power to do, the weak accept what they have to accept."[1] On the other side of the globe, Sun Tzu and his descendent Sun Pin focused on refining cardinal strategic concepts and tactical principles.[2] In *The Art of War*, Sun Tzu draws on the experience of warring kingdoms in China circa 500 BC to generalize about organizing forces as an institution and orchestrating them in battle. Sun Pin's *Military Methods* makes similar arguments, but his writings refer to wars contemporary to his era to bolster his ancestor's claims.

Our purpose, however, is not to review conceptions of war but to provide a frame of reference for the origins of the contemporary international humanitarian system. The spread of the Westphalian system of states and war from the seventeenth century is important background to the story of humanitarianism. Philosophers of this period emphasized war and its connections to states. Niccolo Machiavelli celebrated state authority and sketched ideas for improving armies.[3] Thomas Hobbes preached that war was part of the "state of nature" and that only through designating a powerful sovereign and establishing absolutist states could the individual be free.[4]

The first section of this chapter examines elements specific to interstate war, beginning with its early modern incarnation and continuing through contemporary manifestations. We depict the theoretical model of interstate war (agents, means, political economy, and targets) with historical illustrations. Our objective is to show how early humanitarian institutions corresponded to interstate realities and responded to the armed conflicts produced by them—a marked contrast to the logic of "failed states," "new wars," and the accompanying "crisis in humanitarianism" that is depicted in the following chapters and that has circumscribed much, if not all, future action.

War, States, and Order

War is often either a bellwether or linchpin of changes in international order. The aggregation of people into collective entities that wage war is about both the armed conflicts and the units in a system. Charles Tilly's observation that "states made war and war made states"[5] is apt. Political units are forged in the fires of violence. Armed conflict itself is decisive in the development of units' identities and capabilities. While states often compete and struggle, they are to a certain degree symbiotic: states seek to maintain a stable, state-based system because such a global order supports, if not strengthens, their power. At the same time, respect for the so-called sovereignty of other units is violated as frequently as respected, which is dependent on the relative strengths of the parties. Stephen Krasner has unmasked this fiction as "organized hypocrisy."[6]

The seeds of state formation and interstate war appeared in the late Middle Ages (roughly the thirteenth century) with incipient political entities in Britain and France initiating a process of centralizing authority, developing military capacities, and defining territorial borders. Scholars vary in their emphases regarding the start and duration of this period. Mary Kaldor specifies the uniqueness of the fifteenth through the eighteenth century.[7] On the other hand, Tilly suggests a gradual, uneven process with mounting pressures to form political authority into states.[8] Kal Holsti dates the achievement of an effective state monopoly over violence in Europe to the early eighteenth century, a major component of consolidating state rule.[9]

Whatever the exact timing, the emergence of the international system did not occur quickly or linearly. Before the rise of the state system, confusing, overlapping, and conflicting political authorities fielded a strange mix of irregular military forces with complex agendas.[10] For instance, in seventeenth-century Europe several types of political order existed simultaneously: numerous kingdoms and principalities vied with one another throughout what would become France and Germany; empires dominated in Spain and Austria, as well as much of Eastern Europe; financiers from the city-states of Venice exerted economic authority; the papacy in Rome wielded significant influence; and precursors to modern states such as Britain appeared.

Ultimately, states consolidated their rule domestically, and the state-based system became the defining element of global order. The wars fought from the seventeenth to the twentieth century emphasize the prominent role of states, and scholarship analyzing this period similarly reflects this notion:

- A prominent soldier-scholar of the early nineteenth century, Prussian officer Carl von Clausewitz disaggregated war into three components—people, who pay for war; the military, who fight the war; and the state, which determines interests in war. His model, "trinitarian warfare," shows the complexities of organizing and executing war and situates the central role of the state to war.[11]
- Robert Gilpin has used the term "hegemonic wars" to describe major armed conflicts that determine which state or states would govern the international system.[12]
- "Total war" was an appellation commonly associated with the increase in resources dedicated to fighting war. As states centralized more power and as wars became larger, this modifier became common to describe the monopoly of the state within its jurisdiction to harness resources and the extent to which violence was produced.

In short, much of the era of states implies a particular international political order and type of warfare. Once a state-based order was in place, wars were primarily fought by states, and challenges to order focused on state rivalries, not on trying to unravel the extant state-based order.

States at War

The structural imperatives of war hastened the construction of international order. While wars tend to be seen in terms of violence and victories, underneath are crucial economic aspects. Those who would field the means of destruction must first wield the means of production. Cicero (106–43 BC) called money and resources "the sinews of war,"[13] and Napoleon (1769–1821) is reputed to have said, in addressing the need for resources to fuel military capability, that "an army marches on its stomach."[14] Although he was likely emphasizing not just food but the wider amalgam of logistics, to take the case of nutritional requirements specifically, the availability of food has historically constituted the principal limit on the size of military forces.[15] Additionally, the ability to amass and concentrate economic power into equipping forces not only inflicted greater harm on the enemy but protected one's own soldiers, as signified by comparing casualty ratios of resource-rich forces and their poorer counterparts. Victor Davis Hanson, in his study of why Western militaries were almost always victorious over their non-Western opponents, argues further that economic power continues to be much more important than individual acts of bravery. As a predictive element of military outcomes in battle, "capital, not courage, would determine who lived and who died."[16]

Turning attention back to how this military reality corresponded to the development of polities, Michael Mann has argued that external military competition and its long-term financial burdens were a significant impetus in the emergence of states.[17] The costs associated with fighting wars facilitated the rise of centralized authorities, and states had many advantages in this area.[18] The technological, economic, and political impacts of the artillery revolution of the fourteenth to fifteenth century are prototypical of war's role in state formation. To accumulate sufficient capital to purchase the new cannons and field armies required vast economic resources, and the establishment of territorial administrations to support tax collection furnished the state with additional institutional needs and opportunities to exert authority.[19] An arms race in developing artillery facilitated state claims to direct resources for defense, thereby elevating the political power of the state with respect to rival domestic sources of authority. As states came to wield increasing authority and power, they instituted new methods for organizing military forces, which in turn tightened the state's political and economic grip on society.

A striking case of this transformation is France during its 116-year long conflict (1337–1453) with England in the poetically abbreviated title "Hundred Years War." While fighting, the French kings acquired influence as the importance of feudal nobility waned. Thus, in addition to a struggle with England over French incursions into Scotland as well as territorial claims in parts of southwestern France, the war was also a means for the French monarchy to assert authority. According to Aristide Zolberg, "the Hundred Years War helped free the monarchy from the limitations of previous fiscal and military systems through the abandonment of the seigniorial call to arms and the creation of a paid army, in which artillery was the deciding factor."[20] In effect, the politics and economics of war were conducive to the state in subduing local rivals, and state making became intimately tied to war making. Tilly brands this maintenance of internal order and external defense as a "protection racket."[21]

Other economic aspects of war are suggestive of the power of states. For the most part, economic power under the Westphalian system was harnessed to support the military and political objectives of states. Economic interests of society and elites were not unimportant, but they took a backseat to the overarching political interests of states. In terms of financing state military action, plunder often played a role, but the institutionalization of military actors decreased incentives to engage in the practice.[22] War as purely a vehicle for economically enriching those who could command force was eventually surpassed by the refocusing of economic power to serve state military and political power. Such agendas frequently merge in war, and it is usually impossible to determine which set of interests is paramount. But the scale on which states came to control economies and drive war suggests that throughout the era of interstate war, political power trumped economic interests.

An assortment of military arrangements characterized armed conflicts between and among these entities. There were economically oriented forces as well as ones based on political allegiances to royalty or nation and to religious affiliation. The formation of military actors whose services could be purchased on the market—literally, "free lances" or, more conventionally, "mercenaries"—was ubiquitous, as many political authorities sought ready capabilities when necessary but without the constant investment of maintaining standing forces.

Mercenaries are the oldest form of economically based organized military forces. Their characteristics included purely economic agendas (for treasure, not territory) and an unparalleled degree of professionalism and skill. In other words, the classic mercenary was not a club-wielding hoodlum: he was intensively trained and highly proficient; he represented a substantial capital investment and maintained calm to follow orders in the heat of combat. Perhaps the earliest and most insightful illustration is in *Anabasis*, by Xenophon (430–354 BC).[23] In it he describes "the March of the Ten Thousand," where at the Battle of Cunaxa in 401 BC Greek mercenaries found themselves outnumbered and far from home, as they had been hired by Cyrus the Younger to consolidate his rule of the Persian Empire from a challenge by his brother, Artaxerxes. Moreover, they were suddenly unemployed when Cyrus was killed. Historically, most military forces presented with such a scenario disintegrate. But these Greek mercenaries were professionals, and regardless of their motives their return campaign to Greek areas was an impressive feat of military organization.

Since then, the term *mercenaries* has been commonly used and far-reaching in its application wherever military actors fight for profit. However, upon closer examination, several types of forces are apparent, and the distinctions are important, particularly if we are to understand their actions and implications. Janice Thomson's work on the gradual monopolization of force by sovereign states beginning in the fourteenth century indicates that the key point of difference is in the relations of these organized forces to states and markets in decision making, allocation, and ownership; accordingly, she details eight varieties.[24]

For instance, piracy meets the standards of the broad definition of mercenarism, yet it is unique in that pirates operate without official sanction from political authorities. Privateers, however, were much the same as pirates but worked as a proxy for state naval powers and received official authorization for their actions. Two other significant varieties are more commonly recognized economic actors—military and mercantile companies. Military companies, such as the *condottieri* of Italian city-states, had organized by the fourteenth century and were exemplified by the White

Company of Sir John de Hawkwood. Although not appearing until the sixteenth century, mercantile companies such as the East India Company were even larger than earlier companies of military actors. These entities were perhaps the most organized "mercenaries" in terms of combining economic formality, military power, and eventually even political discretion with regards to states. Although initially created to facilitate conquest, commerce, and colonization at the behest of states, some grew powerful and contested control from their home state. For our purposes— seeing historical antecedents in the production of violence and the nature of different configurations of polities—it is enough to appreciate that mercenaries were common, played militarily significant roles, and often had politically legitimate standing.

In short, political order in the fifteenth through the eighteenth century had a profound lack of clarity or hierarchy, what John Ruggie has called "heteronomy."[25] This reality changed as states became the focal point of order as well as developed and fielded national militaries. And as Thomson notes, the process of disarming NSAs and state monopolization of violence is part of the transition from heteronomy to sovereignty.[26]

The Westphalian order emerged slowly and later, but already in the fifteenth century the state increasingly dominated war making and eventually monopolized violence; in the process, war changed dramatically.[27] The gradual shift from imperial authority, mixed military forces, and religious-based conflict to states can been seen in the signing of treaties. Early agreements between states, such as the Peace of Augsburg (1555) and the Treaty of Cateau-Cambresis (1559), accelerated the construction of order. The former agreement affirmed *cuius regio, eius religio*, "whose the region is, his religion"—that is, the right of princes to decide between Catholic or Protestant religious affiliation for local populations. Not long thereafter, in 1576, Jean Bodin first articulated the concept of sovereignty, or the right of state leaders to rule their populations.[28] However, despite the popularity of such a powerful idea, its practice has been uneven. From a historical point of view, Krasner has correctly noted that the four aspects of sovereignty—domestic, interdependence, international legal, and Westphalian—have been violated repeatedly.[29]

Conflicts between Catholics and Protestants in Western and Central Europe persisted in the sixteenth to the seventeenth century. In the Thirty Years War (1618–1648) religious strife in the context of the slow breakdown of the Holy Roman Empire featured state military forces— for example, Sweden (under Gustavus Adolphus) and Denmark—and mercenaries (German general Albrecht Wallenstein at the bidding of Hapsburgs and those under Flemish count Tilly). The Peace of Westphalia in 1648, comprising the Treaty of Münster (between the Catholic king of France and the Holy Roman Empire) and the Treaty of Osnabrück (between the Protestant monarch of Sweden and the Holy

Roman Empire), ended the conflict and cemented the principle of sovereignty. It recognized the juridical authority of German states, the
Netherlands, and Switzerland to sign treaties and establish their own
political representation.

These political changes underpinned military transformations and the
shift to state-based authority. They also initiated the spread of national
militaries as the predominant form of combat.[30] Although, there are certainly some instances in the eighteenth century that contained heterogenous elements of the earlier period and the more homogenous ones that
defined the interstate system of the nineteenth century. For example, the
American Revolution showcases a mixture of forces and an overlap
between international, civil, and even local conflicts. Nevertheless the
interstate model of war was becoming ascendant: the French Revolution
and its aftermath, as well as the Napoleonic Wars, signaled the strength of
national states in military affairs, displacing previously decentralized
arrangements. At this point, the use of mercenaries began to decline considerably; many political authorities viewed contracted military forces as
being potentially dangerous because their services could be purchased by
the highest bidder and were thus unreliable. Moreover, the growing scale
of violent conflicts questioned whether mercenaries were suited to such
vast military engagements; large national armies were perceived as being
better motivated and cheaper.[31] The political economy of the revolutionary and Napoleonic Wars was harsh on civilians. They suffered greatly
during these conflicts because the limited logistical capacities of armies
meant that military supplies were obtained by looting and taxing local
populations.[32] This scenario likely led to increased support for states and
citizen-based militaries that would be better organized and would not
resort to such economically destructive behavior.

Deborah Avant has examined different explanations for the rise of citizen armies over the course of the late eighteenth and nineteenth centuries
and finds that this outcome was not a foregone conclusion.[33] It was not
only material factors that solidified this change but also ideas. Avant's
analysis is important for two reasons. First, she posits that this model of
war, which was pursued and then thrived, served as the basis for conflicts
whose suffering the international humanitarian system would later be
designed to mitigate. Second, and more important, she demonstrates a
process and logic by polities in organizing force. Given the stakes of the
successful use of military power, those who would command force tested
beliefs, interpreted results, and diffused knowledge. Thus, among the crucial foundations are the substance of change (to state-based citizen
armies) and the dynamic of change (the role of ideas in digesting material
reality and critical junctures).

By the time that Carl von Clausewitz's *On War* was published in 1832,
medieval variations of warfare had virtually vanished in Europe and had

been almost entirely supplanted by a state-based system of organized violence. His logic reflected a continued growth of centralized bureaucracies and interstate rivalries. Clausewitz is known for his dictum "War is a mere continuation of policy with other means."[34] Often "politics" is substituted for "policy" in translations in order to emphasize the grand theoretical proposition behind what, to Clausewitz, was a simple description of his reality, the revolutionary and Napoleonic Wars.

He pinpoints the role of states as drivers of war and highlighted explicitly political motives: "war is an act of force to compel our enemy to do our will."[35] Moreover, he illuminates a distinction between soldiers and noncombatants: "Now, in the combat all the action is directed to the destruction of the enemy, or rather of his fighting powers, for this lies in the conception of combat. The destruction of the enemy's fighting power is, therefore, always the means to attain the object of the combat."[36] Clausewitz's "trinitarian warfare" outlines the contours of the Westphalian system.[37] He stipulates the locus (initiate along borders), agents (national militaries), and targets (official combatants) of war at the same time that he underlines the presumption of state-centric political motivations. In many ways he presages the elements of interstate wars—or as Gilpin terms them, "hegemonic wars"—such as the Franco-Prussian War (1870–1871), Russo-Turkish War (1877–1878), Spanish-American War (1898), Russo-Japanese War (1904–1905), World War I (1914–1918), and World War II (1939–1945).

A final element in this period, the media, also connoted how states channel power to make war. While the cliché asks whether the pen is mightier than the sword, the underlying implication is that powerful ideas and narratives can spur armed conflicts. Indeed the infamous comment by U.S. senator Hiram Warren Johnson (1860–1945) in 1917 that "the first casualty, when war comes, is truth" acknowledges that belligerents also wage war with ideas and that sympathetic narratives and depictions are seminal to war efforts. That is to say, media-influenced perceptions can influence state military capacity by priming the pump of civilian participation. In the context of U.S. actions in the Vietnam War (1965–1975), President Lyndon B. Johnson referred to the media campaign to stoke support for their South Vietnamese allies as a battle for "hearts and minds." On the other hand, media images can also sap states. Wars that are seen as being illegitimate or too costly can lessen popular support and weaken militaries from within.

For the most part during the interstate era, the media served state interests in gathering and maintaining support for war. Media empires of the nineteenth century found many opportunities to boost sales of newspapers by celebrating the spoils and raging against the injustices of war. For example, in 1897 as the Cuban population protested Spanish rule, stirrings of U.S. imperial ambitions manifested themselves. Although there is doubt whether media mogul William Randolph Hearst actually promised to "furnish the war,"[38] when a reporter suggested there was none, the mainstream U.S. media stoked popular support for the 1898 Spanish-American War with slogans such as "Remember the Maine." The development and spread of radio captivated even a wider range of populations hungry for news of wars.

While much more can be said of the relations between the media and interstate wars, what is important here is the media's impact in mustering capability and molding the perception of particular conflicts. The use of images can motivate or deter the political will required to enable military action. Before the industrialized era the shaping of popular perceptions, or even those of more marginal sectors, by state authorities was limited in scale and by technology. Media and its influence on politics grew as the reach of the state was increasing, and thus, one can sensibly conclude that during their infancy modern-media empires created and spread images that supported states. War is prime grist for the media mill—"if it bleeds, it leads" was an implicit theme long before an editor explicitly coined the adage—and states have always had an interest in manipulating media messages. Moreover, during the second half of the nineteenth century and the early part of the twentieth, the creation of inexpensive and widely consumed media—which often produced nationalist and xenophobic images—fomented war. The media is therefore a powerful tool in war. Later chapters examine how the arsenal of media affects the capabilities of armed forces, as well as what it says about those deploying media resources.

We have now outlined the foundations of interstate war. Specifically, this model posits armed conflict between two or more states engaged in territorial conquest by fielding forces subject to the strict command of official political authorities. Perhaps the peak and the most recognizable instance of this form of armed conflicts was the trench warfare of World War I with its relentless and intensive bloodshed. Often branded as "total war" because belligerents ignored restraints on the types of weapons permitted by international conventions, it was by no means total in its range of victims, with soldiers comprising close to 90 percent of combat-inflicted casualties.

However, dramatic cases in the late-nineteenth through the mid-twentieth century deviated from the ideal model of interstate war in at least one significant way: belligerents failed to respect civilians as neutral parties. These events include internal wars, such as the U.S. Civil War (1861–1865); the product of declining empires, such as the Anglo-Zulu Wars (1879) and various Ottoman Empire wars (Greek War of Independence, 1823; Crimean War, 1854–1856; Russo-Turkish War, 1877–1878; Italo-Turkish War, 1911–1912; Balkan War, 1912–1913); and even a combination of internal and international wars, such as the Bolshevik Revolution (1917–1923) and the Spanish Civil War (1936–1939). Overall, however, the major wars of this period dramatize the power of states to direct resources and monopolize force in the pursuit of military objectives against other states. At the same time, the colonial wars of world powers, Sherman's march on Atlanta, and even the ethnic cleansing of Armenians by Turks (1894 to 1896 and more prominently in 1915) bear the hallmark of central state direction and action. World War I, the strife of the interwar period, and World War II further cement the role of states as the principals of war. The dominant body of theory for international relations—both realism and liberal institutionalism in all varieties—is based on this reality.

THE BIRTH OF THE INTERNATIONAL HUMANITARIAN SYSTEM

Long before the formal international humanitarian system, which is usually traced to Henri Dunant and the Battle of Solferino, there was humanitarianism, both normative (an ethical framework that informed action) and material (transfers of resources to those victimized by war). Many ancient civilizations contained precursors to the system that emerged in the late nineteenth century—Greek, Roman, Persian, Chinese, Egyptian, Jewish, Christian, and Muslim. Several of these traditions contained elements of current humanitarian ethics—specifically, doctrine espousing protection of the weak and elements of "just war."[39]

The impulse to assist and protect the innocent and the vulnerable is as timeless as war itself. As Ephraim Isaac has noted, humanitarianism "is a universal phenomenon manifested globally and throughout the ages."[40] However, this impulse took its contemporary institutional form when assistance and protection needs emerging from the interstate system were wedded to the modern faith in a human capacity to manage problems. Furthermore, states and their militaries were eager to foster organizations that served their purposes in many ways. Governments supported relief to ease humanitarian conditions and postwar political tensions but did not usually want to be burdened in spending resources on such endeavors. Thus, private organizations were able to carve a niche for themselves. Before the birth of the international humanitarian system, large-scale systematic operations to improve the welfare of war victims were essentially the sole domain of the military. The unique role and resources of armed forces—experience in war and tending toward being the richest resourced organization within state bureaucracies—had traditionally positioned these organizations to perform humanitarian tasks.[41] Although the military are not humanitarians in the sense of prioritizing human welfare in war above all other interests, to a large extent the organization of armed forces laid the groundwork for organizations dedicated to exclusively focusing on humanitarian efforts. The military's preferred focus on producing violence and supporting separate organizations to provide relief for war victims was instrumental in creating humanitarian norms that led to laws and agencies.

The rise of interstate war and the birth of the international humanitarian system were not coincidental but mutually reinforcing. A good illustration is the treatment of prisoners, starting with the Thirty Years War. As war became more about political relations among states, captured soldiers were seen more as agents of an enemy state and less as personal enemies or booty for the victorious. We see not just an increasing monopolization of force but also the creation of the civic warrior identity, as opposed to a religious, tribal, or economic booty-driven identity. Martin van Creveld notes that prisoners under the interstate model did not become property as slaves but were tended to and exchanged for their own captured soldiers.[42] Thus, institutionalizing the interstate system brought with it a rationality that altered war and made a systematic application of humanitarian principles possible and desirable.

In the West, the values of the Enlightenment produced several legal philosophers whose works laid the foundations of the international humanitarian system. As the Thirty Years War raged, Dutch jurist and lawyer Hugo Grotius (1583–1645), the "father" of international law, formulated the basic tenets of this discipline.[43] But in the late eighteenth and nineteenth centuries, the normative groundwork was laid for the institutions that jelled into a system in the late nineteenth and twentieth centuries. For instance, the work of Emmerich de Vattel (1714–1767) connected principles of natural law to legal arrangements among states and, more important, specified that those not directly involved in armed belligerence be accorded neutral status.[44]

Organizing and institutionalizing norms of war sowed the seeds of humanitarianism. Holsti discusses the norms, rules, and etiquette of warfare that were prevalent in the eighteenth and nineteenth centuries and notes four types of distinctions drawn by states: that between civilians and combatants, that between neutral parties and combatants, that between government actors and designated military agents, and that between peace and war.[45] Notwithstanding that these distinctions were laid down in the context of rationalizing and legitimating war and its institutional proponents, their consequences were seminal to the idea of formal humanitarian organizations and contributed to the establishment of IHL. These taxonomies provide key building blocks for humanitarians by suggesting special needs and protection. The first two suggest that civilians and neutrals be legitimately considered outside the bounds of violent hostilities. The third supports improving the treatment of prisoners and increasing interstate prisoner exchange.

Aiding victims of earthquakes, hurricanes, floods, and fires was also related to the development of the international humanitarian system in times of war. Afflicted regions sought relief, and their political authorities consented to help from outsiders when needs were beyond state capacities. In fact, consent from governmental authorities controlling the territories where victims were located became part of the foundation for the international humanitarian system. After state experiences with humanitarian action in natural disasters, the logic of consent in responding to man-made ones is clear.

The birth of the modern humanitarian system for war victims is usually dated to 1863, with the creation of a new civilian institution and the establishment of international law governing the conduct of armed conflict. Both the operational and the normative dimensions were critically important to the system's emergence and international legal recognition. This first Geneva Convention specifically focused on protections for those sick and wounded in combat. Approaching the problem from the opposite perspective of the convention—the rights of noncombatants initially referring to military casualties but later to include civilians—are the duties and rights of belligerents. Rules for soldiers were codified at two meetings held in The Hague in 1899 and 1907. The resulting Hague Conventions are seen by some as pivotal redefinitions of order—the first truly global gatherings to regulate the decisions to go to war and "civilize" the conduct of war itself by the armies of states.[46]

However, these innovations must be kept in proper perspective; the development of IHL and aid agencies with international sanction and reach did not always have meaningful effects on war. As Adam Roberts has pointed out, many of the conventions were simply brushed aside in World War I. However, "the most difficult challenges" were "the terrible military slaughter caused by great armies engaged in machine-gun, shell, and trench warfare."[47] In short, following World War I, attention was focused on the horrific consequences for those who had served in combat—wounded, shell-shocked, and dead soldiers. Civilians had also suffered in large numbers, but with humanitarian action mostly premised on military battlefields, the international humanitarian system would only later recognize the beginnings of an era in which the state was unable to protect its citizens.

World War II—the next generation of war, which encompassed an ever-wider range of victims—was six times as lethal in terms of lives lost: fifty-five million died, of whom thirty million were civilians, including the six million in the Holocaust. After World War II, earlier commitments were refined and applied to those not directly involved in war, by the 1949 Geneva Conventions and in the 1977 Additional Protocols.[48] The remainder of this chapter follows the laying of these early institutional cornerstones and subsequent structural supports up until the 1980s, when the pressures of the "new wars" (chapter 3) and differences among humanitarians produced what we call the first stirrings of "new human-itarianisms" (chapter 4).

How do humanitarian institutions fit within the larger political-historical context? The first thing to recall is that all of today's primary assistance providers grew from wars—for example, the ICRC, from the Austro-French battle in 1859; Save the Children, from World War I; Oxfam, during World War II, and CARE (Cooperative for Assistance and Relief Everywhere) and the UN system afterward; World Vision, from the Korean War; and MSF, from the Nigerian Civil War. But we are getting ahead of the story. The important thing to note is that the agenda and actions of humanitarian institutions and the development of IHL did not conflict with the power of states—indeed, they served state interests.

Nineteenth-Century Genesis

The international humanitarian system's birth in the late nineteenth century is the product as well as the signifier of several important trends and social movements. As mentioned, states seeking to organize war were a major influence on the construction of the system. At the same time, individuals who embodied the humanitarian impulse created value-inspired organizations to respond to the crises of their times.

As always, material factors of the time allowed for the innovation of social organizations dedicated to war-related humanitarian action. On the side of the military, material improvements in supplying and paying soldiers decreased the needs and incentive to plunder.[49] For humanitarians, improvements in both agricultural and medical science and technologies facilitated their ability to produce and deliver relief. Thus, humanitarianism took root, along with other social movements upholding Enlightenment-era projects and capitalizing on the rising standard of living for the industrialized world—notably, peace movements and those of labor unions (focusing on workers' rights) and women's suffragette associations (working for political rights).

Around the world individuals of different nationalities gave voice to humanitarian concerns. During the Crimean War (1853–1856), Florence Nightingale, who had helped to establish nursing as a profession in England, traveled to Scutari (on the opposite side of the Bosphorus, from Constantinople) in the Ottoman Empire to provide medical assistance, establish hospitals, and upgrade the treatment of casualties. Clara Barton was a nurse in the U.S. Civil War (1861–1865) and tended to casualties from the battles of Antietam and Fredericksburg. In 1870 she delivered medical supplies in the midst of the Franco-Prussian War. Barton would also be instrumental in instituting humanitarian organization in the United States, founding the American Red Cross in 1881. Jean-Henri

Dunant, a Swiss businessman, would establish an aid society in 1863 that would become the International Committee of the Red Cross. Demonstrating the transnational appeal of the social movement, other contemporaries of Dunant were working toward establishing formal guidelines for making the wounded neutral parties and for ensuring humane treatment of POWs: Dr. Ferdinando Palasciano, an Italian physician; Henri Arrault, a French pharmacist; and Anatoli Demidov, a Russian philanthropist.[50]

Notwithstanding the stirring movements and congealing organizations, state-based military actors were also instituting humanitarian principles. The U.S. Civil War was at the cutting edge of war for its time—maximizing the application of industry and drawing on tactics from both interstate and less-conventional models. In the area of humanitarianism, the Union's 1863 published manual of instructions on codes of conduct, developed by Columbia University's Francis Lieber, became a model for European states.

But the real starting point for modern institutionalized aid agencies was that of the Red Cross. After the Battle of Solferino (June 24, 1859), Dunant witnessed firsthand the terrible fallout of six thousand killed and forty thousand wounded. He would later write of this formative experience in *A Memory of Solferino*. His genius was to conceive an international humanitarian movement that operated as private humanitarian organizations within each country, backed by an international treaty to govern assistance and protection of wounded soldiers. In the fall of 1863, Dunant and other Swiss citizens who were anguished at the horrors of war founded a subcommittee of the Geneva Social Welfare Agency: the International Committee for the Relief of Wounded Soldiers. The following August, fifteen states and other representatives gathered for the International Conference for the Neutralization of Army Medical Services in the Field, which produced the Convention for Bettering the Conditions of Wounded Soldiers. With the signing of what became known as the Geneva Convention, the Geneva-based aid organization formally took on duties—promoting knowledge of IHL, monitoring the compliance of belligerents, and deploying relief operations.

Furthermore, the 1864 Geneva Convention codified rights and protections for those not actively engaged in combat. The logic of the treaty is a snapshot of late-nineteenth-century norms: wounded soldiers were neutralized in both a military and a humanitarian sense; the injured were not militarily effective and were thus unimportant, considered protected from further violence, and entitled to succor. Medical personnel and civilians who offered aid to wounded soldiers were also deemed neutral. The line was drawn explicitly at military operations—if military forces were in control of the space or the action, it was not to be considered neutral and thus not subject to the Geneva Convention. Only later would the international humanitarian system expand to cover the treatment of POWs and the protections for civilians caught in war.

An early sense of cosmopolitanism rode the coattails of the Enlightenment and in the later half of the nineteenth century helped promulgate the notion of universal humanism—that all people were equal and worthy of respect. The system, as Michael Ignatieff has poetically iterated, is an attempt to institutionalize "an impalpable moral ideal: that the problems of other people, no matter how far away, are of concern to us all."[51] However, the tension between universalistic human rights and a particularist focus on exclusive and exclusionary communities (such as ethnicity or tribe) has been problematic from the outset.

Indeed, as the aftermath of the Battle of Solferino demonstrates, the politics of humanitarian action were a confusing and tough sell. On the one hand, Dunant saw mangled and starving soldiers. On the other hand, the belligerents (on one side, the French under Napoleon III and Sardinia; on the other, the Austrian Empire) viewed humanitarian relief to war-ravaged populations as potential assistance to those combatants whom they had just overrun and defeated. The perception among many victorious states was that aid of any kind to the defeated would be used to strengthen the opposition. This outcome also raised the possibility that a state could provide assistance as a tool of foreign policy rather than as one out of altruistic concerns. The negatives of allowing humanitarian action were overshadowed by the advantages of cooperation—a ledger of killed and captured was a useful administrative device for states and, as noted, offered comfort to soldiers facing the prospect of death, injury, or detainment. Furthermore, healthy prisoners of war could be exchanged between belligerents to replenish depleted stocks of soldiers. War thus became more "civilized."

The Franco-Prussian War (1870–1871) was the first major case of the international humanitarian system's operating and effectively consolidating a recognized norm.[52] In this armed conflict, the agency that would become the ICRC improved the welfare of many victims through the concerted efforts of national Red Cross societies and the backing of belligerents who had signed the Geneva Convention. While some violations of the convention occurred, immediate successes of the fledgling humanitarian system were evident: the German Red Cross provided for 400,000 POWs; the French society assisted 340,000 casualties; and, in all, fourteen societies contributed to the total effort. The performance of the Red Cross family of agencies during this war, in saving lives while not stepping outside the specified role of neutral aid providers, led to states' acceptance of humanitarians in war.[53]

In 1875 the Red Cross family, which at that point formed the entirety of the international humanitarian system, confronted an armed conflict that did not correspond to the logic and accepted behavior of European interstate warfare, when Christian communities were engaged in a civil war with Turkish populations in the Balkans. Although the status of Bosnia, Serbia, Montenegro, Bulgaria, and Romania would be determined at the Treaty of Berlin in 1878, at the time of hostilities in 1875 and 1876 there were no formal means for dispatching humanitarian assistance to victims of these wars. However, here the creativity of the Red Cross movement was demonstrated, and three innovations emanate from this war and humanitarian action.[54] First, aid was extended to victims of all conflicts, not just those victimized by clearly defined and explicitly deemed international wars with official combatants. Second, the Geneva-based organization that had orchestrated the work of different national societies, the International Committee for the Relief of Wounded Soldiers, incorporated the term "Red Cross" into its official title and became known as the ICRC. Third, the symbol of humanitarianism was broadened to respect Islamic values—the red crescent became an alternative to the red cross.

In addition to sowing the seeds of modern agencies, during this period the first cornerstones of IHL were laid. Earlier efforts had fallen flat. For example, the use of crossbows was briefly viewed by some Europeans as being un-Christian and was therefore deemed morally untenable. Although the Second Lateran Council banned the weapon in 1139, in perhaps a dark foreshadowing of future flexibility in such matters by the powerful, the church refined its ban and allowed its use against non-Christian opponents.[55] In the late nineteenth and early twentieth centuries, several international agreements restricted the ways and weapons of war. Curbs against exploding and expanding munitions, as well as noxious gases and other airborne contaminants, were instituted, but the most emphatic were the restrictions on land warfare.[56]

An unsuccessful effort at Brussels in 1874 to consider a draft on the laws of war drawn up by Russian czar Alexander II met more success later on and formed the basis for the 1899 and 1907 Hague Conventions. As a result, in 1904 American philanthropist Andrew Carnegie gave the unheard-of sum of $1.5 million to make the construction possible of the Peace Palace in The Hague, which became the location for the Permanent Court of Arbitration and then the Permanent Court of Justice under the League of Nations, which then became the International Court of Justice under the UN Charter. The other major international social movement of this era that coincides and blends with that of humanitarians is the peace movement. Several signs of international institution building from the late nineteenth and early twentieth centuries speak of the emphasis placed on peace—the establishment of the Nobel Peace Prize in 1907 and the Carnegie Endowment for International Peace in 1910. Furthermore, they also suggest the power of these social movements when paired with the interests of states to regulate warfare.

Early-Twentieth-Century Developments

In the period between World War I and World War II, the international humanitarian system expanded; norms nurtured during the late nineteenth century were embedded in the establishment of new institutions and legal documents. The scale of violence and victims of World War I, the Russian Revolution, and the breakup of the Austro-Hungarian and Ottoman empires created enormous refugee flows throughout Europe. At this point humanitarians still operated in somewhat of a netherworld of authority—while some international agreements and a few operational agencies existed, international order was fuzzy. Many humanitarian operations of this period, such as Herbert Hoover's efforts as part of the American Relief Administration during World War I and in Soviet Russia during the famine of 1921–1923, were episodic and not engineered to systematically address the broader phenomenon of humanitarian crises. Moreover, humanitarian agencies recognized that many problems were simply too large for agencies to cope with alone, and so they strived to embed themselves deeper in the fabric of day-to-day life by affiliating with more permanent international institutions. The League of Nations (1920–1946, though effectively dead by the late 1930s) was formed in the politically messy aftermath of World War I to prevent nationalist movements from unraveling borders and to collectively secure peaceful relations among states. As the paramount international institution of the day and in light the massive displacement among Russian, Austro-Hungarian, and German soldiers after World War I, the ICRC appealed to the League to organize assistance.

Perhaps the league's most significant accomplishment consisted of establishing the High Commissioner for Russian Refugees (1920–1922), headed by Fridtjof Nansen.[57] The plight of some one million refugees from Russia was exacerbated when the Bolsheviks revoked their citizenship and left them stateless. The success in promoting the cause led to the creation of the "Nansen Passport" in 1922 as a means of identification for the displaced, which was recognized by fifty-one states and thereby allowed its holders to travel, settle, and work. The League also authorized Nansen to widen the geographic scope of his efforts to include not just those displaced by the breakdown of the Russian Empire but also the Austro-Hungarian and Ottoman empires (e.g., Greece, Turkey, Bulgaria). In subsequent years under his leadership, other agencies were devised, such as the Nansen International Office for Refugees (1929–1938) and the High Commissioner for Refugees Coming from Germany (1938). Two of the holdovers from this era, the Intergovernmental Committee for Refugees (1938) and the High Commissioner for Refugees of the League of Nations (1939), would fold together in 1943 to form the basis of the United Nations Relief and Rehabilitation Administration (UNRRA).

Aside from the League of Nations, private agencies also appeared. World War I and the Bolshevik Revolution prompted two sisters, Eglantyne Jebb and Dorothy Buxton, to found Save the Children. As Nazism reared its ugly head in the 1930s, Albert Einstein started the International Rescue Committee (IRC) to provide medical and health care to refugees from Europe.

In terms of international law, progress in establishing and grounding norms was episodic. During the 1920s conflicts between states and rivalries among the ICRC and its national affiliates slowed efforts. However, overall, several important steps were taken in this period. In 1929 a conference in Geneva reviewed existing laws of war (primarily treaties enacted at the Hague Conferences of 1899 and 1907) and produced two conventions—one to address combatants on the battlefield who were injured or ill and another to specify treatment of POWs. Although states had made legal commitments to humanitarianism, the behavior of Axis as well as Allied governments during World War II violated the spirit, if not the explicit letter, of the law. To cite but two glaring examples, Nazi Germany was notorious for its vicious treatment of civilians, especially minorities, and the Soviet Union retained POWs long after violence ceased and peace had been achieved.

Post–World War II Expansion

The plethora of humanitarian crises that accompanied World War II further spurred the development of the humanitarian system. In response a host of new intergovernmental organizations (IGOs) entered the scene— notably, the United Nations family. At the same time, new international legal instruments (e.g., the 1948 UN Convention on the Prevention and Punishment of the Crime of Genocide) were created and other iterations of international humanitarian law were fashioned to reflect the realities of recent conflicts. These updates of the Geneva Conventions in 1949, and again in 1977, elaborated earlier rights and protections and ultimately enlarged those covered to include civilians and civil wars.

We are primarily interested in institutions that had a direct bearing on humanitarian action, but it is necessary to place the creation of agencies and laws within the broader political context of the time. The establishment of the UN family is the most visible and significant barometer of that political-historical moment. Based on the principle of collective security, it underlined idealized norms and the practices of international cooperation that had developed among wartime allies. This normative and institutional framework allowed several crucial components of the international humanitarian system to be nested within world-spanning organizations.

As mentioned, the UNRRA was developed in 1943 to provide assistance to those in Europe who did not plan to repatriate to where they had been initially displaced from. It, too, would be revamped as the International Refugee Organization in 1946, which in turn underwent another makeover into the UN High Commissioner for Refugees (UNHCR) in 1951. The Food and Agriculture Organization (FAO), founded in 1943, was conceived to share information on agriculture and related technology as part of a larger global plan to prevent famines from triggering strife. To specifically address the special needs of children, UNICEF (the UN International Children's Emergency Fund, later the Children's Fund) was founded in 1946.

Private agencies also blossomed during the war and shortly thereafter. A group of Quakers founded the Oxford Committee for Famine Relief (later Oxfam) in 1942 to respond to the Greek famine during the war; Catholic Relief Services and CARE also appeared in this period. Following the cessation of hostilities, other new NGOs materialized: Lutheran World Relief; Church World Service, a branch of the National Council of Churches; and Caritas International, a Catholic charity based at the Vatican. To provide relief to orphans in the Korean War, Christian groups formed World Vision in 1950.

During the 1950s, 1960s, and 1970s, other additions focused especially on emergency needs. In 1961, the World Food Programme (WFP) was instituted to hasten rapid, short-term food aid. The WFP was created to coordinate assistance for and with the FAO, and what began as an ad hoc invention of the moment became a formal and freestanding agency. Beyond food aid, other emergency assistance also required more extensive coordination among UN agencies. In 1971 the UN Disaster Relief Organization (UNDRO) was founded to manage a gamut of tasks—assessing needs, mustering responses, cementing cooperation, and teaching preparedness and prevention.

The historical juncture of the late 1940s also produced other international principles, practices, laws, and institutions that nourished the humanitarian impulse. Most notable were the trials of defeated powers in Germany and Japan. Instead of the preoccupation with the ability of the state to protect citizens against attack from other states, Jews in Germany were subject to depredations by their own state authorities in the 1930s and 1940s. Nazi Germany's vast slaughter of minority populations—its ideological fervor and industrial power threatening to exterminate entire peoples and cultures—led to Raphael Lemkin coining the term *genocide*.[58] The scale of such brutality and Lemkin's work clearly struck a chord with international society. A specialized body of IHL developed to define the characteristics of genocide and define legal responsibilities—the Convention on the Prevention and Punishment of the Crime of Genocide, which was formulated in 1947–1948.[59]

The murder of Jews along with the sick, communists, gypsies, and homosexuals led to a postwar institutionalization of values that are in two ways relevant for contemporary humanitarian action. On the negative side (punishment and deterrence), the Tokyo and Nuremberg trials severely restricted the notion of sovereignty and that of sovereigns hiding behind it as a cover for war crimes and the systematic violation of human rights. On the positive side, the 1948 Universal Declaration of Human Rights—which was, in Michael Ignatieff's words, "designed to create fire walls against barbarism"[60]—and then a host of other international conventions enshrined the notion of common humanity. Geoffrey Best describes these two pillars of the postwar "Temple of Peace" as "the human rights program representing the values of the future, and the war crimes trials symbolizing the destruction of the evil forces of the past."[61]

In addition to the establishment of and innovations to operational agencies and other institutional infrastructure for the system, IHL was updated after the experience of World War II. Given the extent of war crimes committed by numerous state parties, the Swiss government and the ICRC organized another Geneva conference in 1949 to strengthen and expand humanitarian protections. On August 12 four conventions were agreed upon, and they became law on October 21, 1950: the Amelioration of the Condition of the Wounded and Sick in Armed Forces in the Field (first convention), Amelioration of the Condition of the Wounded, Sick, and Shipwrecked Members of Armed Forces at Sea (second), Relative to the Treatment of Prisoners of War (third), and Relative to the Protection of Civilian Persons in Times of War (fourth). Like their predecessors, these four conventions built on earlier principles and agreements but attuned them to the political sensibilities of the post–World War II world.[62] First, the poor treatment of combatants and the captured inspired states to use their power to push for an update of IHL to clarify and develop rights and protections for soldiers and POWs. Common article 13 of the first and second Geneva Conventions stress the applicability of these regulations exclusively to official armed forces and those affiliated or tied to them. This clause also indicates that these provisions cover those who can be and are as accountable as states—meaning that they seek international sanction for their status as legal combatants. Accordingly, they must have a command structure, display distinctive signs and emblems indicating that they are belligerents, carry their weapons openly, and abide by IHL.

Second, the enormous civilian toll of World War II also placed the status of unarmed parties firmly on the agenda and into law. Consequently, although the first, second, and third Geneva Conventions constitute most of the substance of the 1949 renovations, the fourth may actually have more wide-ranging implications, as it is the first international agreement to protect civilians in war. Overall, the widespread popularity of and adherence to the 1949 Geneva Conventions suggests that they effectively embodied the norms of post–World War II world order.

THE FOUNDING ERA IN HISTORICAL PERSPECTIVE

Out of the brew of various Enlightenment-inspired social movements and waves of international institution building to embed the prominence of states, the international humanitarian system emerged in the late nineteenth century. Before and during the early formation of agencies and a system based on international treaty, humanitarianism was fundamentally a movement rather than a chain of organizations and laws. Making the international arena more rational from the point of view of states, coupled with value-based social actors promoting human welfare in warfare, consolidated the international humanitarian system. The interaction of three themes that we introduce in the previous chapter—bureaucratization, politicization, and militarization—encapsulates the major systemic developments of this era.

The most obvious aspect of this period is that of *bureaucratization*, the enormous number of organizations established and consolidated, which at times worked with one other to form the international humanitarian system. The creation of a network of organizations—many private and national societies and some other key international ones—began mostly in Western Europe but spread to other areas, particularly as states became parties to international law. From its beginnings in the 1860s through World War II and its immediate aftermath, the international humanitarian system proceeded to build legal and operational institutions along three fronts. First, different classes of victims in war slowly gained legal status and protections. Second, particular weapons systems were deemed too horrific and were thus banned. Third, the range of wars that were subject to IHL and that served as the locus of humanitarian action eventually expanded from clearly defined international wars to indistinct internal wars.

Beyond improving the welfare of greater numbers of war victims, many humanitarian organizations matured as bureaucracies, growing in size, resources, and visibility. Institutions were designed to respond to temporary crises but became permanent. Agencies found themselves operating in lengthy, drawn-out emergency situations, especially because the armed conflict still raged or even political hostilities among low-level militarized belligerents had not ceased. Previously, we discussed the importance of Nansen and his office in relieving the humanitarian pressures of war and in turn serving humanitarian interests but utilizing means that supported state sovereignty. The Second World War necessitated that the extant international humanitarian system address the problem of transborder flight by establishing camps. This bastion, created for refugees, allowed states that had displaced them to externalize their enemies (physically remove, isolate, and contain them) and shift the burden of responsibility to humanitarian agencies. As it became clear that the modern system of interstate warfare meant that refugees were not a temporary phenomenon, the UNHCR became a permanent fixture of the UN system in 1951 and was further codified in its 1967 protocol.[63] Its mandate was not geared to a particular crisis but was couched generally: to help those "who have crossed an international border because of a well-founded fear of persecution."

Another telling case of a "temporary" humanitarian organization is that of the UN Relief and Works Agency (UNRWA). This agency was designed to assist Palestinians displaced by the founding of the state of Israel and was supposed to last until Palestinians could be resettled in surrounding Arab states or until a political compromise with Israel could be reached that would provide for their return.[64] In the emergency phase of this crisis (during battles and skirmishes from 1947 to 1949), the Palestinian population desperately required immediate relief, and the acceptable course for humanitarians was to establish refugee camps. None could have foreseen that this avenue would prove to be the political expedient course for all states in the region—Israel removed what it saw as a troublesome population, and Arab states had an instant ally against Israel. This agency still exists.

Another major theme is that of *politicization*. Yet by far the most striking aspect of the period covered by this chapter (roughly the century and a quarter after 1864) is the partnership among states, their militaries, and the members of the international humanitarian system. First of all this signals an internationalization of humanitarian responsibilities—that is to say, that states are the parties to these agreements and that states authorize and recognize IGOs and in some cases NGOs to carry out humanitarian work. For example, UNHCR was created because it served the interests of states who feared the destabilizing impacts of refugee flows in Europe following World War II. To that end, it was established more out of practical worries regarding multilateral burden sharing than out of humanitarian concerns.[65]

However, the more prominent aspect of politicization is the actual bargaining and cooperation between governments and humanitarian agencies. This relationship can be seen in the nature of humanitarian space. Over time political leaders and relief workers codified a set of norms that identified noncombatants and their rights to aid. The trick was to avoid politics, be evenhanded, and distribute assistance on the basis of need regardless of their location in terms of battle lines and with the consent of both sides to an interstate war. The norms of neutrality, impartiality, and consent crystallized into guiding principles and became identified with the

ICRC and the humanitarian movement. In a manner of speaking, the dominant politics of the international humanitarian system were to have no politics, or avoid concerns over partisanship and preference in the administration of relief by not threatening states or militaries. Indeed, the authority of many international organizations—and humanitarian ones are no exception—is predicated on a myth that their activities are neutral and serve the common interests of all humanity.[66] This politicization of the system and actions by agencies can be seen in the questions regarding who receives the benefits of the humanitarian system. Fundamentally, in the first hundred years of the international humanitarian system, the answer can be found in the interests and power of states.

The expansion of who receives protection in war is illustrative, and it underlines the point that humanitarian innovations may find their origins in the interests of soldiers, the military agents of states. The power of the military to command the attention of states and international law accounts for the greater focus of the international humanitarian system on the fate of combatants in war than on the plight of civilians. The norm of relief and protection was first afforded to wounded or captured combatants, and only later did civilians attain such status. The military was concerned to fashion a practical solution to its immediate problem—aiding its own soldiers. After this principle had been established in relation to soldiers, it later expanded to cover others. Even then, the pace of progress reflects military priorities—those who come to the aid of soldiers (neutral medical personnel) were the next to be accorded special status. Civilians were the last category of war victims to be considered worthy of humanitarian assistance.

The ICRC during World War II exemplifies the power of states to co-opt humanitarian agencies and exert control when victims receive relief and protection from the international humanitarian system. The ICRC was granted space to facilitate humanitarian operations on the condition that the organization remained neutral and impartial.[67] However, many have criticized the ICRC for witnessing the Holocaust without publicly condemning the Nazis and for not doing much about the misery that Japan was inflicting on China, Korea, and the Philippines. Although concentration camps were mostly separate from the POW camps, the ICRC was granted access. While field representatives may not have had firsthand experience with the Third Reich's "final solution," knowledge of atrocities against minorities did not provoke significant criticism from the ICRC.

The agency subsequently came under criticism for having visited camps in France during World War II, after which inmates were shipped to gas chambers.[68] These kinds of criticisms have a contemporary salience. ICRC's Urs Boegli has remarked on the recurrence of this ugly reality in Bosnia, where "the only thing you can do for them is to make sure they are fed before they are shot."[69] Roberta Cohen and Francis

Deng would later help popularize what were to be called "the well-fed dead" in the Balkans.[70]

The institution's defense was that these compromises were necessary to respect "the rules of the game" negotiated by state parties and to have any sort of access to the victims. In short, the nature of interstate war—that is, the power of states to monopolize access—circumscribed humanitarians and their operating principles. The "father" of the ICRC's principles, Jean Pictet, defined each principle as "a rule, based upon judgment and experience, which is adopted by a community to guide its conduct."[71] In the most infamous instance, the neutrality upon which protection was afforded to the captured and wounded was used by Nazi Germany to inhibit the ICRC from taking any actions that would undermine its war efforts, militarily or politically.

As stated earlier, military forces have always played a role in humanitarian action, and *militarization* is the third theme that emerges. The military is primarily recognized for contributing to humanitarian disasters through the production of violence; however, the relation is much more extensive, and any such modeling should be considerably more nuanced. In fact, on many occasions from the eighteenth through the twentieth century, humanitarian crises were viewed as being sufficiently significant to warrant action that could only be executed with the participation of armed forces. During the Napoleonic era, militaries were used to provide humanitarian relief in conquered lands as a way of building support for the victors among the defeated.[72] Following World War II, the military command of the victorious Allied powers (the Supreme Headquarters Allied Expeditionary Force) provided social services for refugees. Shortly thereafter the Allies would again use the armed forces to deliver aid past the Soviet blockade in East Germany during the 1947 Berlin airlift.

While many examples illustrate how the armed forces have remained a fixture in humanitarian responses, this period more importantly signifies a demilitarization of humanitarianism. The establishment of special organizations to channel humanitarian efforts removed the onus of responsibility that oftentimes fell to less-than-enthusiastic militaries.

Table 2.1 summarizes developments from the 1860s through most of the Cold War. It outlines the parameters of war—where (locus), who (agents), how to sustain efforts and sometimes to what end (economics), at what human costs (targets and victims), with what means (technology), and who will know (media coverage)—and it situates them with reference to their humanitarian implications and the evolving responses of the international humanitarian system. This table exemplifies what we might call the "classic age" of interstate war from the late nineteenth through the late twentieth century, when humanitarianism experienced a profound renaissance—with international commitments grounded in

Table 2.1. Interstate War, Humanitarian Implications, and System Responses

	Interstate War	Humanitarian Implications	System Responses
Locus	Coincide with state borders	Access granted by states	Neutrality, impartiality
Agents	States and their militaries	Mostly military fatalities	Hague and Geneva conventions
Economies	Extraction through domestic tax revenues and conquest of foreign lands	State-based war economy	International law Postwar settlements restricting arms industry
Targets and victims	Mainly combatants	Negotiating protection for defeated soldiers Address displacement of civilians	Geneva Conventions Refugee camps, migration, resettlement
Technologies	Mass-produced conventional weaponry	National-scale humanitarian crises	Hague and Geneva conventions
Media coverage of humanitarian issues in war	Nonexistent to minimal propaganda	—	—

law and agencies established to organize assistance to victims. The contents of this table should be kept in mind as we depict in the next chapter the nature of armed conflicts of more recent times.

From a historical perspective the aggregation of this period's trends produced a particular configuration of war and humanitarianism, and while the building of the system was progress, not all aspects of the system were progressive or forward thinking. For example, the founding of the UN brought about legal and material changes that complemented or made humanitarian action possible, but it also cast them in a particular way that minimized the scope of victims and situations where agencies had sanction to operate. The primary purpose of the UN was to build peace and security among states, and this agenda, as well as the institutions constructed to govern this aspect of international relations, provide many of the major players in the international humanitarian system. The UN Charter's first article states that its purpose is "to achieve international cooperation in solving international problems of an economic, social, cultural or humanitarian character." However, as dramatic as these principles are, other aspects of the charter fundamentally located the nexus of responsibility for crises of all kinds, including humanitarian, within the internationally agreed territorial boundaries of member states. In other words, the establishment of the second generation of world organization took aim at the problem of interstate war, but for humanitarians it only hit part of the target—wars that cross borders and war-affected people (refugees) who do the same. But it did not stem the growing tide of violence within states nor address the victims within them. As long as humanitarian action could conform to the mechanics of interstate war and international relations, access and operations were not imperiled. But human rights abuses and civil wars were another matter.

Of course, the charter also set up a fundamental tension between the protection of human rights (most specifically outlined in article 55) and the prerogatives of state sovereignty on which the world organization was constructed (especially in article 2.7): "Nothing contained in the present Charter shall authorize the United Nations to intervene in matters which are essentially within the domestic jurisdiction of any state." The tension became starker still with the signing of the Universal Declaration of Human Rights.

However, there were already signs of cracks in the edifice predicated on interstate war and temporary agencies. Although the 1949 Geneva Conventions reflect notions of war associated with the nineteenth and the early twentieth century, they also account for some new realities. First, the human costs of civil wars appeared on the international radar screen; article 3 of the 1949 Geneva Conventions was the first international treaty to regulate what were dubbed "non-international armed conflicts," but the very appellation suggests the hold of interstate war and civilian victims on the imagination and vocabulary. However, the real advances in the law governing these wars would await the 1977 Additional Protocols. Nonetheless, even after this next round of updating the laws of war the total number of clauses applying to "non-international" (that is, civil) wars appears in twenty-nine articles—in common, articles 3 and 4 to the Geneva Conventions and Additional Protocol II. This clearly pales in comparison to the 530 articles in the four Geneva Conventions and Additional Protocol I.[73]

The creation of bureaucracies exclusively dedicated to humanitarian goals in the context of a state-based international order truncated humanitarianism to some extent. Although the international humanitarian system achieved a critical victory by insinuating itself as an actor in war and by improving the welfare of many victims, the reins held firmly by states essentially steered the scope of agencies and restricted their actions. However, the usefulness of humanitarian agencies and their successes in saving lives in the first 125-year span after its humble beginnings in the 1860s brought agencies ever-greater resources, responsibilities, and visibilities. In the next two chapters we discuss the armed conflicts to which the "classic" international humanitarian system increasingly responded, beginning in the 1980s (the "new wars"), and the system's performance as a result (the "new humanitarianisms").

3

"New Wars"

Humanitarians focus on the constants of war—death, destruction, displacement, and desolation—but not all warfare has the same goals, means, or consequences. Given that the nature of the sword circumscribes the application of the salve, it is essential to understand the elements that compose what are commonly called the "new wars." In attempting to explain the armed conflicts that do not conform to the textbook patterns of state-versus-state warfare that we spell out in the previous chapter, scholars and analysts have put forth a variety of terms in recent years.

- In a broad sense, "civil war" refers to an internal violent struggle for control of state institutions—but to be more exact, it is over what and where those state institutions will govern. This type of warfare is traditionally distinguished from interstate war by a domestic component, suggesting that all sides in the conflict either have recently been or are currently connected to the same political institutions or community. Similar to the manner in which classic war making of the interstate variety is tied to the manufacture of internal order (state-making), the internal fracture of civil wars can affect international order. Three forms of civil wars illustrate: anticolonial struggles, secessionist movements, and irredentist campaigns. In these instances, various forms of support (from rhetoric and finance to arms transfers or the use of military forces) by outside states can complicate the designation of "civil." For the most part though, civil wars connote a stratum of substate and nonstate actors involved in war making within the internationally agreed boundaries of a state.
- "Insurgency" refers to a widespread armed rebellion against a government (not necessarily the state) or an occupying power and is basically a strategy of an armed belligerent group in civil wars to overthrow or secede a sitting government.[1] The goal of insurgencies is to spark and spread, eventually "liberating" areas and administering them, as a government would. The incumbent regime or occupying power utilizes "counterinsurgency" to quell military resistance and build political support for the government. The degree to which military means substitute for political persuasion is a perennial question. Common to practices of civil wars, insurgency and counterinsurgency highlight a collection of actors operating below the interstate level and a mixture of politics and military power. Examples are widespread, from the communist insurgents in the 1920s and 1930s to the anticolonial nationalist insurgencies beginning in the late 1940s (e.g., the Front de Libération Nationale in Algeria) and peaking in the 1960s and 1970s. Most recently, the term has returned to the headlines with the campaign disrupting the U.S. occupation in Iraq (the

nature of this particular armed conflict is discussed in greater detail in chapter 6).

- The meaning of "guerilla war" as a variety of warfare is distinct from insurgency in its scale of violent opposition; it is usually a phase before insurgency. Whereas insurgencies focus on the growth of their political base, guerilla warriors concentrate on using their small military forces to outmaneuver and unseat the government and eventually develop a broader and sustained following that would qualify as an insurgency. The term "guerilla" was first used to define the "little war" of Spaniards resisting French armies under Napoleon in the early nineteenth century. The phrase "guerilla war" was popularized by Mao Tse-Tung in China during the 1940s and by Vo Nguyen Giap in Vietnam and Che Guevara in Cuba during the 1960s.[2] All three fought in revolutions that had pronounced stages of guerilla war before their efforts produced popular public support, and they were successful in overthrowing central state authorities.

- Underlining the contrast with those campaigns fought to defeat colonial powers—"wars of national liberation"—Leslie Gelb describes more recent internal armed conflicts as "wars of national debilitation."[3] In these struggles the polity is divided over many issues; many actors do not even think in terms of a state or national framework and thereby have radically different perceptions of problems and priorities. The escalation to violence serves not to liberate a society increasingly united against a common foreign foe; instead, it unleashes substantial strife that unravels the polity.

- Edward Rice first used "war of the third kind" to emphasize variations in combatants and that guerilla war did not sufficiently capture the scale of all such conflicts.[4] Kalevi Holsti also uses the term to denote that virtually all armed conflicts do not correspond to classic models.[5]

- "Fourth generation warfare" is derived from the work of U.S. Air Force colonel John Boyd and his OODA theory (observation-orientation-decision-action), which holds that previous innovations in war in terms of organizing manpower, developing firepower, and orchestrating maneuvers are accentuated. And they culminate in a form of war that "is largely undefined; the distinction between war and peace will be blurred to the vanishing point. It will be nonlinear, possibly to the point of having no definable battlefield or fronts. The distinction between 'civilian' and 'military' may disappear."[6] Fourth-generation warfare connects political, economic, and social hubs of power to the battlefield and thus appeals to soldiers analyzing unfolding evolution. "Unlike previous generations, [the fourth] does not attempt to win by defeating the enemy's forces. Instead via the networks, it directly attacks the minds of enemy decisionmakers to destroy the enemy's political will."[7]

- The adjective "asymmetric" before "warfare" denotes fighting on different fronts or in different ways to neutralize the superiority of traditionally configured militaries. While some scholars debate the continuity of this condition with reference to earlier forms of warfare,[8] others concentrate on applying the concept to more recent conflicts, including terrorism and resistance to the U.S. occupation of Iraq.[9]
- While primarily applying to information-based conflicts, "netwar" refers to unconventional warfare spanning not only economic, political, and social forms but also military forms and involving flat, segmented networks instead of hierarchical command-and-control systems.[10] Similarly, some military analysts point to a new model in this genre. Traditional war is seen as following the model of U.S. football, with an emphasis on centralized decision making, tight coordination of forces, and taking of territory; but more recent styles of war more closely resemble European football, or soccer, in which finesse, patience, improvisation, and endurance are at a premium.[11]
- While the internal component is vital to the designation of "civil war," Donald Snow has elaborated on the premise to consider armed practices that appear to be devoid of explicit political meaning: "uncivil wars."[12] Belligerents in these conflicts are also less restrained in their conduct.
- "New wars," earlier terms notwithstanding, has become the most popular and widespread contemporary turn of phrase among practitioners and analysts. Analytical works by Mary Kaldor and Mark Duffield, along with the more popular depictions offered by Robert Kaplan, have made this term almost a household item.[13]

As this topic is the point of departure for this volume, we provide considerably more detail. The ubiquity of the phrase conceals a lack of clarity to what it means and how it is used. Catchphrases are a common analytical hazard, but the simplistic shorthand of "new wars" is among the most misunderstood and hazardous. Labeling an armed conflict as "new" does not advance debate, because it has so many meanings and is so vague that members of the audience can interpret it virtually as they please. For ease of reading but without loss of meaning, from here onward we drop the scare quotes for *new wars*. By now readers should be aware of our unease with the term.

That said, significant changes are afoot in today's wars and world order, and our argument here is straightforward: humanitarians are obliged to unpack the dynamics of contemporary wars in order to move away from entrenched standard operating procedures and principles of the classic interstate period and to adopt strategies and tactics that are tailored to landscapes populated by a hodgepodge of actors with an overabundance of substate interests. The success of the humanitarian enterprise depends on tailoring procedures to fit the peculiar dimensions of contemporary armed conflicts. A refuge in past standard operating procedures is irresponsible for humanitarians and for affected populations.

This chapter dissects contemporary wars with specific reference to the ideal type of interstate war and the shape of global order. Is anything new? And if so, what difference does it make to assisting and protecting human beings ensnared in the vortex of violence?

SO, WHAT'S NEW?

The modifier "new" does not necessarily indicate that an actual armed conflict has begun only recently but rather that the normal dynamics have changed.[14] "Changed" is a more accurate characterization of the transformation at hand, as previous historical instances illustrate similar potential mechanisms. In his *Taming the Sovereigns*, Kal Holsti offers a lucid approach to understanding change, one that holistically integrates factors and historically situates aggregate elements. His subtitle, *Institutional Change in International Politics*, identifies several reasons why new wars could be considered "new." He notes that "a narrow conception of change fails to acknowledge the importance of other *sources* of change (such as ideas and revolutions), other *types* of change (such as the growth of non-state actors and international civil society), and other *consequences* of change (such as global governance)."[15]

The discussion in this chapter demonstrates that it is not so much that new elements have appeared as it is that elements thought extinct or tangential have come to the fore or been combined in ways that were previously unremarkable or unknown. Hence, change is quantitatively significant or the elements are combined in such previously unfamiliar ways that many of the current generation of wars can be considered new.

For example, the number, power, and overall significance of NSAs have grown substantially. The presence of NSAs is novel for two reasons. First, some are in a more prominent position to wage war in an international order principally based on states, certainly since its consolidation as a system in the eighteenth and nineteenth centuries. Second, some are predominant in responding to war, especially IGOs and NGOs—a reality discussed further in the next chapter. This being said, determining the distinctiveness of this phenomenon is problematic. Even the most cursory glance at military history shows that violence by NSAs is by no stretch of the imagination new. The previous chapter details the birth of IGOs and NGOs active in the humanitarian arena and also provides several illustrations of militarily significant NSAs from the early period of state formation. Even in World War II, which in many ways may prove to be the pinnacle of interstate warfare, the case of partisan paramilitary factions in the Balkans suggests that

NSAs have previously inhabited a niche in war, albeit a lower profile one than in the new wars. The rationality and behavior of some NSAs in the wars termed "new" is part of a primordial drive to establish political authority or fashion opportunities for economic enrichment.

These wars are certainly more complex than those of the previous era, which was primarily dominated by interstate wars, but the dynamics of these armed conflicts can be parsed to determine elements of continuity and change. It is also critically important to keep in mind that the same conflict may comprise many wars—depending on the time of the year or the part of a territory where violence is seething. Perception is critical, and the grievances of belligerents are in the eyes of the beholder. For instance, from one perspective what appears as a conflict over political leadership of the state may in fact camouflage other local-level struggles or predation. To capture this reality, the plural form of "wars" is almost always appropriate as it conveys that the structures and agents of war are manifold. Thus, the dissonance between the dynamics of more traditional interstate wars and more recent ones suggests that a more apt terminology may be "uncalibrated conflicts." Carl von Clausewitz reminds generals that "war must differ in character according to the nature of the motives and circumstances from which they proceed."[16] This counsel is equally applicable to humanitarians, as we shall see in the next chapter.

So what exactly is new? Today's prototypical war differs from the archetypical interstate war in six aspects, which are depicted in table 3.1—the

Table 3.1. Comparing "Old" and "New" Wars

	"Old" Wars	*"New" Wars*
Locus	Coincides with state borders	Areas of fragmented political authority; state borders meaningless
Agents	States and their militaries	Increased role of nonstate actors
Economies	Tax revenues underwrite government war effort	Illegal activities, aid, and plunder are crucial
Targets and victims	Mainly combatants	Prevalence of civilian casualties (noncombatants)
Technologies	Large-scale conventional weaponry	New technologies; revolution in military affairs
Media coverage of humanitarian issues in war	Nonexistent to minimal propaganda	Greater coverage Shape inclination toward force

locus of war, the agents of war, the economics of war, the prevalence of civilian victims, the means of war and new technologies, and media coverage. Our discussion disaggregates these aspects for the sake of analytical clarity. At the same time, this typology does not precisely fit any, and certainly not all, real-life armed conflicts. Rather, it is intended to focus attention on different facets of warfare that should be understood as a "potential package," particularly as humanitarian challenges tend to layer and magnify one other. Many, but not usually all, of the characteristics of new wars come together in today's zones of violent warfare. The higher the number of altered characteristics and the higher their frequency, the "newer" the armed conflict. As such, humanitarians need to evaluate the extent to which their traditional operating principles and procedures are useful for assistance and protection within a particular theater.

FRAGMENTED AUTHORITY AND MEANINGLESS BORDERS: A NEW LOCUS

The first and least disputed contemporary characteristic concerns how new the locus of war is. The bloodiest wars of the twentieth century were waged by large and powerful states—the United States, the Soviet Union, Britain, Japan, Germany, and France—across borders for prolonged periods of time in order to gain territory, wealth, and influence. Both World War I and World War II fit the hegemonic war model of interstate conflict among major powers. In the Korean War, although the local population was the focal point of hostilities (a civil war among the political community) with substantial land forces and assistance provided by major powers (the United States to the south, and China to the north), in many ways this conflict was more akin to traditional interstate wars. The result of two hostile and geographically separate states (now independent) engaged in a political stalemate as opposed to one state wracked by persistent civil war underlines that in the early 1950s the sense that national political cleavages would be resolved through interstate war still prevailed.

Other conflicts pitted a major power against a small state that was resisting the influence of the former either through decolonization struggles or manipulating their major rivals as allies. However, whether it is France in Indochina, the United States in Central America, or the United Kingdom in the Falkland Islands (Islas Malvinas), interstate frameworks (and especially defined borders) distinguished belligerents and defined conflicts. In the case of the Western coalition that ousted Iraq from Kuwait in the Gulf War of 1991, a territorial dispute turned into an international war that triggered a short-lived insurgency by Shi'ites from the southern marsh areas and by Kurds in the north against the Saddam Hussein regime. But even after the Gulf War of 1991, the Iraqi state of the early 1990s retained a surprising amount of strength (particularly its military capability) and managed to restore a semblance of authority, though remaining as an international pariah. As will be seen in chapter 6, the scenario of international war giving way to internal war was relatively brief in 1991 compared to the lengthy duration that would commence in 2003.

A larger, if not wholesale, departure from the older model emerges in the new wars of the 1990s, where most battleground states have minimal power, and often even that is contested by internal armed opposition movements that pay no attention to internationally recognized borders. Many have central governments whose sole existence takes the form of UN membership and control of the capital or the main export industries. Although these states claim to be part of the Westphalian order, they bear limited resemblance to Western counterparts.[17] In sum, all illustrate a departure from the conventions of sovereign states in terms of authoritative control over populations and resources. At a territorial level, these states suffer from an "unbundling," a negation of their exclusive authority as states.[18]

Whatever description is assigned to this schema, the frequency of state-versus-state conflict has decreased relative to the upsurge in violence within states—in the 1990s, for instance, 94 percent of wars resulting in more than one thousand deaths were civil.[19] For 2004, one source found twenty-five emergencies of "pressing" concern, twenty-three of which were conflict related—and all of those were in civil wars.[20] The battlefields of new wars do not feature conventional frontlines. Instead, violence gravitates toward resources and opportunities for which borders are meaningless.

The period beginning in the 1990s features varying degrees of fragmentation: the regional wars in western Africa (in Nigeria, Liberia, Sierra Leone, and the Ivory Coast), central Africa (concentrated primarily in the Democratic Republic of the Congo, Rwanda, Burundi, and Sudan), the splintering of societies and states in central Asia (Afghanistan, the Caucasus, and Kashmir), and the growing unrest in South America (Colombia at the moment but with such other Andean countries as Peru and Bolivia perennially on the brink). While interstate elements are part of the mix of these conflicts—historically, their origins or accelerants may reside in an earlier interstate war—these new wars are fought locally (in neighborhoods, villages, and other subnational units), even if modern technologies make external connections easy.

Much of the academic and policy literatures approach these conflicts by looking at the quality of the state (unit-based analysis). These analyses correctly focus on the level of governance, as it is often a prime determinant in making war and making peace. Order at both local and national levels also facilitates the delivery of humanitarian assistance because relief and protection require a central point of organizing efforts and accountability: the state. However, new wars emerge against a backdrop of distorted order, and state institutions often exhibit signs of distortion, corrosion, or incapacity.

The role and importance of the state has been a mainstay of social science since Max Weber wrote at the beginning of the twentieth century about the state's legitimate monopoly on violence and its authoritative position in society.[21] However, our focus is less on theoretical groundings of the state than on the concrete implications of states under duress, particularly as they influence the prospects for humanitarian action. States in the netherworld of fractured order that are the settings for many new wars have been described in a variety of ways:

- "Disrupted states": Amin Sakil applies this term to indicate that states have traditionally consolidated their power within their territorial borders but that disrupted states deviate from the norm of, what he terms, "cohesive states," those that embody Westphalian ideals.[22]
- "Shadow states": William Reno uses this term to define state rulers who seek to exert power through markets despite a pretense of state institutions, making states effectively shadows.[23]
- "Rhizome state": Jean-François Bayart uses this terminology to describe states engineered to enrich private interests.[24]
- "Quasi-states": Robert Jackson aplies this term to describe paper sovereignty, usually a vestige of colonial constructs with little in common with a modern state.[25]
- "Collapsed states": William Zartman uses this description to capture the disappearance of the usual characteristics of a sovereign entity.[26]
- "State death": Tanisha Fazul—looking into the survival rates of buffer states, those caught between powerful rivals—employs this expression to describe the "loss of foreign policymaking to another state."[27] Although her study is addressing the influence of foreign powers, in terms of new wars issues this line of analysis suggests that the erosion of the state occurs at many levels, ideologically and identity-wise as much as institutionally.

While each of the aforementioned descriptions contains insights, for our purposes it makes most sense to discuss a spectrum ranging from "weak" to "failed" states in order to understand the main characteristics that circumscribe central government authority in new wars because such authority is a key variable for outside humanitarians' coming to the rescue.

- "Weak states": The term has been used by many scholars and policy analysts to emphasize how the power of states is shrunk or effectively shaped by other actors. These other actors are mostly civil and domestically based, but stresses also emanate from international and transnational organizations such as the International Monetary Fund and multinational corporations. Internally weak states contend with powerful NSAs, not just armed groups on occasion but civil society and business interests. Joel Migdal deploys the characterization "weak" to suggest that strong societies tend to undercut state power. In reference to the case of Egypt, for instance, he argues that local elites were able to thwart state power and determine outcomes locally.[28] External pressures on weak states tend to focus primarily on immediate international security concerns (threats from other states). Economic influences of the 1970s, 1980s, and 1990s also play a role— neoliberalism advocates the slashing of state budgets, which may contribute to "weakness." Structural adjustment programs that decrease the ability of states to fund basic social services and institutions providing law and order have undermined the already anemic strength of the most economically underdeveloped states.

The shorthand "weak" tends to categorize states that do not measure up to Western role models in international political prestige, wealth, military prowess, and national unity. States can be weak for one of two reasons and sometimes both.[29] First, states may lack the capacity to pursue national interests formulated by an effective leader or bureaucracy.[30] States may also lack the financial resources, technology, skill, population, or political capital to fulfill goals. Many states relied on outside support in the throes of the Cold War and, post-1989, have no patron to fund or provide the maintenance of vital institutions (i.e., those that provide military and tax-collecting capacities). In fact and in an especially poignant change, some weak states in this situation have turned to mercenaries to make up for military assistance.[31]

Second, states may not have the authority to make credible and binding decisions. When a state lacks local resources or when those from abroad dry up, the popularity or even tolerance among local populations is likely to disappear. Without the support of citizens, such states are therefore not perceived as being legitimate. This lack of authority may in turn further undermine capacity. Disdainful populations can be controlled through violence, fear, and other repressive measures. Yet the ability of the state to govern and manage the resources within its borders can be still further eroded in the process of trying to instill fear and repress dissidents, armed or not.

The fundamental measurement of weakness is that some states have ambivalent or hostile relations with the societies that they supposedly serve and govern. In addition, some weak states may be corrupt and predatory or lend themselves to being manipulated by NSAs in the course of war. Recognizing patterns of state-society relationships helps identify states that are weak and in what specific ways, which in turn frame specific challenges for humanitarians.

- "Failed state": This moniker became a staple of analyses since Gerald Helman and Steven Ratner coined the term in 1992 as Somalia caught the attention of decision makers.[32] While "weak" illustrates various types of vulnerability and a range of capacities, the modifier "failed" implies that the illnesses in central authority are so grave as to be politically fatal. The term is contested. Not all weak states actually fail (e.g., Chad), and some weak ones that collapse can make a comeback (e.g., Lebanon).[33]

  Failed-state analysis goes beyond the logic of weak states, emphasizing how fundamental flaws destine a state to implode—indeed, the logic may apply in the future to vast megapolises, or "feral cities," of the Third World.[34] Some analysts have argued that failure stems not only from material pressures (specifically, a loss of capacities) but also from a conceptual shift away from sovereignty—Krasner, for example, emphasizes sovereignty as a politicized social construct backed by the most powerful states.[35] The consequences of weakness result in fragmentation and domestic anarchy. However, a veneer of order can remain or be reconstituted at substate levels.

Shared across the categories is a type of order that deviates from textbook patterns but is still premised on structured arrangements among actors representing political, military, and economic power. Rather than the commonplace descriptions of "anarchy" or "chaos," Mark Duffield's description of "durable disorder"[36] is more accurate. These configurations of war feature a kind of strength facilitated by the processes of globalization. In other words, the same structures propelling economic globalization produce wealth and security in some parts of the world but may also create poverty and conflict in other parts. Moreover, even in these downtrodden areas can one see an enduring quality to the instability. Local situations of new wars may be chaotic but may not necessarily comprise chaos. In spite of the images popularized by Robert Kaplan's apocalyptic views of the future Third World in *The Coming Anarchy*, to the informed observer a different size and shape of order are present. A freefall of authority is associated with the crumbling capacities, but so is a "malorder," whereby order is intentionally manipulated or concocted to benefit a particular group.

In reference to patterns representing continuity with earlier historical periods, as early as the late 1970s, Hedley Bull described the return to overlapping authorities as a "new medievalism."[37] He argued that over time the gradual development of a society among states is crucial to international order, but late-twentieth-century patterns of unraveling authority have reversed this historical arrangement in at least some parts of the globe. More recently, scholars have drawn parallels between today's wars and those that accompanied European state formation, particularly with the contrasts between power located in governments (states) versus power residing in looser structures of governance (poly-archical networks).

Picking up on Bull's packaging, Jessica Matthews notes that the post–Cold War power shifts among states, markets, and civil society resemble the dynamics of the Middle Ages.[38] Mohammed Ayoob, draw-ing on Charles Tilly's work, goes so far as to argue against those who try to halt humanitarian emergencies by pointing out that armed conflict was an essential ingredient of European state making and that similar kinds of humanitarian disasters are the invariable by-product of comparable processes at work in much of the Third World.[39] Blood has always been the lubricant of political power and the currency of military victory, even in internal military conflicts. However, the fragmentation of authority and the relative meaninglessness of borders in the new wars, while a depar-ture from nineteenth- and twentieth-century international political order, epitomizes a historically familiar reality.

What is not familiar, however, is the central challenge to international peace and security, as Holsti reminds us: "the major problem of the con-temporary society of states is no longer aggression, conquest and the obliteration of states. It is, rather, the collapse of states, humanitarian emergencies, state terror against segments of local populations, civil wars of various types, and international terrorist organizations."[40] Tradi-tional humanitarian thinking may be skewed by unhelpful assumptions about progress because in responding to challenges of what is a pre-Westphalian order in certain parts of the globe, the principles and tactics that have worked well in the past for humanitarians dealing with inter-state wars are undoubtedly of limited utility. As a practical matter, the deinstitutionalization of sovereign central authorities mean, at a mini-mum, a vastly diminished role for international law. As David Kennedy writes, "Those seeking to bring law to bear against warfare have also enchanted their tools, overestimated the significance of legal pronounce-ments, and mistaken legal warfare for humanitarian warfare."[41]

THE PROLIFERATION OF NONSTATE ACTORS: NEW AGENTS

The significance of key actors behind the convoluted order endemic to con-temporary conflicts marks a dramatic shift away from state-centric per-spectives. For at least the past century, war has fundamentally been filtered through the lenses of state belligerents, which James Rosenau has dubbed "sovereignty-bound."[42] However, these lenses no longer provide a clear focus for new wars because organized violence and humanitarianism are not beholden only or evenly mainly to state authorities. Hence, the second defining characteristic of current armed conflicts consists of the rising multitude of unconventional political units with dramatic security implications (militarized NSAs).[43]

The end of the Cold War resulted in disengagement and withdrawal by superpower patrons, and this loss of support weakened the state in parts of the Third World.[44] Moreover, many NSAs became dominant locally by providing essential social services, and some even consolidated political power by using resources provided by humanitarians. In Sudan, for instance, the Sudanese Liberation Army controlled access and aid distribution, thereby increasing over time the authority and legitimacy of a movement that in late 2004 became part of the government. In Lebanon, Hezbollah made an international name for itself and earned worldwide condemnation in dispatching suicide attacks against Israel. At the grassroots level, however, the organization burnished its image and built concrete political support by funding and organizing hospitals and schools.

Some NSAs in effect usurp the roles and realms of states. Stephen Stedman and Fred Tanner use the expression "pseudo-states" to denote crafty belligerents that manipulate the presence of refugees to attract and exploit humanitarian resources for their political agendas.[45] In an even more apt image, Beatrice Hibou refers to powerful criminal NSAs as "parallel states."[46]

For humanitarians, a direct challenge ensues because NSAs can be impediments or assets to immediate relief as well as to development and peace in the longer term. The weakening and disappearance of central political authority has been a boon to NSAs of all stripes. Where vacuums of authority exist, humanitarian agencies are obliged to negotiate memorandums of understanding with a variety of NSAs, instead of working out a single one with a government. Moreover, agencies must devote resources to get to know the actors on the battlefield because their predisposition and power shape operational environments of humanitarians.

NSAs can be rated in many ways—by military capabilities, economic resources, and official or informal relations to state or foreign influences. But as the primary agents in new wars, their intentions toward humanitarian action, coupled with their capacities to inflict violence, are probably the most accurate ways to measure their most critical implications for aid agencies. Does an NSA present a threat to access or assistance? The destructive behavior of "spoilers" dispels the "romance" of any idealistic notions of the private sector.[47] As stakeholders in complex emergencies, the interest of spoilers in humanitarian assistance derives from its potential to perpetuate rather than mitigate profitable violence. After a negotiated peace, the onset of reconciliation, the establishment of the rule of law, and—worst of all—the prospect of a peacetime economy, perennial spoilers risk being marginalized. "Make war, not love" is their slogan.

Once a crisis has subsided, resources brought from outside a war zone by aid agencies—goods, jobs, rents, and contracts—can no longer be manipulated to help sustain patronage relations with supporters, and soldiers and racketeers who committed serious crimes cannot return to their communities. They often disdain liberal values and operate without reference to or even knowledge of international conventions on the rights of civilians in war, much less broader human rights agreements.[48] Protracted wars and state collapse do, as William Reno points out, "give a comparative advantage to sociopaths."[49]

At the same time, the crises that are engendered are not exclusively populated by misanthropic gunmen whose behavior and interests can be dismissed merely as maniacal or beyond calculation. Many spoilers pursue interests that appear "irrational" to outsiders when measured by the aggregate welfare of afflicted societies. However, the narrower calculations by those who benefit directly (employment, booty, and power) make such wars quite "rational."

Although NSAs are neither historically new nor completely absent from the margins of major interstate armed conflicts, their presence and scale as political authorities and primary belligerents, coupled with their influencing the inability of agencies to carry out humanitarian action, are most certainly new. Three general groups of NSAs—many of whom are a composite—are of particular concern for their ability to spoil what otherwise passes for laudable humanitarian action. The first consists of armed belligerents, whether they be local militias, paramilitary groups, former military, or the followers of warlords. All pose the potential to inflict greater suffering and prevent humanitarian access.[50] In the wake of dissipating state authority, the monopoly on violence is broken and the use of force largely privatized. The key characteristic of this group of NSAs is the autonomy of their military and political power, which is tied to society but not subordinate to it. As John MacKinlay notes, "like the baron and the chieftan, [the warlord's] power rested on the possession of military forces, he occupied territory in a strictly predatory manner and his social activities seldom enriched the lives of civilian families in his grasp. Warlordism involved the use of military force in a narrower, more selfish way than the baron or the chieftan. It implied protectionism, racketeering and the interception of revenues, without any mitigating cultural or religious commitments."[51] In brief, armed groups have a political base that rests firmly on persistent insecurity, fear, and division. They seek not to establish legitimate political order but to provide protection primarily for security or political payoffs and economic gains.

The second group is composed of those whose primary economic interests are served by violence. Ranging from mafia, criminal gangs, and illegal business to opportunistic profiteers, they may seek to sustain war and a humanitarian crisis, which promote an economic atmosphere conducive to their own profits.[52] In addition to such usual predatory economic practices as driving up food prices and manipulating markets, humanitarian emergencies produce a class of war merchants whose activities include killing competitors; pirating; and trafficking in arms, people, drugs, and toxic wastes. For instance, agencies often encounter problems tendering bids for transportation and money exchange with criminals who are well positioned to reap the fruits of aid.

The third group of spoilers consists of hybrids that blend military and economic agendas, including mercenaries and a distinctly new creation, private military companies (PMCs).[53] They too can spoil aid operations. Mercenaries tend to be less formalized and more of a danger than PMCs. Fitting the profile of mercenaries are such notorious characters as former British soldier "Mad Mike" Hoare and ex-French military man Bob Denard, both of whom essentially fought for the highest bidder in various African wars. PMCs, on the other hand, seek official acknowledgment, if not sanction, from political authorities and function as legal business entities. The most commonly cited example of PMCs is that of Executive Outcomes (EO), a firm that formed following the demobilization of soldiers in the late 1980s and early 1990s, when the Cold War ended and many foreign forces were withdrawn from proxy conflicts in Africa. EO arrived on the scene and immediately began to turn heads with its ability to defeat dangerous guerilla groups and bring security to war-torn areas.[54] In Angola from 1993 to 1995, EO deployed only five hundred men and yet basically routed the União Nacional para a Independêcia Total de Angola (UNITA).[55] Even more striking was in Sierra Leone in 1995, when two hundred military contractors from EO pushed ten thousand rebels out of the capital and back into more remote regions of the country.[56]

With greater military resources seeking private employment and governments and businesses in need of security, PMCs such as EO found a solid niche in the strategic doctrine of feeble states and in the international markets for military services. Indeed, over the course of the 1990s expenditures on global military service skyrocketed and by some estimates reached $100 billion per year.[57] Although the growth of the private military sector is usually correlated to increasing concerns over security—in fact, neoliberal pressures and globalization also spurred development of this industry. PMCs officially work on behalf of other actors, and when they pose an obstacle to agencies, it is usually their contracting agent that is ultimately crucial in propelling conflict.[58]

Further complicating our understanding of spoilers is their possible opposition to humanitarian action and their complex dual role as victims and agents of war. Whereas some are viscerally opposed to humanitarian action, others are more expedient. It is not always clear whether an NSA has crossed a point of no return and is intrinsically a spoiler as opposed to simply being opportunistic and capable of responding to altered incentives.[59] That is to say, some spoilers are certain beyond a doubt while others take a more tactical approach and, depending on the situation, are open to possible co-optation.

Moreover, some spoilers both spur and suffer from armed conflict. Often, a NSA assumes the role of gatekeeper to victims in a geographically defined area (even a refugee camp), but on occasion such spoilers themselves become victims. In these situations humanitarians frequently work with people who have been forcibly moved to refugee or IDP camps, despite the fact that many such victims may either be loyal supporters of a government or an armed political faction or, indeed, be partisans. The manipulation of outside humanitarians in the camps of what was then eastern Zaire in the mid-1990s tragically illustrates this point.

Aristide Zolberg, Astri Suhrke, and Sergio Aguayo have labeled externally displaced populations who have engaged in organized violence "refugee-warriors."[60] However, not everyone who suffers actually crosses a border (e.g., IDPs), and war is executed and sustained by a wider variety of actors than just those who perform frontline acts of violence. In many new wars those who have received aid have used it to make war. For example, during the Soviet occupation of Afghanistan, refugees were not manipulated or coerced into joining the resistance; they willingly supported militarization of the camps.[61] Perhaps the term "belligerent-victims" would be more accurate in some contemporary cases.

An essential bottom line for humanitarians should be not only whom to help and how, but how to do so in a way that does not propel war. Perhaps the most noteworthy illustration of the need to understand "belligerent-victims" is the phenomenon of "child soldiers," who tend to be coerced and conditioned to participate in war or activities that support conflict.[62] Some child soldiers are like other combatants, subject to an incentive structure that promotes participating in organized violence under the direction of strong leadership. But child soldiers also present additional challenges already affecting their adult counterparts because often they lack useful skills, such as farming, and may have lingering physical, mental, and emotional wounds. Hence, the challenge is not "reintegration" into an existing society but integration into a society that has to be created, perhaps from scratch.

If child soldiers were the only aberration in the provision of aid, humanitarians could be forgiven for their willingness to rely on previous standard operating procedures and principles. Unfortunately, child soldiers are only one part of a larger pattern of problematic actors in new wars.

ILLEGAL ECONOMIES, PLUNDER, AND AID: NEW ECONOMIES

The third salient characteristic of contemporary armed conflicts concerns idiosyncratic economies in war zones. Earlier we note Clausewitz's celebrated dictum that war is the continuation of politics, but David Keen goes as far as to argue that economic agendas in today's warfare have become so pronounced that "war may be the continuation of *economics* by other means."[63] Economic conditions and structures of new wars allow some to pursue war and many to profit from it. While states are failing or rebuilding, unusual economic opportunities abound. Local balance sheets have always been important in fueling war, and certainly, captains of industry from Krupp to Boeing to Halliburton have been more than willing to help the national cause and simultaneously enrich corporate and personal coffers.

But in contemporary wars, the local economy plays a quantitatively and qualitatively different role than that previously seen.[64] The society as a whole suffers while isolated individuals benefit. With cash, arms, and power flowing into their hands, the leaders of warring factions have no incentive to proceed to the bargaining table; their interests are served by prolonging war.

Some suggest that economic interests catalyze violence, while others contend that economic agendas are an add-on—that is, more a complicating than a propelling factor. States traditionally included calculations of long-term wealth in pursuing war (i.e., their economic prospects in military crises). Indeed, historically, state bureaucracies have generated revenues for war making through "extraction" of resources from their citizens. The location of taxation can in many ways prove to be as much a commentary on the nature of war making by states as it is on the political economy of the state. States that rely on internal taxation tend to deploy their military forces abroad to defend state interests. However, states that rely on taxing revenue earned through exports (e.g., customs, duty) usually have to use their military power internally to crackdown on internal opposition.

In the new wars, NSAs similarly often apply their military capacities to suit their economic interests, but their time frame is much shorter, and their economic interests are certainly more parochial. Accordingly, instead of the euphemistic designation of "extraction" that states use only with reference to themselves or other states, this behavior—borrowing from the terminology of analysts of Mafioso groups—warrants the moniker "extortion." Whereas earlier war was driven primarily by national or imperial conflicts with a long-run perspective, in new wars unusual economic opportunities and predatory practices with immediate payoffs are pervasive. Whatever their explanatory power, the role of rapacious economic interests in driving war and hindering humanitarian efforts has grown dramatically in three ways: a market for protection services, illicit and destabilizing commerce, and aid manipulation.

A prominent form of predation is the sale of protection. Whether called "extraction" or "extortion," the process is fundamentally the same for military or paramilitary elements that provide security to commercial agents.[65] A related but different phenomenon involves instances where military forces *are* private commercial interests—some informal irregulars (mercenaries) and others acting as formal business institutions (PMCs). As the aforementioned illustrations of various operations carried out by EO demonstrate, the extent to which PMCs are predatory or essential providers of protection in insecure environments can only be determined case by case.

In conventional international relations theory, the control of territory is essential to maintaining political authority, but the political economies of the new wars impel actors to concentrate their energies on controlling commerce in a few resources, such as diamonds or tropical timber. Much of spoiler behavior—before, during, and oftentimes after wars—can be explained by their economic interests, with "taxing" for protection a prime tactic for sustaining and enriching local actors. Global demand for many commodities also contributes to this incentive structure by providing an outlet for these goods and by stimulating markets for military services.

Commercial activity in many of today's wars is premised on the continuation of violent conflict or is used to fuel it, or both. In the first instance, profiteers manipulate markets to benefit from the high prices common to war economies.[66] Necessities such as grain and gasoline are "priced" to account for the expense of production and distribution but have also been inflated to enrich speculators and intermediaries ("middlemen"). A second form of criminal, distorting, and debilitating commerce is often the product of the exploitation of natural resources by private interests. Sometimes the formal economy of the state is manipulated for private gain—an "economy of plunder."[67] At other times criminals, especially those operating as part of transnational networks, foster the erosion of state power to prevent regulation and taxation.[68] The opportunities for personal rewards and a means to finance war lead many NSAs to focus their efforts on securing access to natural resources, which frequently results in still more violence and heightened humanitarian crises.

Despite the obvious economic advantages inherent to a rich resource endowment, the armed conflicts that occur as a result of struggles over their control—what Michael Klare calls "resource wars"—may be fundamentally disadvantageous.[69] Indra de Soysa uses the expression "resource curse" to describe how abundant mineral wealth correlates with a greater frequency of economically based conflicts.[70] Examples of natural resources that fall into this schema and have financed the newest generation of wars include minerals (diamonds, cobalt, bauxite, gold, and oil) and agricultural commodities (tropical hardwoods and certain fruits and vegetables).[71] In an oft-cited World Bank study of conflicts from 1960 to 1995 that involved "natural resource predation," Paul Collier found that countries with such "lootable resources" were four times more likely to experience war than were those without them.[72]

Humanitarians provide additional elements for local economic analysis because emergency aid itself has inadvertently contributed to fueling war. Not only does aid allow belligerents to pursue armed conflict by saving resources that they would otherwise spend on food or medicine, but its distributional impacts can also provoke violence.[73] Wars foster scarcity, and humanitarian assistance is a prize that can easily become an object for struggle among war's agents and victims. Illustrations span the last few decades. In the late 1970s and 1980s armed factions routinely vied for control of humanitarian assistance in refugee camps along the border between Cambodia and Thailand, a pattern repeated again in camps straddling the Afghanistan-Pakistan border.[74] In the early 1990s, belligerents in Sudan (both government forces and the Sudan People's Liberation Army) used a variety of tactics to manipulate or monopolize aid—diverting aid, raiding staging areas, and feigning being noncombatants.[75]

Charity always seems worthwhile. But food, clothing, and shelter are fungible—that is, they can be used interchangeably with some of the resources used to fuel soldiers and war and therefore free other economic resources that can then be applied directly to the war effort rather than to keeping noncombatants alive. Moreover, humanitarian aid can be used to curry favor among supporters because elites receive credit for ensuring international assistance.

Bogus local nonprofit counterparts are widespread and can be little more than institutional fronts for rogues. They are often created to satisfy the political correctness of "local control." But what has been cynically dubbed a "Doxfam" (donor-created Oxfam) or an "UNONGO" (UN-organized NGO), for instance, is not a genuine local product but rather a local attempt to "capture" agencies, monopolize jobs and resources, and prevent assistance from being distributed to adversaries. In the worst cases, external agencies inadvertently become a virtual logistical support unit for militias. Their local armed guards—the most notorious example being the "technicals" in Somalia who were employed by many agencies—may simply be local militiamen on foreign payroll.

"Aid economies" must be large enough to warrant being a point of violent contention despite the other costs of waging war. Also, aid economies do not require high levels of violence to prosper; the threats posed by unstable pre- and postwar conditions are sufficient to keep aid flowing and profits booming.

The most compelling analysis of how aid economies interweave with the dynamics of war is Peter Uvin's dramatic treatment of the runup to the Rwandan genocide.[76] He explores the contradiction between a country considered to be a "model" of development and the unspeakable tragedy of 1994. Development assistance in this instance ignored and then reinforced the characteristics of structural violence within the local economy that permitted Hutu extremism.

Hoarding and parallel markets are another way to distort relief efforts by undermining local producers. For instance, in Afghanistan, the economic power of Pashtuns is based on their connections to markets in Pakistan, which have tilted the benefits of assistance and reconstruction in their favor.[77]

War can benefit state or NSA authorities, or both. States that host humanitarian disasters are normally the conduit for international financial and food assistance.[78] Government authorities can then manipulate the allocation of these resources, thereby helping advance their own agendas—overt or hidden. Belligerent NSAs operate in a similar fashion although they tend to profit most politically and economically when states are weakened or crumbling.

However, state failure can create onerous expenses of a different type for war profiteers. For instance, a lack of a central government may mean fewer controls and tolls, which benefit spoilers, but it can also mean a lack of rule of law and security that results in costs that reduce the bottom line for spoilers. Increased economic opportunities are correlated with diminished governance by the state, up to a point; but complete collapse of central authority can alter the equation substantially for the worse, even for thugs.

In short, the new wars present several overt and direct means of enrichment (protection and plunder) at the same time that they also hold the prospect of infusing fungible resources (an aid economy). Humanitarians simply cannot continue "business" as usual, even their own.

THE PREVALENCE OF CIVILIAN CASUALTIES: NEW TARGETS AND VICTIMS

Since the inception of the international humanitarian system the lengths that military force has been used against civilian populations has varied considerably. At the most extreme is the intentional killing of civilian populations with genocide—the attempt to destroy ethnic populations—being the worst variant of these bloody strategies. But extermination of noncombatants is not the only extreme strategy, because forcibly moving them can accomplish many of the same heinous aims. On a lesser but still horrifying scale, militaries have committed acts of violence to coerce populations to flee and relocate outside the territorial bounds of the state. As history demonstrates, it is often the connection that military forces have with political authorities that may lead to the targeting of civilians. In the new wars of the 1990s, NSAs often operate without concern to humanitarian responsibilities and seek to target civilian populations, thereby producing an elevation in the proportion of civilians killed in combat as well as the toll from less-direct but war-related fatalities (e.g., famine). Tragically and ironically, although humanitarians have made progress in garnering greater protection for civilians through legal means and in some instances more robust operational tools, there appears to be an inverse correlation between the institutionalization of the law of war among states and the growth in violations perpetrated by NSAs in new wars.

Although combatants were the main casualties of armed conflicts, civilians have constituted an increasing percentage in this century, currently approaching 90 percent or more. Estimates vary, but they all seem to point in the same alarming direction. The Carnegie Commission found that 90 percent of those killed in new wars of the 1990s were civilians, while only 15 percent comprised such fatalities at the turn of the century.[79] Mary Kaldor claims that civilians account for 10 percent to 15 percent of total combat deaths at the start of the twentieth century, 50 percent during World War II (falling at the middle of the century), and 80 percent in new wars in the late 1990s.[80] Holsti's data depict a slightly sharper increase— only 5 percent of casualties were civilians in World War I, 50 percent in World War II, and in recent wars near 90 percent.[81] Virgil Hawkins goes even further in that civilians now constitute 95 percent.[82] While researchers may debate the actual motives for targeting civilians, this painful reality is a perennial in today's war zones.[83] The "total war" model associated with World War I, whose "totality" was predicated on the range of weapons permitted to be used against other soldiers, was greatly surpassed in overall fatalities by wars that were all encompassing in the sense of routinely targeting civilians.

Historically, there have always been episodes in which civilians were targeted, but changes that place civilians at the center of military strategy have become widespread in the 1990s. As noted earlier, other episodes of the late nineteenth and the early twentieth century showcase features of what are now called "new wars," including the intentional targeting of civilians. However, the shift from military to civilian casualties took on significantly greater proportions during the buildup to World War II. In World War I (1914–1918), 8.3 million soldiers and 8 million civilians were killed;[84] but the approximate 1:1 ratio of civilians to combatant casualties overall did not last, with an increasing number of civilians dying not just as the result of war but specifically in combat. Despite fundamentally being an interstate conflict, World War II (1939–1945) brought huge numbers of civilians into the fray—the most egregious examples of which being the German air blitz of London, the Allied firebombing of Dresden, atrocities perpetrated in Japanese-occupied Nanking and Manila, the Holocaust inflicted against European Jewry and other minorities, and ultimately the use of the atomic bomb by the United States against the residents of Hiroshima and Nagasaki. In the end, twenty-three million soldiers and over fifty-seven million civilians lost their lives.[85]

Technology accounts for some of this shift because the ability to inflict greater damage and casualties from a greater distance increased the range of possible targets. That is to say, technology has also facilitated a change in strategy that flies in the face of IHL and humanitarian action—namely, targeting civilians. However, as discussed later, technology has also been used by some of the advanced militaries to limit civilian casualties, particularly in urban areas. But only a few states possess "smart" munitions, and even then there have been criticisms that the technology is still not "smart" enough—consider the North Atlantic Treaty Organization (NATO) in Sarajevo and, more recently, the United States in Baghdad. On the whole, civilians in the new wars have more likely suffered from advances in military technology than benefited.

Civilians were always viewed as an asset in warfare, but since the late nineteenth century, and more so with the passing of the 1949 Geneva Conventions, they have been considered assets more political than military. But the blurring politics and military in the new wars contribute to the direct targeting of civilians. They have often been accorded prominence in the overall strategies for winning wars and, in the 1960s, became part and parcel of military strategies, as typified by U.S. "pacification" projects, "strategic hamlets," and other attempts to win "hearts and minds" in Vietnam. At the same time, the use of civilians as cover by Vietnamese guerillas meant that distinctions between combatant and noncombatant were almost completely lost. Norms associated with the interstate model of war had posited that civilians contribute to the fighting capacity of the enemy but were seen as fundamentally secondary to the threat posed by enemy military forces.

Entering the period of the new wars, civilians played an even more prominent position and often as frontline combat casualties. As noted in chapter 2, intentionally displacing or driving out minorities was not unheard of historically. However, in the post–World War II period, this practice was extremely rare, with the notable exceptions of riots and population transfers that resulted in the division of India and Pakistan in 1947 and the violence that displaced Palestinians and produced Israel's consolidation as a state in 1947–1948. The Balkan wars of the 1990s tragically illustrate that the "cleansing" of noncombatant populations from a defined territory has become a primary aim in the new wars. Shock met the first reporting of gaunt European faces behind barbed wire in 1992. That, however, is no longer the case. The string of reports from the UN secretary-general on the protection of civilians epitomizes the growing prevalence of civilian victims—as the 2001 report put it, "affected civilians tend not to be the incidental victims of new irregular forces; they are their principal object."[86] International advisory groups such as the Carnegie Commission on the Prevention of Deadly Conflict and the International Commission on Intervention and State Sovereignty reach similar conclusions.[87] Overall, the trends of new wars suggest that innocents have become targets, shields, resources, and objectives.[88]

Lastly, the nature of civilian casualties has changed in a definitional sense. Previously, the idea of victims was tied to the dynamics of interstate war, but with the geographical boundaries of states being less meaningful in determining victimization, another reflection of systematic structural shortcomings becomes evident. The spectacle of IDPs, or those who remain within their own countries rather than cross a border because of a legitimate fear of persecution, was formerly a blemish but has become a major scar on the international humanitarian system. IDPs are refugees in everything except name.[89] Indeed, the fact that they do not fall under international jurisdiction and have no formal statute or UN agency on their side may make them worse off than refugees.[90]

The tally of refugees declined over the 1990s, but IDP numbers soared. The number of refugees at the beginning of the twenty-first century was generally agreed to have shrunk to below that of fifteen million;[91] but the number of IDPs is considerably larger and at least twice the number— depending on who is counting, from twenty million to thirty million displaced by wars and a similar number by natural disasters. When IDP data were first gathered in 1982, there were only a million, at which time there were about 10.5 million refugees. This stream of data suggests that IDPs increasingly constitute a larger share of displaced populations and merely looking at the numbers of refugees as a measure of humanitarian needs can be misleading.

Refugees and IDPs are both civilians for the most part, but the latter do not have the same legal and institutional infrastructure, which was designed to help the victims of interstate wars. This historical anomaly is a concrete indication of the lag in thinking about the nature of suffering from most contemporary wars; it also reflects a lack of institutional design to address the main victims of the new wars.[92]

THE REVOLUTION IN MILITARY AFFAIRS: NEW TECHNOLOGIES

and of CW→ no ideological affinities

The fifth characteristic concerns the means of war and new technologies available to states and nonstates alike. The resources mustered to fight wars often draw on the most advanced technology of their times but not always. This section sketches the consequences of ongoing "revolution in military affairs" (RMA) for the new wars.

There have been several major revolutions in military affairs, or transformations in the organization of armed forces and the execution of war. The move from bronze to iron and the spread of the bow and catapult involved not only an increased ability to produce violence but also reciprocal social changes. The artillery revolution of the fourteenth to fifteenth centuries assisted the centralization of political authority into states. Contemporary military technologies still provide a gauge of the quality of armed conflict and possibilities for international order.

A view of military technology of the twentieth century shows three levels of actors: a top echelon comprising a handful of the most powerful states; a second tier consisting of those middle- and small-power states with competent national militaries; and a bottom rung of low-tech fighters relying exclusively on small arms. Military logic dictates shaping the battlefield to gain strategic and tactical advantages, and the conditions of interstate war dictate using the latest technologies and concentrating forces to hammer enemy soldiers. But the new wars favor unconventional, often asymmetric approaches. Our analysis therefore suggests that a fourth and motley stratum is likely to emerge—an actor from the third level with access to weapons derived from the first.

In the late twentieth century the application of the most sophisticated technology to military matters was limited to a few states actively capable of financing the latest RMA. Derived primarily from the U.S. experience in the Persian Gulf War and NATO's operations in Kosovo, the bases of RMA in the 1990s were improvements in the informational aspects of war, finding targets and hitting them with greater accuracy.

In terms of framing humanitarian issues, several aspects of this RMA are relevant. The first is that the improvements in destructive power have increased the scale of humanitarian challenges. More firepower for the military often means more death and displacement to populations for aid agencies. Even in cases where civilians are not the intended targets, the use of more lethal weapons can increase so-called collateral damage and civilian casualties or such damage to infrastructure that survivors will suffer. Furthermore, the proliferation of nuclear, biological, and chemical weapons technology—weapons of mass destruction (WMD)—represents an alarming possible future challenge for humanitarian action. Humanitarian agencies have no experience with WMD, but the diffusion of such technology and weapons intimates a looming nightmare.

A second historical change that accompanies RMA is the increase in the distance over which violence is projected. War has long ceased to be exclusively a hand-to-hand affair, and many technological improvements have emphasized creating space as a buffer from retaliatory strikes. Gunpowder and air power continue a trend that began with fabricating longer blades and placing them on longer poles. From the perspective of advanced national militaries, the territorial range of their power has expanded greatly. Since 1950, "air craft range has quadrupled from 2,000 to 8,000 miles, aircraft speed has increase from 500 miles to 2,000, maximum aircraft payload has quintupled from 10 tons to 50 tons. Navigation precision has fallen from a tenth of a mile to a thousandth of a mile, and radar resolution and range have improved by ten thousand-fold and five hundred-fold respectively."[93] For militaries the trade-off is between projecting force in a way that keeps their own soldiers at a safe distance and losing immediate oversight and control over who is victimized by the use of force.

The implications of RMA for the new wars are unclear, as are those of any sort of high technology. Given that many major powers are not directly fighting in new wars, these essentially intrastate conflicts do not reflect RMA or deploy the most advanced weaponry, at least not yet. The majority, if not the entirety, of actors in the new wars are of the nonstate variety, and thus their military capacities are ordinarily based on rather low-tech hardware that is readily available and cheap. The military forces of NSAs tend to practice asymmetric warfare—following strategies that favor relatively weak military units, such as targeted hit-and-run operations by guerillas against large, heavy, widely dispersed forces. Small arms are the backbone of militarized NSAs, and their availability has increased the ability of NSAs to destabilize weak states, set off humanitarian crises, and obstruct the delivery of assistance and protection. Furthermore, the will to violence is often a more essential factor than that of technological sophistication—the bloodiest and most rapid of recent humanitarian crises was carried out by the machete-wielding extremist Hutu militias of Rwanda, who killed over eight hundred thousand during an eight-week rampage beginning in early April 1994.

The spread of advanced weapons technologies is just beginning to penetrate the logic and practice of the new wars. The amalgamation of Kalshinakovs and cellular phones underpins the feasibility for smaller, less-formalized, and very deadly military units to wreak havoc. Again, the lesson for humanitarians is to keep abreast of developments that circumscribe their ability to provide aid and determine who is in their care.

WINDOWS ON WAR: NEW MEDIA POWER

Visibility can be instrumental in shaping how war is viewed; as a result, media tools are part of the arsenal of new wars. Among both high-technology and low- to no-tech actors, information management is critical to shaping the political and military battlefields. In describing war or particular wars, how the media portrays the rationality and violence of the conflict can influence the strategies and resources available to belligerents.

The dissemination of IHL or knowledge of humanitarian legal responsibilities in war was an important building block in developing and expanding compliance by belligerents. When states were the sole political authorities, with their monopoly on violence intact, negotiations for acceptable conduct in war centered on the leadership of states who were charged with ensuring that their military forces adhered to IHL. However, the media has also played a considerable role in providing information or images of war, and although the media sometimes catered to state interests, other times it offered a distinctly different picture. In the 1990s the conduct of war tended not to be informed by IHL; rather, the media provided inflammatory images.

Media resources for low-technology belligerents may be limited, but the creation and dissemination of hostile rhetoric help grease the wheels of some wars. Not only is propaganda the product of high-technology and highly centralized state authorities like Nazi Germany, but it can also emerge from less technologically and organizationally sophisticated NSAs. Exemplifying this element in some new wars was the use of hate radio in Rwanda to drum up support for genocide at the community level.[94] Official media broadcasts and telecasts were part of the arsenal in Belgrade and Zagreb, for instance, in mobilizing nationalism in the respective Serb and Croat populations.

In high-technology states, especially the United States, improvements in military technology that are magnified by media coverage may create an impression that victory will be quick, clean, and easy. The mid-1970s witnessed the demoralized condition of the U.S. public's unwillingness to support military actions abroad following the ignominious U.S. withdrawal from Southeast Asia—a media scenario better known as the "Vietnam syndrome," which lingered until the first Gulf War, in 1991. The 1993 *Black Hawk Down* scene of U.S. soldiers dragged through the streets of Mogadishu during an ill-fated attempt to arrest Somali warlord Mohammed Aideed temporarily revived this syndrome. Following such traumatic events reshaping perceptions is important to gaining support for the use of force. If violence is more precise and intimidation engenders victory more quickly with fewer casualties, then the viewing public may be more inclined to accept the use of force.[95] Images of laser- and satellite-guided munitions and pictures, such as the "highway of death" in the first Gulf War, may help to convince citizens in the top tier of states that war can be fought at a very low cost on their end. Hence, humanitarians should get a handle on the media, or they will underestimate problems in the field and at home. When combined with the other five elements of the new wars, analysts and practitioners confront a distinctive new set of challenges.

"NEW WARS" IN HISTORICAL PERSPECTIVE

This chapter has analyzed the elements of the new wars in detail, but it is important for one to place them in the context of the long-term historical evolution of war in order to understand more precisely the extent of change and the sources of humanitarian challenges. Here we briefly connect cases to prototypical elements and highlight what the elements of new wars illustrate about broad historical trends and processes (i.e., systemwide change).

New wars are internal armed conflicts primarily waged by NSAs who subside on illicit and parasitic economic behavior, use small arms and other low-technology hardware, largely prey on and victimize civilians, and are media savvy. Instances of such have ignited and cooled in almost every region of the world. Decolonization and postcolonial struggles accounted for some of the strife in the decades following World War II. However, since the end of the Cold War, starting in 1989, there has been significant upswing in the occurrence of new wars. Table 3.2 provides thumbnail sketches of selected cases and their textbook elements. Many other cases could be analyzed in a similar fashion to underline the features of new wars. This collection is clearly illustrative and not exhaustive. Yet both the simultaneity of elements and their magnitude suggest such unusual challenges as to constitute a distinctly new kind of theater for humanitarian action.

We are principally concerned with the development of the international humanitarian system and the parsing of the environmental contexts in which humanitarian agencies deploy field operations. They are imperative to framing the practices and challenges of the "new humanitarianisms." The elements of the new wars show the nuts-and-bolts aspects of the period, but they also express two of our major trends.

The first is that of *politicization.* Although some might confuse the lack of states and publicly espoused political agendas as suggesting a dearth of politics, this is far from the case. The politicization present in new wars takes the form of rebelling against the predominance of states and may be indicative of a fragmentation in global governance. The devolution of political order within states and the flourishing of nonstate authorities within areas hosting new wars are part of a larger historical shift from militarized disputes between the clearly distinguished armed forces of states, an area of international relations subject to an array of established norms and organizations.

The emergence and growing significance of NSAs is political, but the *privatization* of warfare is also intimately tied to *marketization,* the second trend. Economic agendas and interests have perennially shaped the evolution of war, but, coupled with a strong private and a large informal sector, business and profit-motivated actors have thrived in new ways. Plunder and other illicit activities have always existed but never with the outlets and markets offered by the global economy at the dawn of the twenty-first century.

These trends and the other major ones identified in chapter 1 are echoed in the "new humanitarianisms" but encompass not only the battlefield in which agencies operate but also the boardrooms in which debates and donors are center stage. It is to these challenges, those born of responding to the new wars, that we now turn.

Table 3.2. Elements of "New Wars"

	Locus	Agents	Economics	Targets and Victims	Technologies	Media Tools
Somalia	Internal civil war	Militias, warlords, U.S.	No state taxes; extortion; aid economy	Civilians	Small arms	—
Liberia	Internal but crosses borders	Warlords	Plunder	Civilians	Small arms	—
Sierra Leone	Internal but crosses borders	Militaries, rebels, UN, mercenaries, militias	Plunder	Military personnel, many civilians	Small arms	—
Bosnia	Breakdown of state led to civil war	Yugoslav military, Serb militia, Bosnian militia	Aid economies	Military personnel, mostly civilians	Some heavy weapons, mostly small arms	Widespread propaganda
Rwanda	Civil war with genocide, cross-border violence by neighbors	Tutsi rebels, Hutu militias	Plunder in Congo; aid economies	Mostly civilians	Small arms, machetes	Hate radio
Kosovo	Secessionist region, part of civil war	Yugoslav military, Serb militia, Kosovar guerillas, NATO	Trafficking in illicit goods financed Albanian rebels	Military personnel, a large proportion of civilians	Heavy weapons (Serbs), small arms (guerillas), hi-tech munitions (NATO)	Serbian media

4

"New Humanitarianisms"

81

The previous chapter emphasizes the problems created by war, and here we study the particular problems associated with responses by humanitarians. The new wars—sometimes with only a few of the prototypical components but often with the cumulative impact of several—have spawned distinct breeds of humanitarian crises, and several strains of humanitarianism have emerged in response. This chapter examines developments over the post–Cold War era in order to determine the extent to which the international humanitarian system corresponds to current predicaments or remains outfitted to address the challenges of an earlier period. To what extent do the salves of our times soothe the wounds of today's swords? The analysis teases out what appears new in many humanitarian responses—legal, institutional, and operational—and spotlights what appears to be lacking.

Violence has few consistencies, so humanitarian responses should thus reveal little if any pattern. A "humanitarian pluralism" is required, which, for us, means that different approaches may be necessary to different wars or even to different phases or geographical parts of the same war. Nonetheless, we are not setting up a straw man: the mantra of traditional humanitarians remains "more of the same." Indeed, in Stockholm in June 2003 at a meeting to pursue "good humanitarian donorship," "donor governments agreed that humanitarian action should be guided by the principles of humanity, impartiality, neutrality and independence." But then shortly thereafter, they promptly disagreed about the operational and political meanings of trying to respect the traditional terms.[1] The challenges to the effective delivery of humanitarian services posed by the divergence in agency perspectives and codes are discussed in greater detail in later chapters, but here we generalize about the range of efforts by the international humanitarian system in the 1990s.

The cases analyzed in this chapter underline the argument that the off-the-rack humanitarian suit (neutrality, impartiality, and consent) may fit some but certainly not all contemporary armed conflicts. Furthermore, this ideal type does not reflect how some agencies have tailored their principles and actions. Hence, to assess the whole spectrum of efforts, we need to chart the elements of humanitarian action in the 1990s—a look at the host of responses to new wars that set the stage for a host of "new humanitarianisms." As we did in the previous chapter, we cease using scare quotes around *new humanitarianisms* because readers are now familiar with our particular use of this term. This chapter is mostly descriptive, but the material informs the prescriptions in chapter 7.

SO, WHAT'S NEW?

The horrors of war (the dead, disabled, and displaced) are constants, as are the demands placed on agencies (for resources and access), but the conditions under which they operate have changed, in many cases sharply. The fusion of many elements of new wars in a single context certainly means that time-tested recipes no longer necessarily produce the desired results.

Nothing that we have written here should in any way cast aspersions on the members of the honorable humanitarian profession who have worked heroically over almost a century and a half to succor those suffering from warfare. Rather, our purpose is to indicate how the elements of new wars can react and ultimately distort traditionally cast humanitarian efforts and feed into new humanitarianisms. Not only did the new wars produce multiple humanitarian crises of a magnitude and simultaneity that dwarfed those of previous generations, but they also led to debates among humanitarians about the purposes and practices of their collective endeavors. Earlier humanitarian agencies had faced some of the elements found in the new wars. For example, the confusion of humanitarian responsibility and access in internal as opposed to international wars was seen in the U.S. Civil War (1861–1865). The 1949 extensions of the Geneva Conventions included noninternational armed conflict and considered those in unrecognized governments or in resistance movements as being subject to restrictions and protections. In 1967 with Biafra engaged in a secessionist struggle against Nigeria, the international humanitarian system experienced the first thrust of the new humanitarianisms, a new approach taken as the result of assistance being misused.

The plethora of wars in the 1990s hastened the extent to which previous orientations in the international humanitarian system were dated with respect to the challenges at hand. The performance of agencies created anxiety and doubts among many humanitarians. A strong advocate for humanitarian action, David Rieff, characterized the responses of the 1990s as putting "humanitarianism in crisis."[2] This chapter depicts disconnects between traditional principles and operational contexts of the new wars and, as a result, the span of humanitarian actions mounted over this duration. In the next chapter we more fully parse how the character of new humanitarianisms has revealed long-festering collective action problems.

A helpful starting point is to recognize the formidable role of aid agencies in war-torn societies. First, the scale of human suffering and needs ranges from being enormous to being overwhelming. During the first decade of the post–Cold War era (1989–1999) wars, mainly civil but some international, killed over 1.5 million people and wounded many more.[3] More than the numbers of fatalities and wounded, the number of people forcibly displaced by armed conflicts perhaps gives a better indication of how ample the challenge is for those coming to the rescue. Though the numbers of displaced had decreased somewhat at the end of the 1990s, approximately 1 in 135 of the world's population required international assistance and protection as a result of wars at the peak of the flows. The sheer volume of these numbers represents a staggering burden on humanitarians, not to mention that on war-torn societies themselves. And the depressing numbers have continued growing in the first half of the next decade—indeed, since 1998 deaths in the Democratic Republic of the Congo (DRC) alone approached four million.[4]

Second, with states weakening or collapsing, outside agencies became the main lifeline for many distressed populations,[5] which sometimes replaced traditional structures and coping capacities, hardly a sustainable proposition. As the need for humanitarian services grew, established institutions increased in size and scope; and new agencies sprang up with each new crisis. The unprecedented growth in the resources and activities of IGOs and NGOs can be gleaned in the fivefold increase in humanitarian aid in the first post–Cold War decade, from about $800 million in 1989 to some $4.4 billion in 1999.[6]

Moreover, the system is increasingly diverse in its approaches. Experiences with aid deliveries and their negative impacts led to diverse operating principles.[7] Variations have always existed in interpreting how best to operationalize humanitarian values, but they have become far more prevalent in recent years as both crises and institutions have proliferated.

The fractures in the international humanitarian community are apparent to many observers. Abby Stoddard, for instance, has distinguished between three strands of humanitarianism—religion based (those who understand humanitarianism as part of religious values), "Dunantist" (those advocating a humanitarianism distinct from state interests), and "Wilsonian" (those who see a bond between humanitarianism and U.S. foreign policy).[8]

The basic divide in the late twentieth century centered on the political implications of humanitarians' work, as depicted in figure 4.1.[9] On one

Figure 4.1. Spectrum of Humanitarians and Operational Principles

Classicists		Solidarists
Neutrality	◄──────────────────►	Take sides of selected victims
Impartiality	◄──────────────────►	Skew distribution of resources
Consent	◄──────────────────►	Override sovereignty

side are the "classicists," who continue to uphold the principles of neutrality, impartiality, and consent. On the other are the "solidarists," who emphasize and side with selected victims, publicly confront hostile governments, advocate partisan public policies in donor states, attempt to skew the distribution of aid resources, and ignore on many occasions the sovereignty of states.

For many on this end of the spectrum, humanitarianism no longer is viewed as being "pure," and universal acceptance of neutrality, long a cornerstone of humanitarianism, is seen as being naïve or at least unrealistic. Proponents of this school believe that aid should not be merely palliative and given without regard to political context; rather, it should be ameliorative and address structural problems that foment humanitarian crises in the first place, and it should also be useful in terms of cementing peace processes. According to this logic, good intentions do not mitigate perverse consequences, and the distribution of aid is loaded with economic and political implications that should be reflected in programming decisions.

The founding of Doctors Without Borders is among the earliest and most dramatic instances of the division in the humanitarian community over the politicization of aid. This movement emerged in the war between Nigeria and its Ibo inhabitants in the oil-rich eastern province of Biafra.[10] A group of dissidents led by Bernard Kouchner—later humanitarian minister in several socialist governments in France and the UN's first representative in Bosnia—refused to keep quiet in what they saw was the systematic slaughter of a people. Rather than pretending that working on both sides was essential and that silence was an operational advantage, the dissidents sought to publicize the plight of one side and work to help them. To that end, they took issue with the ICRC's unconditional adherence to principles and formed Médecins sans Frontières in 1971 to signal a clear break from the orthodoxy of the ICRC's Geneva headquarters.

Although the breach between "classicists" and "solidarists" first appeared in the late 1960s, when war was still primarily characterized by Clausewitzian logic, a new and even more controversial cleavage appeared with the advent of perhaps the most politicized strain of humanitarianism—the use of military force for human protection purposes, or "humanitarian intervention." A lack of central political authority in war-torn areas often translates into a severe security problem for humanitarian agencies as well as local populations. In the 1990s, the spread of new wars and massive crises in Africa and the Balkans spawned a hot topic: whether the use of force could legitimately be advocated on humanitarian grounds and, if so, whether its use did more harm than good to war victims.

The bookends around the 1990s were interventions in northern Iraq in 1991 and Kosovo in 1999. The beneficiaries or losers, depending on one's perspective, were both war victims and the humanitarian enterprise. In one sense, such actions represented a victory for humanitarian norms and distressed populations, as both gained a newfound respect in international politics. At the same time, however, violence is bloody and destructive and never produces winners, only varying degrees of relative losers; this generalization applies to humanitarian intervention as well. Indeed, in the introduction to an MSF-commissioned set of essays, Jean-Hervé Bradhol questions to what extent "the recent enthusiasm for ethical and humanitarian values benefited populations exposed to mass violence."[11]

Over the course of the last fifteen years, the goalposts of debates among humanitarians have moved on several occasions. Within the international humanitarian system, the onset of the new wars has spurred calls to rethink consent, impartiality, neutrality, and the use of force.[12] Alongside these developments within the humanitarian community, international norms to protect and assist civilians in war were passionately debated among diplomats.

Figure 4.2 depicts that some humanitarians have espoused a more "muscular" stance and have pushed for military resources to help. For the most part, aid agencies take advantage of military action to secure humanitarian goals but from a somewhat defensive and begrudging posture—as a last resort. In delivering relief and protecting local populations, however, armed aid convoys or security for refugee camps have demonstrated themselves to be vital objectives. Hence, humanitarians on occasion also support the use of force to militarily defeat those who have caused or worsened a crisis. Indeed, some "human rights hawks" go so far as to call for force to overthrow governments that violate the rights of their citizens and to enact a political transformation of afflicted states and societies—a right of humanitarian intervention and regime change.

On the other side of the spectrum, classicists still see military force as the antithesis of true humanitarianism or at least wishful thinking without the presence of substantial national interests to stay the course—which is rarely in evidence. Again, the categories in this figure are fluid

Figure 4.2.   Reconfigured Spectrum of Humanitarians and Operational Principles

Neutral		Political	Enforcement
Neutrality ◄――――►	Take sides of selected victims	◄――►	Use of force
Impartiality ◄―――►	Skew distribution of resources	◄――►	Trusteeship
Consent ◄――――――►	Override sovereignty temporarily	◄――►	Regime change

NOTE: The asymmetric presentation of this figure consciously suggests that neutrality is further away from the political than enforcement is.

and are designed to shed light on the nature of differences and not necessarily to portray the behavior of any agency at a particular moment.

When classicist sentiment did not prevail, the increased use of outside military forces for humanitarian intervention and peace enforcement felled barriers to entry. As a result, in the 1990s many more organizations became involved in active war zones than ever before. Mark Bowden, a senior OCHA official, has somewhat undiplomatically described the "explosion in the number of actors involved in humanitarian response, in particular non-governmental and quasi-governmental organizations and the more recent phenomenon of increasing private sector involvement."[13] During the Cold War there were fewer moving parts, but "the ICRC's and UN's monopoly on humanitarian action was broken by the mid-1990s," according to Joanna Macrae.[14] Being where the action is in war zones became an option for any international NGO, as evidenced by the fact that in the immediate aftermath of the Rwandan genocide there were some two hundred such entities and that in Kosovo during 1999 even more NGOs populated relief activities, which Ian Smillie and Larry Minear have called "the humanitarian free-for-all."[15] Therefore, the use of military means to provide protection not only became an issue of debate and values but had the effect of opening up the aid marketplace to many agencies that had either no presence or one of little significance.

Table 4.1 delineates the contours of the new wars spelled out in chapter 3 along with their implications and responses to date by the international humanitarian system. In spite of some rethinking and evolution, the system remains fundamentally geared to solve, or at least cope with, the types of interstate armed conflicts and crises for which it was created. Although agencies mostly respected the consent of sovereign state authorities, these long-standing rules were broken by instances of cross-border operations, aid that helped only some victims, and advocacy for the use of military force to come to the rescue. Agencies continued to work through governments, and it is important to keep in mind that states were still the primary authorities with humanitarian responsibilities: states had established IHL, and most continued to respect it. However, some agencies found other avenues for expressing humanitarian impulses. An agency could specialize in addressing particular needs in humanitarian crises (medical, food, housing, etc.), and its staff could also develop unusual relations with partners to gain access. In the process of focusing on different tools and interlocutors, agencies became more individualized and less interchangeable in form and functions.

The rest of this chapter analyzes the peculiar humanitarian implications of new wars and identifies the international system's responses to date. They include political-legal innovations, operational practices, and unresolved struggles. A lag always exists between unusual challenges and institutional adaptations, but the gap between new problems and old

Table 4.1. "New Wars," Humanitarian Implications, and System Responses

	"New Wars"	Humanitarian Implications	System Responses to Date
Locus of war and relief	Areas of fragmented authority; state borders meaningless	Difficult to monitor, relieve, and protect in areas without clear authority	Creation of humanitarian space by military
Agents of war, relief, and peace	Increased role of nonstate actors	Engagement dilemmas: access versus abuse; Legal status of belligerents	Humanitarian intelligence; Creation of International Criminal Court
Economies	Illegal activities, skewed aid, and plunder are crucial	Greed- and grievance-based war economies; Aid economies	Codes of conduct for "conflict resources"; Humanitarian intelligence; local capacity building ("Do no harm")
Targets and victims of war	Prevalence of civilians	Increased scope of humanitarian crisis; multiple crises, many "permanent"; Violence against aid workers	Human security agenda and the responsibility to protect; Special action taken for internally displaced; Protection and security tools
Technologies	New technologies; revolution in military affairs	Increased lethality of force may increase casualties, worsen crises; Transportation and logistics innovations improve speed of response	Ethics of war issues (humanitarian war, landmine ban); Disconnect between calls for action and investments in rapid response capabilities
Media coverage of humanitarian crises and action	Intermittent coverage, only when geopolitics disturbed	More resources for visible crises, others ignored ("forgotten emergencies"); Political will for humanitarian action obviates responsibility for political intervention	Dramatic crises attract resources; agencies follow; Response to less-visible crises vulnerable to ebbs in donor financing

solutions is a gaping chasm in today's international humanitarian system. The disconnects between each of the respective challenges and the lack of institutional adaptation is serious enough, but when several separate challenges appear concurrently, they compound one another. The international humanitarian system as presently constituted is ill-equipped to address contemporary man-made disasters.

CREATING SPACE AND ACCESS

In areas of fragmented political authority, state boundaries do not readily suggest where humanitarian responses will be required—that is, where the investment of limited resources will save the greatest number of lives. Once a state ceases to maintain political authority or have a monopoly on violence, borders lose meaning as the locus of war. These same states afflicted by the new wars of the 1990s may also be unable to effectively muster or manage responses to humanitarian disasters. At mid-decade then UN secretary-general Boutros Boutros-Ghali noted, "The new breed of intra-state conflicts have certain characteristics. . . . They are usually fought not only by regular armies but also by militias and armed civilians with little discipline and with ill-defined chains of command. They are often guerilla wars without clear front lines. Civilians are the main victims and often the main targets. Humanitarian emergencies are commonplace and the combatant authorities, in so far as they can be called authorities, lack the capacity to cope with them."[16] The legality as well as the actuality of access are in doubt and may have little or nothing to do with the authorities who occupy central government offices in the national capital—the usual interlocutors for outside humanitarian agencies.

The focus on people or resources more than on territory or formal boundaries creates challenges for a system responding to conflicts that cross borders while being based essentially on the consent of territorially defined belligerents. UN organizations are bound by their constitutions to deal with member states, and NGOs have usually operated in a similar fashion, although their terms of incorporation are not really linked to states. Finding victims, securing access to victims, and delivering relief to victims has led to the creation of humanitarian space in law and practice—that is, room to maneuver and help in providing protection and relief to war-ravaged populations. Humanitarian space was guaranteed by states (including belligerents) in many interstate conflicts of the twentieth century and by the Geneva Conventions.[17] But in most new wars, victims do not have this luxury. Belligerents often do not provide consent, allow for the passage of relief, or respect international agreements—they are often unaware of them and are not signatories.

Hence, the most elementary struggle in the new wars is for aid agencies to actually carve out secure space in which to operate.

Beginning with northern Iraq in the early 1990s, the Security Council authorized safe areas without the consent of belligerents—indeed, oftentimes against their expressed wishes.[18] The concept of opening humanitarian space inside war zones without such approval developed gradually. The dynamics of the new wars and, specifically, the need to engage NSAs did not appear with sufficient regularity to generate support for new international humanitarian legal mechanisms and operational principles until late in the twentieth century. With the exception of 1977 Additional Protocols to the Geneva Conventions, the Cold War had hamstrung the development of the international humanitarian system to address the violence produced by NSAs.

Although humanitarian agencies, many within the UN itself, struggled to find operating space, the Security Council was largely missing in action regarding humanitarian matters. No resolution mentioned the humanitarian aspects of any conflict from 1945 until the Six-Day War of 1967, and the first mention of the ICRC was not until 1978.[19] However, humanitarians were able to focus attention on wars and relief operations that did not threaten the United States and the Soviet Union to bring about supplementary legal protections.

Despite the narrow scenarios for humanitarian action that were the product of Cold War power politics, on the legal front humanitarians were making greater and more permanently grounded institutional strides toward ensuring space. In 1974, the Red Cross convened an international conference to hammer out another series of conventions.[20] The 1977 Additional Protocols are representative of the slow but sure sea change by humanitarian agencies in recognizing dramatic shifts in who was fighting wars and where, as well as specifying contemporary norms regarding who is entitled to the rights and protections afforded by the international humanitarian system. Both protocols legally sanction the military forces of national liberation movements (guerilla groups fomenting decolonization), which had gained legitimacy and stature in international politics since the 1960s. Article 1 of Additional Protocol I states that the convention also applies to "armed conflicts in which peoples are fighting against colonial domination and alien occupation and against racist regimes in the exercise of self-determination." In section 2, articles 43–47 similarly allow combatants to be lawful so long as they do not pose as civilians or fight for private gain (i.e., are mercenaries).

Furthermore, the Additional Protocols continue the development of norms to protect civilians. As the international humanitarian system is geared toward states and international armed conflicts, the provisions regarding civilians afflicted by these wars are more specific and elaborate.

Additional Protocol I, article 48, establishes the "Basic Rule": "In order to ensure respect for and protection of the civilian population and civilian objects, the Parties to the conflict shall at all times distinguish between the civilian population and combatants and between civilian objects and military objectives and accordingly shall direct their operations only against military objectives." However, regulations (Additional Protocol II) to protect civilians trapped in "noninternational" wars, or civil wars, remain small in comparison to those referring to interstate conflicts—as mentioned earlier, only 29 versus 530. Although the Additional Protocols did not anticipate the magnitude or the scale of changes in warfare in the 1990s, they demonstrate a degree of foresight in breaking legal ground in the protection of civilians, especially those victimized by their own governments. As David Forsythe reminds us, "the ICRC was one of the first, and no doubt the most persistent, in trying to expand humanitarian protection from international to internal wars."[21]

These innovations in IHL did not begin to have an impact on the ability of agencies to create space until the Security Council did so, as a focal point for decision making about international peace and security. The transformation of the humanitarian landscape from the 1970s to the 1990s was dramatic. Ted van Baarda notes that in the 1970s and 1980s, "the Security Council gave humanitarian aspects of armed conflict limited priority . . . but the early nineteen-nineties can be seen as a watershed."[22] In the late 1980s, traditional UN peacekeeping was supplemented by a host of new operational tasks—including disarmament, election monitoring, human rights observation, and humanitarian help. The terms "multidimensional" and "second generation" peacekeeping, or what militaries refer to as "operations other than war," appear at this time and suggest the flexibility of adapting to new tasks the major existing operational security tool of the UN.[23] It was a logical step to extend classic UN peacekeeping to facilitate humanitarian action.[24] With East-West tensions dissipating, humanitarians became more successful in lobbying for political and legal support in international organizations for the creation of room to succor and protect victims. By the time of the 1991 operation in northern Iraq, the use of military force for human protection purposes was considered a feasible policy option.

In 1989 Operation Lifeline Sudan became important in bridging the fading politics of the Cold War and the more impassioned and robust responses of the 1990s. First, the UN negotiated with rebels from the Sudanese Liberation Army as well as with the central government in Khartoum. Second, while a "permanent crisis" was continuing with armed conflict raging (as more and more years passed since its beginning, in 1983), "corridors of tranquility" were agreed that opened up a new kind of space for humanitarians. Within it, they could come to the rescue.[25]

Interestingly enough, the UN as an intergovernmental body continues to confront difficulties in dealing easily and openly with NSAs. A 2004 OCHA report on the treatment of IDPs, for instance, points to the continuing "need for the UN to have contact with all actors affecting the protection of the civilian population" and asserts that such success "should be non-negotiable."[26] What could be more obvious?

An important development took place on the fringes of the French government because the socialists named a new minister of humanitarian affairs: the founder of MSF and later Médecins du Monde, Bernard Kouchner. In collaboration with international lawyer and Sorbonne professor Mario Bettati, Kouchner laid the forward-looking framework for the expansion of space at the 1987 Humanitarian Law and Moral Conference that produced the controversial notion of humanitarian intervention.[27] Although David Rieff now dismisses these efforts as being "millenarian" because the performance of the system has been riddled with flaws, both the operational and normative advances represent concrete steps toward a system to improve access to victims.[28]

The last decade of the twentieth century represents a turning point—in wars themselves and in responses by the international humanitarian system. During the first half of the 1990s, twice as many resolutions were passed as were those during the first forty-five years of UN history. They contained repeated references, in the context of enforcement under Chapter VII, to humanitarian crises amounting to threats to international peace and security, as well as repeated demands for parties to respect the principles of IHL. Although the vocabulary varied, the overall thrust was to advance the international norm of human protection.

Beyond action in the Security Council, General Assembly resolution 182/46 (1991) further substantiated the right of agencies to have access to victims. This resolution brought to light how the lack of centralization and the policy of the UN's ad hoc naming of lead agencies inhibited the overall effectiveness of the international humanitarian system. This resolution also led to the establishment of the Department of Humanitarian Affairs (DHA) and a UN "czar" in the form of the emergency relief coordinator. Jan Eliasson, the Swedish ambassador who had steered the resolution through the minefield of sovereignty-sensitive developing countries, became the first to hold this position. In 1998 this unit became the Office for the Coordination of Humanitarian Affairs and is part of the secretary-general's inner circle.[29]

One of this period's innovations is the creation of physical, instead of merely legal, space where relief could be administered. While not entirely, and in some instances not remotely, effective in creating secure space, such areas represent the grandest reaches of the system. Building on the example of the "corridors of tranquility" in Sudan, other examples of safe spaces established in the 1990s include the following:[30]

- *"Safe havens" in northern Iraq (1991–2003)*: In Iraq the Security Council demanded that "Iraq allow immediate access by international humanitarian organizations to all those in need of assistance in all parts of Iraq" and furthermore declared that Iraqi refugee flows "threaten international peace and security in the region."[31] While the council authorized this action, it was predicated on U.S. airpower's deterring Iraqi interference.
- *"Safe areas" in Bosnia and Herzegovina (1993–1995)*: Consent was initially obtained from the government of Yugoslavia to protect civilians.[32] UN Protection Force was to "deter attacks against the safe areas, to monitor the cease-fire, to promote the withdrawal of military or paramilitary units other than those of the Government of Bosnia and Herzegovina and to occupy some key points on the ground, in addition to participating in the delivery of humanitarian relief to the population."[33] When UN personnel were threatened and calls for recognizing obligations under international treaties were defied, the Security Council issued stronger resolutions authorizing more robust measures, such as those to create safe areas and ensure humanitarian action when parties refused to give consent.[34] However, as the massacre at Srebrenica demonstrates, these "safe areas" did not ultimately afford safety to civilians.[35] In a memorable one-liner about what had happened, Fred Cuny looked around a devastated Sarajevo in 1993 and quipped, "If the UN had been around in 1939, we would all be speaking German."[36]
- *"Secure humanitarian areas" in Rwanda (Opération Turquoise, 1994)*: The Security Council did seek the "establishment and maintenance, where feasible, of secure humanitarian areas."[37] The council later authorized the French-led Opération Turquoise to use "all necessary means to achieve the humanitarian objectives" of previous resolutions.[38]

The space in which humanitarians have conventionally operated was dictated by territorially based units, states. The need for relief and rescue where states would not or could not allow action led humanitarians to try to expand their operational space. More concerned about the welfare of populations than about territory, aid agencies will normally stomach a bittersweet bargain if access affords the delivery of assistance without a designated area.[39] One essential aspect of the new wars is that the locus of violence is murkier than it is in places clearly covered by the laws of interstate wars. Creating space and access, never easy, has become a constant operational challenge, especially because of the size and the complexity of the main actors in the system. This theme is central to understanding the collective action problems in the next chapter.

ENGAGEMENT DILEMMAS:
NEGOTIATING ACCESS WITH AGENTS

As humanitarian agencies deployed in areas lacking state authority and encountered menacing Nsas, access became increasingly problematic. In situations where the state is under stress or is essentially nonexistent, agencies have always been on dubious legal ground, and this uncertainty carries over into operational arrangements with NSAs.[40] Negotiations previously centered on state authorities. However nebulous or cumbersome the follow-through, at least the channels, the official web of interlocutors, were clear. To the extent that wars no longer follow the contours of interstate borders and shift onto more uncertain political, economic, and social terrain, agencies have no choice except to widen the range of actors with whom they negotiate access to affected populations.

Mary Anderson rightly points out that aid is both an economic and a political resource, meaning that it not only materially enriches but also often confers legitimacy.[41] For a long time, it was difficult for a UN agency to relate openly with NSAs because such overtures lent an element of international recognition by an intergovernmental body. However, UNICEF was well placed in the turning point in Sudan because "women and children" were topics that were supposedly unquestionably neutral and the space created by Operation Lifeline Sudan did not imply international legal recognition.[42] Thus, despite legal concerns and political reservations, the prevalence and proliferation of actors gradually made it an operational imperative for many agencies to negotiate access directly with authorities controlling an area. What had been exceptional became conventional in the 1990s.

States, even when they are mere shells of the Westphalian ideal, frequently remain key players in armed conflicts. But their lack of ability to provide security and other significant social services render them but one actor among many. Now that belligerents have proliferated and often control substantial areas of national territory, NGOs and UN agencies are required to relate directly to NSAs as well as central governments. Although agencies have always interacted informally with local actors, the importance and the number of interactions with subnational units have become commonplace.

We categorize NSAs in the operational theaters shared with humanitarian agencies as being helpful, harmful, or heterogeneous.[43] Table 4.2 illustrates how these three types of actors in new wars affect humanitarian action, noting the potential for assistance and abuse.[44] A new handbook for humanitarians laments that humanitarian negotiation "involves negotiating the non-negotiable . . . from a position of relative weakness . . . [with] only hope for second best outcomes."[45]

Table 4.2. Local Actors Encountered by Humanitarians in Delivering Relief

Civil Society	*Situational Spoilers*	*Certain Spoilers*
Nongovernmental organizations	Local militias Private military companies Business	Warlords Mercenaries Mafia

Unpacking the politics of war-torn societies reveals two major problems for humanitarians: understanding sources of violence and tailoring responses to individual actors. Doing so, of course, requires admitting that some NSAs are more worthy than others and establishing priorities—in effect, to abandon any pretense of neutrality and impartiality as a desired ideal or a necessary tactic. "One size fits all" is neither a tenable philosophical position nor operational orientation.

Analysts using the label of new wars tend to aggregate too many types of violent armed conflicts under a common rubric. Despite an understandable tendency to look for a central dispute and a clear cause, agencies must also be aware of regional and local dimensions that give most armed conflicts a multifaceted character.[46] The difficulty of "getting it right" is perhaps best illustrated by the DRC, which combines the best, or the worst, of ideological, tribal, national, and regional parties. It also reflects involvement by neighbors and by issues that run the gamut from exploitation of natural resources to the recruitment of soldiers, from the composition of the national government to who constitutes a citizen, grievances from political to personal, and motives from patriotic to parasitic. Yet this diverse mixture is too often analytically lumped into a single macrocleavage in the budgeting and annual reports of aid agencies.

Many popular narratives of the DRC suggest that the violence, which has increasingly wracked the country since the early to mid-1990s (though starting in the 1960s), is principally a civil war pitting stalwarts of the Mobutu regime against guerillas seeking to institute a government that would devote more national resources to the mostly neglected populations in the east. While these tensions ran deep and triggered major military activity from 1994 to 1996, this struggle was only one episode in a long and bloody series. With the Cold War–era regime overthrown and a new leader installed (Laurent Kabila), the new government opted for a cosmetic change in the state. The country would no longer be called Zaire but the Democratic Republic of the Congo. Yet this change in name could not wipe out the numerous and diverse conflicts that lurked beneath the national horizon.

What may have once been seen as a civil war between parties (the Mobutu government and the Kabila-led guerillas) obscured multiple armed conflicts, and the defeat of the incumbent regime opened the door wide for numerous subnational agendas to play more prominent roles in propelling violence. Even before the fall of Mobutu, the genocide in neighboring Rwanda illustrated that war in the DRC was not simply about a struggle for state power between two political factions supported by rival Cold War patrons. The conflict had no single comprehensive or collective grievance, and the wars—and there were many—were expressions of a variety of interests (political, economic, ethnic, and economic) on many levels (local, national, regional, and transnational). Such new wars represent an enormous challenge to understanding conflicts (gathering and utilizing research, even when it is on target), let alone to crafting suitable tactics for engagement with NSAs.

Agencies have three needs in fashioning appropriate operations with local actors. The first is identifying and promoting those actors that facilitate humanitarian operations—in short, nurturing those civil society actors involved in emergency assistance. The second is limiting relations with and curtailing the influence of rogues that profit politically or economically from war—marginalizing and navigating "uncivil" society or spoilers. The third is distinguishing those that have the potential to contribute to humanitarian action and then finding strategies and tactics for transforming their interest structures toward fostering peace—assessing and cultivating ambiguous partners. Hence, the aim of abandoning any pretense at neutrality and impartiality is not only to maximize those local actors who are helpful and to minimize those who are hurtful but also to assess those heterogeneous ones and co-opt the best candidates to be helpful in the medium term.

Blanket pronouncements and binary distinctions are comforting but ultimately misleading. The absence of subtle distinctions is understandable—humanitarian action requires a clear-enough message to move ahead vigorously. At the same time, a black-and-white perspective fosters a cookie-cutter approach to many actors in new wars that are anything except uniform. As one policy group making recommendations to the German government put it, "An analysis of the capacities of all security-relevant actors, their popular legitimacy and acceptance is recommended. . . . However, it is inappropriate to idealise these actors. When developing a support or containment strategy, the key question is whether they help, rather than hinder, state-building."[47] The same can be said of humanitarian action.

Existing analytic frameworks and methodologies based on working with proven, clearly identified "good guys" and "bad guys" are not helpful when dealing with the mixed agendas, evolving interests, and actions of less-predictable local actors. In associating with "gray" actors, humanitarians often risk clouding principles and consequences, which raises the specter of a "gray humanitarianism." One problem is that by working with spoilers, humanitarian organizations may grant legitimacy to otherwise illegitimate actors. Formal relations with spoilers implicitly acknowledge their authority, and a relief role bolsters their claims of legitimacy.[48] The problem discussed earlier—of the UN's collective hesitancy to negotiate with NSAs because some member states were wary of the precedents of lending legitimacy to the claims of armed belligerents—has thus not totally disappeared. Yet, there is simply no other choice.

The consequences are ambiguous. Locally affected populations receive relief but often must acknowledge or support those who allowed access and, in the process, may be seen as taking sides in the conflict that ushered in the humanitarian crisis in the first place. NSAs allow assistance that may ultimately undermine their power, but in the short term they receive in exchange legitimacy and influence as well as resources. Agencies fulfill mandates to provide aid, but actions that confer legitimacy or sustenance to questionable NSAs can risk the reputation and legitimacy of humanitarians.

A review of humanitarian agencies demonstrates a diversity of approaches to determining who receives assistance and where humanitarians deploy. When and where agencies require engaging local actors to attain access to victims, they face a choice: either gain consent of interlocutors or, when confronting them, be prepared to carry out the option of withdrawing from the area. Examples of consent-based techniques of this period include the establishment of the Ground Rule in South Sudan, Memoranda of Understanding in Afghanistan, and Principles of Engagement in the DRC; risk-avoidance approaches—cases of confrontation leading to withdrawal—are quite rare, though the ICRC left Liberia in 1994 and MSF pulled out of the Goma camps for Rwandan refugees in 1995.[49]

From a strategic point of view, over the course of the 1990s the following general types of tactics can be discerned: neutrality and impartiality; co-optation and pragmatic adaptation; and confrontation. While not all agencies intend to help all victims and not all agencies consider all options, the selection of intended recipients and goals influences tactical decisions. Table 4.3 depicts the trade-offs that agencies make in the selection of tactics for interacting with local NSAs. The row labeled *Helpful* denotes operations with clear benefits for agencies and a general lack of distasteful compromises; however, these are possible only with a limited group of local actors. The *Heterogenous* row illustrates a significant area where the overall implications of tactics are uncertain to the point of being troubling. The *Hurtful* row suggests situations that are intrinsically losing propositions because aid is wasted while the continued abusive, often violent behavior of belligerents is rewarded and more lives are lost than saved.

We unpack the spectrum of engagement tactics in the following sections, but even this quick sketch suggests only a limited number of decisions for clear-cut applications of traditional principles and demarcates

Table 4.3. Engagement Tactics and Trade-offs

	Tactics			
	Neutrality and Impartiality	*Co-optation*	*Pragmatic Adaptation*	*Confrontation*
Helpful	+ Access + Build local capacity	—	—	—
Heterogenous	+ Access - Opportunities for exploitation of aid	+ Access + Contribute to peace - Legacy issues, may entangle war criminals	+ Access - Legitimacy for obstructionist actor - Compromise humanitarian mantle	- Access - Hostility, possible violence toward aid workers + "Do no harm" + Protect humanitarian mantle
Hurtful	- Aid manipulation - Politicize assistance; compromise humanitarian mantle	- Aid manipulation	- Aid manipulation	—

which instances merit obvious rejection. It is the gray areas that aɪᴄ ... numerous and most problematic, where continual monitoring, weighing alternatives, and carefully adapting to circumstances are required.

Neutrality and Impartiality

Although the ICRC is the "prophet" of the classic approach, Hugo Slim tells us that there are many other "priests."[50] Distancing itself from politics and calling for a division of labor with other agencies (human rights advocates as well as aid purveyors) and military forces, the ICRC is protective of its classic doctrine and suggests that neutral agencies still have a role to play. The ICRC is open to engaging belligerents on all sides, but it is not inclined to develop a partisan relationship toward one. Other organizations pursue what might be labeled "nonpartisanship"—that is, attempting to engage all belligerents but also exhibiting at times favoritism to one side.

This strategy is clearly sensible for interactions with the helpful members of civil society, just as it is for virtually all local counterparts in natural disasters, such as the tragic tsunami of December 2004. But in the new wars, where some NSAs wish to sabotage peace efforts and others may or may not, can humanitarians remain oblivious to incentive structures and spoiler behavior by local actors whom they are helping?

In spite of protestations by traditionalists, "business as usual" is not a viable option for dealing with many actors in today's humanitarian disasters. While apt in earlier periods and still practical in many interstate wars (as well as natural disasters), neutrality and impartiality are of limited applicability in "stateless" complex emergencies. Working on all sides and staying clear of politics is not only impossible but may actually make matters worse. Consent has little meaning when outside military forces intervene to enforce decisions. One summary of a discussion on this topic by prominent private agencies concludes, "Many within the NGO community who initially believed that their organizations could play neutral roles in complex emergencies have begun to revise their views."[51] Even such a faithful proponent of neutrality as Larry Minear has acknowledged that the experiences of the 1990s "have placed on the defensive people who have sought to preserve the consensual and civilian character of humanitarian action."[52] Within the halls of the UN, where the mandate of agencies is premised on taking a neutral stance in conflicts, the 2000 Brahimi report (analyzing the future of peace operations) argues that neutrality is inappropriate where one side violates the UN Charter.[53]

Despite the apolitical ideas that gave birth to the enterprise, even the ICRC's humanitarian action is, as David Forsythe reminds us, innately and intensely political.[54] Although the ICRC is neutral, it advocates on behalf of IHL and may take public positions toward violators. This attempt to stand outside of politics and push for humanitarianism is itself a political act. Even when actions are not intended as such, they are perceived as being political. The evidence of armed conflicts and responses from the last fifteen years suggests that maintaining artificial barriers between the humanitarian and the political thwarts effective programming.[55] Indeed, Mark Duffield and others have called for a more avowedly political posture. The "new or political humanitarianism" is an integral part of a set of relief, development, and reconstruction activities required by the new wars.[56] In short, while neutrality and impartiality remain useful in dealing with members of "civil" civil society, they may be ineffective or even counterproductive in dealing with some situational spoilers and all certain spoilers. While this conclusion may reek of schizophrenic institutional principles, in such unstable situations these approaches are not a malady but an operational necessity.

Co-optation and Pragmatic Adaptation

Opposing or defying NSAs can work against aid agencies and risk the lives of expatriate and local personnel. An agency's bargaining relationship is normally weak, whether measured by military power or willpower. Ratcheting up measures implies the willingness to withdraw, but NSAs usually calculate that the aid agencies' need to be present in a crisis will outweigh the costs of being entangled with various species of spoilers.

Hence, confrontation is a strategy saved for only the most certain of spoilers or clearly "uncivil" civil society. Heterogeneous NSAs have two options: in the best cases, they can become permanently helpful and be co-opted into "civil" civil society; or, for a fixed period their cooperation can be secured to help victims by changing incentives as part of a pragmatic adaptation by aid agencies. In short, faced with extortion from situational spoilers and obstructionists, aid agencies may opt for a time to sup with the devil in order to aid at least some needy populations. Determining the terms and duration of the agreement requires knowledge and courage to keep abreast of daily developments. For instance, common tactical concessions include agreeing to diversion at the point of entry as well as employment and contracts for individuals specified by warlords. These measures are temporary instrumental calculations. Those doing the math, however, should be clear that the compromise is for a moment and should not labor under the delusion that they are building civil society in the longer term.

Still, the threat to withdraw is a common tactic, often born of frustration, fatigue, and, increasingly, insecurity. A temporary suspension of operations can be useful if an agency can convince recipients to blame spoilers and not the agency itself. But permanent withdrawal is a step beyond what most agencies can contemplate, for three reasons: tangible numbers of lives saved immediately, political strings, and economic interests of the organization. For some agencies getting any assistance through is preferable to witholding aid, regardless of the politics of victims or the actual outcome of efforts.

Moreover, IGOs operate under orders from political masters, and unless a governing body of states approves confrontation—for example, the UN's Security Council in invoking its Chapter VII powers or the Governing Council of the United Nations Development Programme (UNDP) in setting priorities—field personnel or even heads of agencies have little room to confront belligerents. When High Commissioner for Refugees Sadako Ogata tried to suspend operations in Sarajevo after particularly egregious behavior by Bosnian Serbs in 1992, UN secretary-general Boutros Boutros-Ghali overruled her, presumably because the intergovernmental United Nations had no choice but to be there.[57] While the UNHCR did not want to reward atrocities committed by Bosnian Serbs, the Secretariat framed the problem with an eye more toward the overall international significance of the United Nations rather than toward the humanitarian situation on the ground, as confronted by its operational agencies. According to this perspective, the world organization had substantial political capital invested in Bosnia. Failing to act, as well as being perceived as incapable, would have dealt a serious blow to the organization as the embodiment of collective security. Many inside the UN and in national capitals thought that, for the world body to play a meaningful part in post–Cold War international politics, it had to prove itself by addressing major sources of instability—once commitments were made, the credibility and viability of the world organization were at stake.

In addition to political considerations, resource mobilization also can trump principles. Headquarters can press staff to remain in a particular crisis to foster fund-raising and media objectives, even if the actual field mission is dysfunctional in the eyes of those on the ground. The economic rationality is to have and maintain a presence in disasters. A presence leads to a high profile that attracts donors and therefore generates the resources necessary for action in the crisis in question or elsewhere. The power of the purse and the economic appetites of agencies may compel an agency's staying when humanitarian sensibilities suggest leaving.

Utilitarian logic always operates on a slippery slope; at some point the good that an aid agency is doing may be offset or overwhelmed by the damage wrought by compromising tactical bargains. That harm can be measured and may include the weapons procured by warlords with the relief aid handed over as a "tax," the precedents set for future transactions, and the empowerment of thugs. As an expedient and risky way to manage the short-term problem of spoilers and variable NSAs, however, tactical bargains remain an option.

To ensure that pragmatism is not sheer opportunism, some NGOs have experimented with subcontracting to merchants. Allowing private sector elements to participate in the economic activity associated with relief in grain and transportation markets can engage otherwise resentful actors and facilitate relief operations. By paying only for what was delivered— that is, making recipient communities responsible for distribution— agencies advance restorative incentive structures. In some instances NGOs have bargained as a group to limit extortion—that is, agencies do not outbid each other for access or otherwise reward "gatekeeper" taxation schemes.

For those NSAs who are more obstructionist than spoiler, behavior is driven by short-term economic calculations and survival rather than an intrinsic opposition to humanitarian action. To the extent that external actors possess carrots and sticks, they sometimes can reshape interests and modify behavior. Hence, effective policies focusing on co-opting NSAs may become an option that requires input from the field and head-quarters.

Shifts in the structure of interests are not amenable to quick fixes, but perhaps among the exceptions to this rule are demobilization programs, which can provide skills training and financial incentives to armed belligerents to put down their weapons. Nonetheless, success is more likely during genuine economic recovery; otherwise, efforts to co-opt armed belligerents are likely to lead to disgruntled unemployed men who return to banditry or insurgency if there is no meaningful paid employment. Contracting delivery of food aid to business is another instance of successful co-optation.[58] The essence is to create stakeholders in law and order, an arduous but not impossible aspiration in some postconflict war zones.

To repeat ourselves, it is relatively easy to make decisions to sustain the helpful members of civil society, but it is extremely hard to decide how to co-opt heterogeneous actors in the long run or make instrumental decisions about short-term compromise. In the context of spoilers, rigidly adhering to neutrality and impartiality limits agencies from working in some areas where they might have access. There are times and places that call for agencies to practice co-optation or pragmatic adaptation. In them, a traditional resort to neutrality and impartiality becomes a hollow justification to act without reflection and without weighing potential costs.

Confrontation and Withdrawal

Transforming warlords into elected officials, bandits into security personnel, and Mafioso merchants into legitimate entrepreneurs is usually beyond the capacity of aid agencies. Hence, a tactic of confrontation definitely belongs in the humanitarian toolkit, which requires weighing short- versus longer-term benefits. For some agencies this tactic is perfectly sensible, but others view it as being inherently problematic. The perception of a small window of time in which to accumulate benefits leads decision making to be shortsighted, and NSAs ask themselves, "Why work with an agency controlling substantial wealth and goods if they are likely to depart shortly?" The short-term nature of emergency responses—many disbursements must occur within three to six weeks—invites local actors to behave expediently, confiscating as many resources as quickly as possible.

Limiting the tactic of temporary suspension or a longer-run withdrawal is the decentralization and redundancy in the international humanitarian system. Such tactics would be more effective under a united front. When a sole agency departs, it may be viewed as the result of its misunderstanding and mishandling of local dynamics. If collective bargaining were undertaken by major agencies, the message would be unmistakable. However, such unity is difficult in that humanitarian agencies often have mixed feelings for one another as well as diverging agendas, ideologies, governing boards, and donors. Selective suspension or withdrawal has more symbolic than practical implications because other agencies can almost certainly make up the loss.

Lonely defectors may temporarily occupy high moral ground, but they increase the demand for other agencies, whose boards and staff are conscious of "market share."[59] Their leaving may in turn lower their media profile, which can affect fund-raising and programming for activities in other parts of the world. Indeed, such a stance may jeopardize the future of the agency—agencies without field operations have limited or almost no appeal or donors. Furthermore, although by withdrawing, an agency may prevent its own efforts from being corrupted in a particular crisis, it cannot compel other agencies to follow suit. Thus, confrontational behavior is unlikely "in today's humanitarian world," which Smillie and Minear describe as having "a dog-eat-dog competition that is relentless as it is unproductive."[60]

Perhaps the most powerful argument against withdrawal, from the perspective of humanitarians, is that relieving suffering is why their organizations exist. However, some agencies have reasoned that in certain situations they were doing more harm than good and thus left the scene. For example, over the past twenty years MSF has withdrawn at least four times—Ethiopia, 1985; Goma (Rwanda crisis), 1993–1994; Burundi, 1996; North Korea, 1998. But these cases indicate that there is often no consensus among different sections of the agency as to when such tactics should be used.[61] The ICRC has also faced similar situations and is often hit with the criticism that neutrality wastes resources in dealing with symptoms and leads to subsequent violence against those aided—or worse yet, that those who were given aid used it or were sustained while committing or supporting acts of violence.

The prospect of the "well-fed dead," those who received aid but were not sufficiently protected to survive the duration of violence, epitomized the worst-case scenario of such limited, misconceived humanitarian efforts. As there is no shortage of crises and demands for help, according to the logic of confrontation, resources should be channeled to contexts where aid is not frittered away or used to fuel conflicts. In practice the ICRC has no precise policy on conditions for engagement but is usually committed to staying in crises. When the ICRC feels its efforts are largely successful in providing relief to victims (such as in Somalia, 1991–1995), it remains engaged, but when abuses of aid seem substantial and systematic (as in Liberia, 1994), the agency departs.[62] The question becomes not just to stay or go but whether such tactics meaningfully change the behavior of obstinate, manipulative interlocutors. Confrontation may be a feasible strategy for a limited number of malleable NSAs in special circumstances.

Some humanitarian organizations have long-standing experience in war-torn communities. In these instances, long-term interests in maintaining an agency's presence can build civil society, neutralize or even attract obstructionists, and help isolate and transform certain spoilers.[63] However, an ongoing presence in communities is impossible unless donors are in a position to make financial commitments for the longer term and are not going to penalize aid agencies for running unnecessary risks and putting the welfare of their organization above those of locally effected populations.[64] To facilitate the calculations and maneuvers discussed here, donor flexibility will have to increase and criteria will have to change. This seemingly obvious reality has yet to sufficiently penetrate donor capitals or the Development Assistance Committee (DAC) of the Organisation for Economic Co-operation and Development.

ECONOMIES OF WAR, ECONOMIES OF AID

The preceding discussion should make clear the extent to which new wars are characterized by a cast of characters different from those on-stage or in the wings in interstate wars. The prevalence of NSAs of various shapes, sizes, and sensibilities with economic interests served by continued violence poses a host of distinctive engagement dilemmas for aid agencies. While spoilers have been present in previous armed conflicts, the current generation is both more numerous and better equipped to wreak havoc. The synergy of local and global economic conditions coupled with relatively inexpensive arms allows NSAs to assemble military capacity without much difficulty or investment.

Laurent Kabila reportedly said that to have an "army" in Zaire, one need only have $10,000 and a cell phone. Aid agencies face a steep learning curve in negotiating access in such contexts. What is clear, however, is that reflection is increasingly more valuable than visceral reactions. Humanitarian impulses and goodwill are simply inadequate.

We have just outlined the trade-offs and a range of strategies for altering the ways to conceive and approach NSAs in war zones. Here we address a specific subset—those who use economic means and have economic ends, that is, those who exploit war or aid economies. As discussed earlier, two general types of economies influence war and humanitarian action. First are "war economies," or economic interests that directly profit from armed conflict. In his farewell speech in 1961, U.S. president Dwight D. Eisenhower warned, "we need to guard against the acquisition of unwarranted influence . . . by the 'military-industrial complex.'"[65] The new wars do not operate with the sophisticated organization or technology of the U.S. military-industrial complex, but the similarity results from a network of economically calculating actors who profit from the production of violence. The second type of economic system that surrounds humanitarian action is that of "aid economies," or economic interests that are primed to benefit from the provision of external aid. Despite overlap the challenges for and the responses by humanitarians differ.

Humanitarian responses to war economies have two tracks: controlling means and controlling ends. The former approach seeks to prevent or limit economically based actors from developing their means to wage war. Two examples of which are the international efforts to restrict the spread of small arms and the regulations banning mercenaries. Several studies have spotlighted the former, and humanitarians have worked to limit the production and distribution of these weapons by targeting arms sales.[66]

Impeding or stopping the use of mercenaries is also crucial but less prevalent in recent analysis. In many new wars, commercially inspired military actors have become standard fare. Bad memories of colonial intrusion in the Third World have shaped perceptions of guns for hire, and international bodies have taken action to thwart such hiring. Several international agreements have been reached: article 47 of Additional Protocol I to the Geneva Conventions of 1977;[67] the 1977 Convention for the Elimination of Mercenarism in Africa;[68] and the 1989 UN Convention against the Recruitment, Use, Financing, and Training of Mercenaries.[69] The UN has also created the position of a special rapporteur to monitor developments and create guidelines.[70] Furthermore, many national governments have legislation to ban mercenaries and regulate security firms.

Nonetheless, mercenaries and the more corporatized PMCs continue to play important roles in the new wars. Despite bans, mercenaries have appeared throughout the world, mostly in Africa but also in the Balkans,

Latin America, and Southeast Asia. The war zones in which PMCs tend to be deployed are also those in which IHL has not been a major considera-tion of belligerents on either side—for example, PMCs have had sizable operations in such diverse sites as Sierra Leone, Bogainville, and Borneo.[71] We pick up this aspect in chapter 6 in reference to post–September 11 Afghanistan and Iraq.

The second track is ends oriented and seeks to regulate the resources over which parties struggle in the new wars. The UN has attempted to emphasize the role of the plunder of natural resources, with particular emphasis on Africa.[72] Earlier we examined the role that a variety of such lootable resources play in sustaining wars—gold, silver, coltan, timber, copper, titanium, and diamonds—of which the last was the first resource to garner such attention. It is worth noting the progress made since the early 1990s regarding the formulation of "blood diamonds" to signify how widely this phenomenon has been embraced. Codes of conduct are becoming increasingly important in the diamond industry. The Kimberley process began in May 2000 with a meeting in South Africa after NGOs such as Global Witness have pressured the diamond industry to accept regulation and clamp down on an illicit trade responsible for fueling wars.[73] The Kimberley Certification Scheme came into effect January 1, 2003, to control trade in over forty countries. However, many diamond operations are not covered by this agreement and thus, under the newly created Diamond Development Initiative, NGOs, multinational diamond companies, and governments are working together to expand the scope of the program.[74] These efforts have led to broader efforts to regulate "con-flict resources" pertaining to a wider array of agricultural commodities and mineral deposits that often provide the funds for financing civil wars. Experts on civil wars have long been aware of the links between preda-tion of natural resources and financing violence, but now efforts to control such economies have become more widespread.

However, powerful external commercial interests that are vital to development—such as oil, mining, and timber companies—can some-times constitute additional obstacles to relief efforts or even spark con-flicts that trigger humanitarian crises. Foreign oil companies in Africa alone—whether operating in the "scorched earth" area of southern Sudan, in the charged ethnic environment of the river delta of Nigeria, or in deposits that funded guerillas and governments in Angola—demonstrate the significance of their impact on economies and political governance. Mining interests in the Congo, Sierra Leone, and Indonesia also typify how large multinational corporations become powerbrokers in resource-rich countries. While oil represents the most substantial loot, other natural resources represent substantial funds—illicit diamonds in Angola are believed to generate some $700 million per year and in Sierra Leone probably $350 million.[75]

Connected to "war economies" are "aid economies," where the focus is not so much on benefiting from violence as it is on taking advantage of efforts to relieve suffering. Aid agencies are concerned to find ways to avoid the manipulation of markets that benefits profiteers and fosters dependency. Providing aid can facilitate exploitation by creating greedy intermediaries, speculation, and hoarding, as well as generate conditions conducive to breeding future resentments and exacerbating local tensions. Furthermore, outside aid can also be an unfortunate disincentive to the creation and development of indigenous institutions.

Among humanitarians the response has been a modified Hippocratic oath. In fact, the consequences of ignoring or eroding local capacities, long a theme in the work of Mary Anderson,[76] has led to the adoption of "do no harm" criteria in aid manuals and operations. The idea behind such efforts is to aim to deliver emergency relief in a fashion that helps improve the ability of communities and public authorities to take control of their own destinies, begin development, and be in a position to react better to future disasters. In the "do no harm" approach, preserving or facilitating local capacities helps determine how humanitarian relief resources are allocated.

Local commercial interests constitute a blend of promise and pitfall that are pivotal in shaping the operating environment for aid agencies. Merchants and traders are stakeholders in the price of basic commodities, which can be undermined by the availability of relief goods in local markets. Private sector providers of key services in veterinary medicine, vaccinations and health care, agricultural supplies, and even potable water see profits dwindle when aid agencies provide goods for free. One of the more astute measures used in Somalia in 1993 was to make foodstuffs commercially available, rather than gratis, which forced hoarders to dump their commodities and which enticed legitimate traders back into business.[77] Similarly, the ICRC cooked rice supplies to decrease their economic value and inhibit predatory economic behavior. Well-intentioned relief can make enemies of legitimate local businesspeople, prompting them to sabotage wells, drive food convoys away, or even incite violence against aid agencies.

A related category of potentially problematic actors in aid economies are employment seekers. They may be amenable to co-optation or at least open to pragmatic compromise. Although these individuals tend to be the greatest threat when scarce resources or other frustrations lead them to join a militarized faction, they can also present a challenge on purely economic grounds. When unemployment approaches 100 percent and people are desperate for work to feed themselves and their families, external aid agencies may constitute virtually the entire formal monetized sector. Stories of drivers working for external agencies who earn ten times the salary of senior government officials are accurate and highlight the problems of skewed incentives in aid economies. When hiring procedures are perceived to have been unfair, aid agencies can be confronted with spurned applicants. In other cases, local staff who are fired or whose contracts are not renewed can become a security problem in and of itself. Other negative factors for the local economy include skyrocketing rents and inflation, prostitution, and parallel markets.

To add to the list of possible woes, agencies have also been criticized as being the primary beneficiaries in aid economies. When operating expenses—including such big-ticket items as salaries, transportation, equipment, housing, insurance, and security—rival the aid delivered or when international aid workers live lives of luxury next door to feeble shanties and squalid refugee camps, the humanitarian enterprise not only appears to waste scarce resources but also tarnishes its reputation. Alex de Waal and Michael Maren stridently criticize outside humanitarian agencies as enriching themselves from the needs of local populations on the dole.[78] MSF's Fabrice Weissman notes that "aid agencies [are] ever sensitive to the preservation and growth of their budgets."[79] Mark Duffield goes a step further and singles out Western aid agencies that require to have wars to respond to as part of a new international political economy.[80]

Our discussion of the economies of war and aid suggests the uncertain terrain on which aid agencies walk while trying to help. Again, many of these elements were evident in previous armed conflicts. However, the magnitude of outside aid and a globalizing world economy create an unusual witches' brew of challenges for humanitarians. They are so quantitatively different as to constitute a qualitative change.

THE RESPONSIBILITY TO PROTECT
WAR VICTIMS AND AID PERSONNEL

The presence of vulnerable displaced populations in tenuous political and security environments has been the usual consequence of war. The number of civilian victims is mounting, with the percentage of such casualties approaching 90 percent; in fact, the ratio of civilian-to-military deaths nearly tripled from the 1980s to the 1990s alone, according to Mary Kaldor.[81] As such, the new wars have also come to feature a growing number of lethal attacks on aid workers. Agency personnel have often been inadvertently caught in the crossfire, but growing politicization has also meant intentionally placing aid workers in the crosshairs of violence. This section elaborates the arguments presented earlier of UN support for the creation of humanitarian space, by examining political-legal developments for protecting civilians—the human security agenda and the "responsibility to protect" agenda—and agency personnel.

Early responses to the new wars on this front revolved around the successful negotiation of the 1977 Additional Protocols to the Geneva Conventions of 1949. Starting in 1974, the ICRC held a series of conferences to examine changes in war and to retune the international humanitarian system. By 1977 supplemental texts were adopted. Additional Protocol II is particularly important to the new wars because it grants protection to victims of wars that are not explicitly or exclusively international. In many ways Additional Protocol II is an attempt to bridge laws of war and human rights. It establishes mechanisms that do not exclusively reflect the Westphalian state system, and it emphasizes the specific rights of noncombatant (or civilian) victims of all wars, including "noninternational armed conflicts." In other words, whereas IHL was primarily predicated on victims being POWs and civilians under the rule of an occupying power, Additional Protocol II acknowledges that states may victimize their own populations. The overall emphasis of the international humanitarian system clearly remains grounded on states and their command over armed forces—earlier, we note the vast discrepancy between the numbers of paragraphs devoted to international wars versus intrastate wars—but this recognition was a noticeable and significant reorientation.

The experience of the 1990s underscored the relevance of human rights expectations on sovereign political authorities and revealed, as well as shaped, the formulation of the human security agenda. The dramatic growth in the weight of humanitarian values to justify diplomatic and military action is clear to seasoned observers of world politics. "In the 1990s," summarizes Adam Roberts, "humanitarian issues have played a historically unprecedented role in international politics."[82] Political momentum came to a head in the late 1990s in NATO's campaign to protect civilians in Kosovo—including what many agencies found to be a true oxymoron, "humanitarian bombing." Ultimately, the growing violence led the Security Council to pass resolutions shoring up the protection of vulnerable populations and securing access.[83]

But violence persisted and many humanitarians pleaded for military intervention. Although the UN did not authorize NATO's actions in Kosovo, "its legitimacy," according to Michael Ignatieff, "[depends] on what fifty years of human rights has done to our moral instincts, weakening the presumption in favor of state sovereignty, strengthening the presumption in favor of intervention when massacre and deportation become state policy."[84]

Whether one takes issue or not with Edward Luttwak's disparaging remarks about "Kofi's rule . . . whereby human rights outrank sovereignty,"[85] humanitarian intervention was undoubtedly the most controversial topic within UN circles by the end of the 1990s. Three of the secretary-general's speeches at the decade's end were widely debated because what was aptly called "the age of humanitarian emergencies" had led to policies of "saving strangers."[86] Regardless of political quarrels, the growing visibility of humanitarian needs constituted growing pressure for a new international framework to address the situations that led to emergencies.

The review of UN actions in Rwanda underscored the lack of suitable legal and operational tools. At the time of the genocide, the commander of UN troops, Roméo Dallaire, recognized how unprepared the UN was to act, and his pleas eventually led to Opération Turquoise, a force that promised to protect endangered civilians.[87] Only years later did a hard-hitting UN investigative report find that "while the presence of United Nations peacekeepers in Rwanda may have begun as a traditional peacekeeping operation to monitor the implementation of an existing peace agreement, the onslaught of the genocide should have led decision-makers in the United Nations—from the Secretary-General and the Security Council to Secretariat officials and the leadership of UNAMIR—to realize that the original mandate, and indeed the neutral mediating role of the United Nations, was no longer adequate and required a different, more assertive response, combined with the means necessary to take such action."[88] Moreover, the Brahimi report built on these sad conclusions and pointed to the UN Security Council as the focal point for making humanitarian action possible: "The Security Council has . . . established, in its resolution 1296 (2000), that the targeting of civilians in armed conflict and the denial of humanitarian access to civilian populations afflicted by war may themselves constitute threats to international peace and security and thus be triggers for Security Council action."[89]

As mentioned earlier, an academic cottage industry grew; but, more important, governments sponsored a host of policy initiatives and published reports on the topic. *The Responsibility to Protect* of the Canadian-inspired International Commission on Intervention and State Sovereignty is the most comprehensive statement to date of the *problématique*.[90] This report followed findings from a Swedish initiative, the Independent Commission on Kosovo;[91] the previous U.S. government's overview by the Policy Planning Staff and a report from the Council on Foreign Relations;[92] and major inquiries into the legal authority for intervention by the Dutch and Danish governments.[93]

The ICISS extended the approach pioneered by Francis Deng's work on IDPs, beginning in the early 1990s. "Sovereignty as responsibility" emphasized the rights of victims and the responsibilities of outsiders to protect them when their own governments could not or would not. The status of state sovereignty is not challenged per se but reinforced. However, if a state is unwilling or unable to protect the rights of its own citizens, it temporarily forfeits a moral claim to be treated as a legitimate party. Its sovereignty, as well as its right to nonintervention, is suspended, and a residual responsibility necessitates vigorous action by outsiders to protect populations at risk. The threshold conditions identified by the ICISS are large-scale loss of life and ethnic cleansing, both actual and apprehended. In brief, the three traditional characteristics of a state in the Westphalian system (territory, authority, and population) are supplemented by a fourth (respect for human rights). This norm was then blessed by the secretary-general's High-level Panel on Threats, Challenges and Change in its December 2004 report, which frames the UN's twenty-first-century agenda.[94] The secretary-general further endorsed the emerging norm in his report in preparation for the UN's sixtieth anniversary, and the 2005 World Summit supported this overall approach.[95]

It is worth reiterating an earlier point—namely, the irony that the fastest-growing category of war victims needing the implementation of the "responsibility to protect" norm, IDPs, still has no legal or organizational home. In spite of the overwhelming growth in such populations, the international humanitarian system still treats them, legally speaking, more as an aberration than as the norm.[96] This lacuna is perhaps the clearest institutional indication of the extent to which existing humanitarian machinery is engineered to respond to the crises of another era: interstate armed conflicts. In other words, even though NSAs that do not cross state borders as belligerents are bound by IHL, international institutions and conventions still do not fully acknowledge the formal impediments to succor victims who are not defined according to the parameters of interstate conflicts and the international system.

In addition to local populations victimized by war, agency personnel themselves are increasingly targeted. Targeting relief personnel has both its tactical and strategic reasons. At the operational level, humanitarian agencies may undermine NSAs by presenting an alternative source of vital resources to war-ravaged populations. From a strategic point of view, NSAs may view attacking humanitarians as a means of sending a political message to international organizations and outside military forces. A review of aid workers killed in recent years attests to a disconcerting upswing: from 1992 to 2000, 198 UN civilian staff were killed, and in 1998 alone more civilian staff were killed than military peacekeepers.[97] As seen in chapter 6, this situation is even more critical in the newest of the new wars, those in Afghanistan and Iraq.

Although the humanitarian mantle has in the past afforded a meaningful modicum of physical protection, the danger to and the loss of personnel during the new wars has prompted humanitarians to push for legal protection. In the early 1990s the Security Council began to take note of the increased violence directed toward aid workers. During humanitarian operations in Somalia in 1993, the council passed a resolution to respond to "acts of violence against persons engaging in humanitarian efforts."[98] Shortly thereafter the UN adopted a convention criminalizing attacks on such international personnel, which entered into force in January 1999.[99]

This discussion highlights a paradox in the story of an ever-expanding international humanitarian system: on the one side, the positive normative development to ensure access to and protection of victims; on the other, the growing number of victims—the civilian populations as well as their rescuers. The extent of this paradox reached new heights during the new humanitarianisms of the 1990s, when protection for civilians in particular received greatest attention with widespread support of the "responsibility to protect" norm. Whether this quantitative change in number of victims in relation to calls for civilian protection constitutes a qualitative one is debatable; nevertheless, the new wars clearly presented dangerous challenges with few precedents. The responsibility to protect is part of humanitarians' reckoning with crises associated with state failure and evidences the normative context of the 1990s. As more horrifying atrocities with large numbers of civilian victims erupted—Somalia, Bosnia, Rwanda, Kosovo—these traumatic events produced a dramatic shift in international political norms regarding intervention. Thus, the paradox of greater protections and greater likelihood for victimization encapsulates a tragedy of the new humanitarianisms: rethinking the norms of protecting civilians in war is born solely of bloody failures.

TAMING DEADLY TECHNOLOGIES

Technology may help humanitarian action, as well as pose grisly dangers to victims, as well as aid personnel. Improvements in airlift capacity, for instance, assist the projection of violence but hold the potential for more effective international humanitarian responses. The bombings of Kosovo and Serbia in 1999 and Iraq in March 2003 are not unrelated to the delivery of help to Banda Aceh and other areas rendered inaccessible and hosting vulnerable populations in the aftermath of the December 2004 tsunami. Both the bombings and the delivery of aid reflect the formidable technological and organizational prowess of the U.S. military.

Muscular humanitarians, who advocate the use of force for human protection purposes, are obliged to face issues about how technological innovations have added ethical complexity. Proponents of humanitarian intervention suggest that new technologies inspire confidence in military capacities to help resolve political and humanitarian crises. The ethics of "humanitarian war" refer to the justness of the cause but are rarely, if ever, used to highlight how war is fought.[100] Critics emphasize that the means in which a noble cause is pursued are as important as the intent, and they remind us that "the construction of a 'better world' invariably comes at a price—the lives of others."[101]

Thus, available technologies and possible reactions are closely linked. High-altitude precision bombing in Kosovo spawned the idea of "humanitarianism from 15,000 feet," but this depiction may be more of a commentary on the conditions under which major powers engage in military action than a doctrine for merging humanitarian efforts and military tools. That food and medicine are pushed out the back of cargo planes has created the sense that advances in airlift capacity might somehow signal the end of ethical dilemmas.

For humanitarians the change in technology as filtered through the new wars at once calls for greater resources in responding to the increased levels of lethal force and at the same time promises that such wars may be shorter, have fewer civilian casualties, and entail easier responses. New technology creates greater opportunities to act quickly and vigorously in responding to humanitarian disasters but does not tackle the fundamental political, economic, and social problems endemic to the endeavor. As Michael O'Hanlon notes, "It cannot resolve the political challenges that outside countries always face in conducting these types of missions, such as whether to take sides in a conflict, simply create safe havens, impose a partition line, or forcibly disarm all combatants even at the risk of having to fight them to do so. . . . While an advanced military can use airpower to punish an aggressor, and limit its ability to conduct mechanized warfare, it can not defeat small arms from long distances or stop the violence perpetrated by them."[102] Moreover, optimism should be tempered by the recognition that only a few states have these capacities and that decisions to devote expensive resources to humanitarians are hardly a foregone conclusion. The fundamental questions of political mobilization remain as responses are more likely to be restrained by a lack of will than a dearth of capacity.

Our discussion here is designed to tease out the implications of technology for "old" or "new wars." The key issue is how precisely technological innovations can be applied to improve the capacities of the international humanitarian system and not just the hands dealt to wielders of violence. In short, how can the healing powers of the salve keep pace with the destructive ones of the sword? And is it possible to use the same building blocks as the sword in order to sew stronger sutures and forge sturdier shields?

MAXIMIZING MEDIA ATTENTION TO HUMANITARIAN CRISES

At the same time that local media can be wielded by belligerents and their allies to facilitate support for and willingness of populations to engage in war, the international media can pluck the heartstrings of outsiders to respond with assistance or even military force. In fact, the media is a look-ing glass in which humanitarians see themselves, and it is a lens through which others view the enterprise. Humanitarian action can be romanti-cized and eulogized or depicted with warts and criticized.

Portraying humanitarian disasters has inherent difficulties: the press seeks the drama that makes for a good story, and humanitarians hope for a message that opens pocketbooks. Together these orientations com-bine to paint narratives of humanitarian action as being laden with mas-sive suffering and failed responses. Never does the media portray a cri-sis that did not happen, downplay its severity, or celebrate the success of humanitarians—it simply has little, if anything, to gain from this type of representation.

The so-called CNN effect was, for a time in the mid-1990s, a preoccu-pation in the analysis of what were not quite yet labeled new wars, but it did have consequences for humanitarianism. As Andrew Natsios has argued convincingly—and he should know as the director of the U.S. Agency for International Development (USAID) in the George W. Bush administration and of the Office of Foreign Disaster Assistance in the George H. W. Bush administration and as a vice president of World Vision in between—"the so-called CNN effect has taken on more importance than it deserves. . . . The truth is most complex emergencies get little media attention at any stage."[103]

Earthquakes, hurricanes, and tsunamis readily make headlines, but the cleanup following such ordeals is unlikely to be deemed newsworthy in light of limited public attention spans. However, the situation in man-made emergencies is markedly different. If important geopolitical inter-ests are threatened by a humanitarian emergency, then the media is prob-ably pushing on an open door and is irrelevant in terms of mobilizing political will. If such interests are absent, then media attention will not illicit a robust response but may influence the availability of public and private funding. Indeed, if an area is truly peripheral, then the media will have to work hard merely to overcome the active opposition of diplomats, the military, and parliamentarians.

Telling are the simple statistics regarding international responses to vis-ible or "loud" emergencies versus those of "silent" emergencies. The UN's Office for the Coordination of Humanitarian Affairs calculates total per capita resources available to victims of wars in various regions. When wars were raging in the Balkans, for instance, it was approximately ten to twenty times better to be a victim in Europe than in Africa. In another instance, almost half of the humanitarian funds for the European Com-munity Humanitarian Office from 1993 to 2000 were spent in Europe. OCHA reports note that consolidated appeals for 2000 varied wildly—from about $10 per capita for North Korea or Uganda to $185 per capita in southeastern Europe.[104]

This discrepancy is deeply unsettling to many observers, practitioners, as well as analysts. The largest donors to most major humanitarian agencies are states, and international political considerations often command funding priorities. Smillie and Minear, for example, have found extremely wanting "the charity of nations" because of the discrepancy between the actual "needs identified by people in distress" and the response by the international humanitarian system. The latter reflects "what humanitarian agencies think the political traffic will bear and what they think donors will provide."[105]

The explanation for the differences clearly reflects the calculations by donors—what the IFRC summarizes as "Global aid tracks political priorities"—but it is also often tied to publicity and the politicized media prism.[106] Three tiers of humanitarian crises can be distinguished: high profile, visible, and forgotten. In the first instance, powerful geopolitical interests fuel humanitarian concerns, and agencies rapidly mobilize. Under these circumstances, humanitarian interests are often conflated with political objectives. Proximity and the presence of troops make for powerful headlines and footage, as U.S. troops in Somalia or Haiti in the early 1990s or in Afghanistan or Iraq today aptly demonstrate. In such crises, attention from international media along with aid monies is in abundance, leading often to a discussion about "limited absorptive capacity," or the inability to administer and use well the abundance of resources that flow into such high-profile emergencies.

At the second level are war-related crises that receive attention solely as humanitarian disasters; they lack the additional layers of concerns that may be decisive in mustering more muscular military responses as well as aid allocations. Oftentimes, these crises may receive more attention than resources. As a result these second-tiered crises are addressed purely as a humanitarian issue, meaning that states tend to substitute humanitarian action to cope rather than dedicate greater amounts of political and economic resources to address the larger issues, those which produced the crisis in the first place.[107]

The breakup of the former Yugoslavia and the first few years of the emergency in the Balkans provide excellent illustrations. It was not really until later—in autumn 1995, to be exact—that Croats took matters into their own hands and forced Western political and military responses. Until the arrival of NATO forces in large numbers after the Dayton Accords, the media focus was elsewhere. The "humanitarian alibi" seemed enough: why act militarily or politically when the application of the humanitarian salve was doing so much to lessen suffering?

On the bottom tier are those emergencies that suffer from both a lack of response and a lack of media or any other kind of attention. In such cases, states do not provide sufficient capacities, and the disaster churns on in woeful anonymity. Media images especially associated with the bottom tier may also be conducive to a narrative that such crises are unavoidable and waste resources, specifically implying that cultural factors make out-side interest and meaningful humanitarian action impossible at best and foolish at worst.[108] The disappearance of Somalia and Haiti from today's screens and pages, in spite of substantial U.S. military involvement ear-lier, suggests that action is simply beyond the pale at present.

Once again, this discussion of media coverage of the new wars has not revealed a distinctive set of contemporary problems, except that fatigue—after two decades of a steady diet of covering humanitarian crises with print and pictures—is undoubtedly a problem for a journalist attempting to get stories of humanitarian need in the DRC or Liberia into print or onto screens. In fact, we should not delude ourselves, because media coverage may also hurt the humanitarian cause. "We cannot have misery without aid workers. They conjure away the horror by suggesting that help is at hand," writes Michael Ignatieff. "Coverage of humanitarian assistance allows the West the illusion that it is doing something; in this way, coverage becomes an alternative to more serious political engagement." He continues that the real story is thus one of disengagement "while the moral lullaby we allow our humanitarian consciences to sign is that we are coming closer and closer."[109] A similar comment comes from the BBC's Nik Gowing, who dis-tinguishes between quality journalism and the "noise" (different from "loud" emergencies that require in-depth treatment), which does not add any analysis but rather "imperfect real-time reality."[110] John Hammock and Joel Charny have described the media's treatment as "a scripted morality play" whose simplified images contribute to compassion fatigue and a fail-ure to educate the public and politicians about root causes.[111]

Hence, the conventional wisdom that media coverage drives policy and intervention—that is, "something must be done"—is off the mark. Images and coverage can be important in eliciting resources and galvanizing humanitarian responses when they align with or are nurtured by political power. How humanitarian crises and action are viewed matter—locally and internationally. Those deemed politically crucial receive the lion's share of attention and resources.

"NEW HUMANITARIANISMS" IN HISTORICAL PERSPECTIVE

Here we connect to relevant themes in order to situate the elements of new humanitarianisms historically as well as within the broader configu-ration of the post–Cold War period. They represent the various responses of different humanitarian agencies to the transnational and nonpermis-sive environments of new wars, the dangerous and manipulative actors within them, the surge in civilian casualties on the battlefield, and the potential opportunities afforded by recent technological improvements.

Table 4.4. Crises and Traumas Shaping "New Humanitarianisms"

Crisis	Trauma	Issues for System
Somalia, 1991	*"Black Hawk* down"	Humanitarian mission too politically engaged Use of force insufficient to end hostilities
Bosnia, 1993–1995	"Well-fed dead"	Aid without protection is meaningless
Rwanda, 1994	Genocide and militarized refugee camps	Aid can be manipulated by belligerent victims
Kosovo, 1999	Legitimate but not legal use of force	Use of force can backfire and undermine legitimacy

The evolution of the new humanitarianisms illustrates that shocking humanitarian crises of the 1990s have shaken agencies and provoked policy reactions. Table 4.4 provides a thumbnail sketch of the key disasters and the traumas that led to altering long-standing practices in the international humanitarian system.

These traumas in particular shed light on three themes that characterize the new humanitarianisms. The first is that of *politicization*. From the founding of the international humanitarian system up through the final stages of the Cold War, humanitarian action has been essentially predicated on state consent and support. Indeed, much like that of previous periods, state interests were implicit in shaping the decision making of agencies entering the era of new humanitarianisms. For example, the UNHCR's practice of forcibly repatriating refugees violated the principle of *nonrefoulement*—that endangered populations not be returned to menacing states or those that afford no protection—and was standard procedure in the 1980s.[112]

However, to cope with the causes and scope of crises common in the 1990s, the system had to distinctly depart from the interstate logic that had framed its existence since its inception. The actions and policies of agencies such as MSF and UNHCR were instrumental in pushing out the political envelope of humanitarianism by making choices that would reverberate throughout the international humanitarian system. Working with NSAs and sometimes even without the consent of belligerents occurred with increasing frequency during this period and thus brought to the surface the politics on which the system hinges. The myth of depoliticized humanitarianism was thoroughly dispelled by the new humanitarianisms—first by the political strings of states but later by the absence of consent from credible and powerful nonstate authorities.

The second trend concerns *militarization*. The huge increases in civilian fatalities heightened humanitarian calls for interjecting military resources to render physical protection. Sometimes, such as in the case of Kosovo, military interjection leads to securitization or a sense that population flows and human rights violations are a threat to international security. Other times the sheer inhumanity of massacres greases the gears of a humanitarian response and with it a militarized component that is sanctioned by humanitarians. The responsibility to protect is predicated on military resources' being available to ensure humanitarian access and to protect human rights. However, as the case of Kosovo demonstrates, military utilization is still quite a few strides behind military penetration of humanitarian action. Thus, the major strand of militarization of the new humanitarianisms signals that humanitarians are much more likely to authorize force than have it under their command and then author its use.

A third theme that underpins the transformation entailed by the new humanitarianisms is that of *coordination/fragmentation*. Its complexity has such significance for this period that an in-depth analysis is required, which we turn to in the next chapter.

5

Humanitarianism
and Collective Action

- 🌍 The Panacea of "Coordination"
- 🌍 Three Threads of Collective Action: Cooperation, Centralization, and Integration
- 🌍 Divergent Perceptions of Needs, Priorities, and Sequences
- 🌍 Differences in Tactical Engagements
- 🌍 The Value of Independent and Diverse Operations
- 🌍 The Blowback from Insecurity
- 🌍 Institutional Rivalries
- 🌍 Collective Pursuits and "Atomized" Action

Providing relief and protection amid the hostile fire of war while eluding the predation of local NSAs is central to the contemporary humanitarian *problématique*. As if this scenario were not challenging enough, an additional layer of structural impediments has resulted from the extreme decentralization of the so-called system. The complexities of effectively applying the salve to counter the impact of the sword in the new wars raise prodigious collective action problems that speak to the net effects of new humanitarianisms.

Mustering sufficient resources to fund programming is of course essential to the enterprise, but the tunnel vision of individual agencies often blinds their decision makers to the collective dimensions of their work. Mancur Olson's classic work on the difficulties of collective action is instructive. Although his case studies concern cooperation among states, a similar logic applies to relations between aid agencies. Olson demonstrates that a variety of units sharing common goals often end up operating in ways that undermine presumed intentions.[1] Negative results do not reflect bad faith but rather ingrained, improper incentives as well as poor knowledge of how the system functions as a whole. Humanitarian organizations often publicly espouse altruistic objectives but essentially pursue more self-centered ones not only to address the emergency needs of distressed populations but also to thrive as institutions.

It is important to bear in mind some key recent developments that have heightened traditional collective action problems—namely, the growth in resources and institutions. Over the 1990s, substantially increased resources flowed into the international humanitarian system, creating more and larger actors, many with diverse agendas and interpretations of humanitarianism. In 1991 overall assistance was $4.5 billion, and although this figure dropped to $3.8 billion in 1997, it climbed back up to $5.8 billion by 2000 and, as we will see later, reached some $10 billion in 2004.[2]

Second, the infusion of resources has poured not just into the mainstream—UN agencies and the Red Cross movement—but to an ever-growing number of NGOs. Indeed, Alexander Cooley and James Ron point out that, as barriers to entry in the market have fallen, "there is little doubt that the transnational world is increasingly dense. Between 1960 and 1996, the number of INGOs [international nongovernmental organizations] grew from 1,000 to 5,500. This growth has been particularly dramatic in the transnational aid sector, as private aid agencies expanded their operations by 150 percent from 1985 to 1995."[3] It began with the famine in Ethiopia and Operation Lifeline Sudan in the 1980s. By the 1990s, NGOs had become major players in their own right, and the UN and the ICRC no longer dominated relief efforts.[4]

The overall impacts of more resources and more players were to widen and increase humanitarian operations in war zones. Competition naturally increases with the stepped-up jockeying for resources by a wider array of actors, and the harshest of critics have pointed to abuses and perverse funding patterns, including the humanitarian industry that benefits from providing aid to war-ravaged populations.[5] David Rieff draws a parallel between delivery in war zones and the December 2004 tsunami: "For all the talk of coordination and accountability, the need to maintain market share continues to trump sound humanitarian practice."[6]

The plethora of NGOs has made the international humanitarian system unwieldy and eroded whatever potential there was for meaningful coordination—an omnipresent solution that is often put forward and that is discussed here to start this chapter. What follows is an examination of several other components of the current conundrum: divergent perceptions of needs and sequences, differences in tactical engagement, the value in independent and diverse operations, the blowback from insecurity, and institutional rivalries. By the end of the chapter, it is evident that the laudable Good Samaritan culture is inadequate. The enterprise is "atomized"—competitive individual units, rather than partners, often end up "defecting" from a common approach.

THE PANACEA OF "COORDINATION"

It is essential to recognize how the crises growing from the new wars frame the peculiar collective action problems of the new humanitarianisms. We begin with a hard look at how coordination is preached versus how it is practiced.

Language itself indicates how conceptual changes penetrate institutions or fail to do so. The literature on the current historical stage of warfare comes with its own vocabulary. To the list of terminology describing contemporary phenomena, humanitarian affairs has added "complex political emergency." By the early to mid-1990s, concepts circulating to capture new wars congealed into the necessity for humanitarians to confront a "humanitarian crisis in a country, region or society where there is a total or considerable breakdown of authority resulting from internal or external conflict and which requires an international response that goes beyond the mandate or capacity of any single agency and/or the ongoing UN country programme."[7]

The UN's definition suggests that coordination is the most significant issue and presumes that the central problem is determining which agency should perform which function at which stage. But the meaning and significance of "complex political emergency" to agencies is open to interpretation. With no central power of the purse and no wherewithal to ensure compliance, it should come as no surprise that collective action in an atomized system is the exception rather than the rule. It may be evermore necessary as a result of the new wars, but it remains unlikely within an atomized system.

Figure 5.1 illustrates the species of governmental, intergovernmental, and nongovernmental aid agencies that flock to emergencies, along with other external actors. While it portrays accurately the various decentralized sets of outside actors that arrive on the scene, it cannot convey the complexity and confusing reality that each type of actor contains a bevy of totally decentralized units that fly to a war zone. Hence, the label "IGO" fails to capture the complexity of the European Union or the dizzying acronyms and connections of the UN system—with the main abbrevi-

Figure 5.1. The Humanitarian Network: Significant Actors in Humanitarian Crises

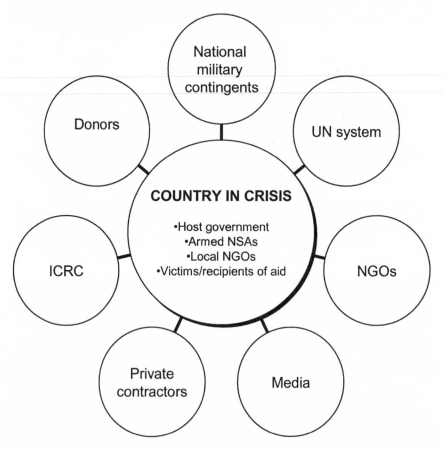

NOTE: ICRC: International Committee of the Red Cross; NGOs: nongovernmental organizations; NSAs: nonstate actors.

ations being UNHCR, UNICEF, WFP, UNDP, and OCHA. And the hundreds of international NGOs—some with budgets comprising hundreds of millions of dollars, others "mom and pop" operations—are hidden behind the "INGO" label.

Figure 5.1 also can only suggest the extent to which calls for enhanced "coordination" are usually sung by a passionate chorus of bureaucrats, but actual behavior is accompanied by more tepid decibel levels that reflect administrative inertia and dominant economic incentives pushing in the opposite direction. As one former military officer summarized, "the need for a concerted approach . . . contradicts the current independence of each responding agency and organization in an international response."[8]

The widespread shorthand for the delivery of humanitarian action is the international humanitarian "system." This label disguises the fact that all agencies subscribe to common philosophical premises, when overall performance reflects the sum of individual actions rather than a planned, singular, and coherent whole. The use of another image, international humanitarian "family," might be more apt in that it allows for several eventualities, including being extremely dysfunctional.

The need to make better use of the many moving parts of international humanitarian machinery has been a preoccupation for some time, but the need for enhanced coordination was pushed by donors with responses to the new wars of the 1990s. As the international system increasingly confronted war-torn societies in which civilian humanitarian organizations interacted routinely with military operations under UN or other auspices, the perceived need for coordination was reinforced—especially as the numbers of NGOs and private contractors grew substantially. Improving the effectiveness of the development system has been on hold since the UN's 1969 capacity study, but the necessity to have less waste and more impact at least within the humanitarian part of the international delivery system seemed especially compelling when huge numbers of lives were at stake in humanitarian disasters.[9]

The real problem is that everyone is for coordination as long as it implies no loss of autonomy. One practitioner, Antonio Donini, who spent much of the last fifteen years of his career in Afghanistan, drew distinctions among three broad categories of coordination within the United Nations:

- Coordination by command—in other words, coordination where strong leadership is accompanied by some sort of leverage and authority, whether carrot or stick
- Coordination by consensus—where leadership is essentially based on the capacity of the "coordinator" to orchestrate a coherent response and mobilize the key actors around common objectives and priorities

- Coordination by default—where, in the absence of a formal coordination entity, only the most rudimentary exchange of information and division of labor takes place among the actors[10]

These distinctions should be viewed not as airtight categories but rather as points on a spectrum. Given the feudal nature of the UN system and the ferocious independence of INGOs, coordination by command is clearly unrealistic, however desirable, particularly in the context of coercive military operations. The experience of the DHA under the best of circumstances—for instance, during the first six months after the Rwandan genocide, when agencies were especially sensitive to concerns over net impacts—could undoubtedly be described as coordination by consensus. The experience of its successor, OCHA, under the worst of circumstances—for instance, in the uncharted chaos of Liberia or Afghanistan—demonstrated the absence of meaningful coordination, and what little existed could accurately be labeled as coordination by default.

Many critics and practitioners argue that, without central authority, all UN coordination mechanisms constitute a hindrance rather than a help. To them individual creativity that spawns chaos is better than the damage from botched efforts at coherence. The process is better self-regulated than poorly coordinated because one less layer of bureaucracy is preferable to one layer more. Moreover, some ardent proponents of laissez-faire humanitarianism argue that a coherent strategy is unwise because it works against the magic of the marketplace in which individual agencies pursue independent strategies but magically arrive at a sound division of labor. As no one is really in charge and no one can be sure what will work, so the argument goes, why not make the best of it rather than merely add a ceremonial layer? Still others maintain that failures to address collective action dynamics are not only an organizational nightmare but can also potentially exacerbate or contribute to conflict.

However, throwing in the towel is unacceptable. The essence of the collective action problem is that, to apply Gertrude Stein's unkind characterization of Oakland, there is no there there. It is simply not apparent who is in the collectivity and what actions they are capable of taking to prevent counterproductive tendencies. The clearest theme emerging from our descriptions of the new wars and new humanitarianisms is the urgent need for fewer outsiders and for better orchestration among them when coming to the rescue—the central players in figure 5.1 include the military; IGOs; and, especially, the members of the UN system, international NGOs, private contractors, and the ICRC.

No expression in the international public policy lexicon is more used and less understood than that of "coordination," which is the reason why it appears so frequently in donor, UN, and NGO documents. It is also why they employ a host of other "soft" words (in meaning, not pronunciation) beginning with "C"—cooperation, cohesion, complementarity. These need to be replaced by words that start with a hard "C" and have a hard and meaningful edge—consolidation, command and control, and compulsion—or by one that starts with a soft "C" but that has a harder edge, centralization.

It is precisely such "hard"-content "Cs" that would improve international responses to war victims and help address collective action problems. The charade continues as the stakes get higher (in terms of human lives and resources). Donors and aid agencies speak out of both sides of their mouths. Autonomy, not meaningful coordination, is the key goal of proprietary UN agencies and market share–oriented NGOs. Crocodile tears shed by officials who lament waste and the lack of effectiveness should be replaced by serious efforts to forego financial and operational independence in the interests of the humanitarian enterprise and addressing seriously its collective action problems.

THREE THREADS OF COLLECTIVE ACTION: COOPERATION, CENTRALIZATION, AND INTEGRATION

We begin with a discussion of three threads of collective action in order to be in a position to parse more carefully several interwoven possibilities to improve performance in the new wars. As should be clear from the preceding section, the relaxed bias of coordination connotes an ideal without indicating the unlikelihood of its being actually achieved.[11] We use three terms—*cooperation, centralization,* and *integration*—to distinguish between how agencies can work together, be orchestrated, or become part of other nonintrinsically humanitarian efforts.

Cooperation refers to nonbinding, usually informal arrangements among humanitarian agencies. The term suggests that each makes its own decisions regarding policy but that on occasion they are willing to work with other agencies. Sometimes referred to as "complementarity," this approach recognizes that the efforts of different agencies may be harnessed without forcing agencies to subscribe to a single goal or mandate.[12] On the best days, this is the prevalent SOP within the enterprise.

Illustrations of the mechanisms that promote cooperation can be found among NGOs and IGOs. InterAction in Washington along with the International Council of Voluntary Agencies and the Emergency Committee for Humanitarian Response in Geneva are the largest and best known NGO coordinating bodies. Similarly, within the UN, the Inter-Agency Standing Committee is a forum in which agencies have an opportunity to coordinate efforts within the UN as well as with the ICRC and NGO consortiums. However, the existence of such institutions does not guarantee coordination but may facilitate meaningful cooperation.

Beyond the looseness of cooperation is a higher degree of coordination that is more formalized and rigid: *centralization*. This notion implies that humanitarian action is most effective and efficient when there is a formal institutional way to centralize the planning and execution of efforts within the world organization. In many ways, the UN has struggled with and promoted this idea since its earliest experiences in responding to humanitarian crises. Historically, the International Relief Organization, UNRRA, UNHCR, UNDRO, and DHA all typify attempts to pull together resources to better administer humanitarian assistance.

The most recent incarnation was the creation of OCHA in 1998.[13] By making use of several mechanisms (e.g., the Consolidated Appeals Process (CAP), which brings together the needs assessments of different UN agencies and allocates funding), OCHA is at the apex of the planning pyramid for UN humanitarian agencies. However, as the CAP demonstrates, compiling a joint statement with various agencies' wishes is not the same as effective coordination. As a recent analysis of the CAP process noted, "the phrase 'shopping list' has long been synonymous with many of the early appeals, pointing to the fact that they were little more than a series of different projects bound together in one document, but not under a coherent and unifying strategy."[14] In short, the limitations of the planner without the power of the purse are that any meaningful centralization still reflects the willingness of financially independent units to cooperate on the plan.

A further impediment to promoting sectorwide cooperation is that fewer and fewer amounts of money are channeled through CAPs (around 30 percent), while more and more resources are administered through NGOs.[15] Although NGOs are notorious for their decentralization and operational independence, there are also centralizing aspects within this subset of humanitarian actors. One aspect is the size of the market controlled by a handful of NGOs or families of them—including familiar ones such as CARE, MSF, Oxfam, Save the Children, and World Vision and less-familiar ones such as APDOVE (Association of Protestant Development Organizations in Europe), CIDSE (Coopération international pour le développement et la solidarité), and Eurostep. Typically, the members of this oligopoly account for 45 percent to 55 percent of the total $10 billion of global humanitarian assistance.[16]

The idea behind *integration* is that the actions of humanitarian agencies should serve the broader need to resolve political differences and address the root causes of conflict. In the parlance of the UN, an "an integrated mission" is defined as "an instrument with which the UN seeks to help countries in the transition from war to lasting peace, or address a similarly complex situation that requires a system-wide UN response, through sub-suming various actors and approaches within an overall political-strategic crisis management framework."[17] Although humanitarian assistance focuses on emergency aid to victims, those advocating the integration agenda argue that this focus cannot be separated from rehabilitating society so that war does not return. Accordingly, humanitarian agencies and their actions must not undermine peace processes and postconflict peace-building. They should only devote their resources where they do not jeopardize political reconciliation or establish incentives that promote or profit from violent hostilities.

The move to integrate humanitarian action into wider political efforts to end wars and foster conditions for rehabilitation and reconstruction gained momentum in the 1990s. Three trends lay behind this develop-ment: attempts to redefine security more broadly to include humanitarian disasters (securitization); organizational philosophies pushing manage-ment to unite means and thereby make international efforts more effi-cient; and recognition of aid as a tool for promoting political change.[18]

Furthermore, the actual effects of humanitarian relief in crises moved integration to front and center of the agenda. The debacle of providing aid to those who carried out the genocide in Rwanda and continued to desta-bilize the region was a formative experience for many agencies. Although traditional humanitarian principles demand that assistance be given to all victims, practices that rigidly follow this course limit humanitarian oper-ations from being integrated into broader international political action.[19] Consequently, by the mid-1990s many agencies began to admit the limits of humanitarian solutions for humanitarian problems and leaned toward more consequentialist practices.[20] Later in the decade, with multiple ongoing responses to the long-running civil war in Afghanistan, the inter-national assistance community mounted its greatest attempt at integra-tion in 1998, the Strategic Framework for Afghanistan. This arrangement among different branches of the UN and various humanitarian agencies was intended to place a concentrated set of projects on par with other responses to the conflict.[21]

This sentiment gained ground outside of addressing the war in Afghanistan when in 2000 the Brahimi report advocated greater coher-ence across all UN mandates and agencies.[22] In spite of the "back to basics" passion of traditionalists in the ICRC and the MSF and elsewhere who wish to keep their distance, during the last decade integration has moved from the drawing boards of a few humanitarians to being squarely on the agenda and in many programmatic decisions.[23]

The next five sections identify possibilities for "defecting" from com-mon actions. Each contributes to weakening these three possible threads that are essential to overcoming collective action problems and keeping the fabric of the international humanitarian system from unraveling.

DIVERGENT PERCEPTIONS OF NEEDS, PRIORITIES, AND SEQUENCES

The first monkey wrench thrown into the collective humanitarian works results from agencies' assessing and addressing different requirements of war-torn populations and societies. When violent conflict erupts and visible streams of victims seek to satisfy their most basic needs, it is clear that humanitarian action should initially emphasize the delivery of food, water, and medicine as an urgent first step toward recovery. However, this sequence and these priorities presume clarity in the start and finish of hostilities and aid programming. They miss the reality that war can ebb and flow, much as responses do. Accordingly, one agency may stress food to sustain populations, while another may already be stabilizing food production and grain markets and reviving development efforts.

Table 5.1 depicts the diversity of actions that have come to fall under the rubric of "humanitarian," to illustrate the temporal and substantive dimensions of the complete humanitarian agenda in war zones. All directly or indirectly improve human welfare in the short or long term. While the elements may dovetail, their doing so is unlikely.

Problems begin with trying to ensure proper sequencing and priorities. Long-term indigenous capacity building or elections always sound sensible but often ring hollow and are close to impossible in the throes of war. Moreover, the new wars present a confusing array of stages of conflict because their impacts are sporadic and nonlinear across time and space in war-torn societies, leaving new humanitarianisms to address a variety of requirements without a clear template.

For instance, if an agency moves toward investing in the long term, it is not "defecting" from improving human welfare in the immediate future.

Table 5.1. The Length and Width of the Humanitarian Agenda

Width	Length	
	Short Term (Emergency Phase)	*Long Term (Postconflict)*
Legal	Protection in war (Geneva Conventions)	Foster human rights
Economic (material resources)	Provide food, medicine, and shelter	Social and economic development
Security (physical protection)	Supply armed protection by military actors	Build army, police forces, and judiciary
Political (stop war)	Foster and enforce cease-fire agreement	Build national institutions

Nonetheless, by rendering such assistance, it may inadvertently create opportunities for actors seeking to manipulate aid in the short run and continue war. The injection of aid when other components of the international humanitarian system are trying to stem destabilizing resource flows and improve local accountability can backfire on all projects.

This example underlines the unfortunate reality that effective action requires more and harder coordination among agencies than that required in wars in which there is more of a countrywide pattern to needs and a cleaner beginning and end to the emergency phase. Earlier, the central debate about the "relief-to-development continuum"[24] focused on how to move as quickly as possible from life-sustaining relief to rehabilitation and development after a peace process, which included thinking creatively about building local capacities even during the emergency phase.[25] In armed conflicts as diverse as those in Colombia, Sudan, and the DRC, for instance, certain parts of the country can be functioning reasonably well and with a degree of security while elsewhere violence and insecurity require emergency sustenance. Consequently, in recent years, there has been talk of broadening the continuum to link humanitarian relief to security.[26] Exemplifying this trend is the DAC's reformulated definition of overseas development assistance (ODA) to include security assistance.[27]

The problem is not just the plethora of needs but also the simultaneous implementation of multiple partial solutions within areas in which virtually every need is a priority. Although humanitarians often think of programming in terms of a "continuum," in reality they operate as a "simultanuum"—not a clear and discrete progression but a jumbled mass of inputs and approaches with the hope that somehow most urgent requirements will be satisfied. A lack of agreement on principles and on what goals must be achieved by humanitarian assistance in specific areas critically weakens the ability of the system to function, let alone to do so coherently.[28] The new wars in particular exacerbate this problem in that chaos and stability may come and go, or they may be present or absent in one locale or another. With the staggering growth of the international humanitarian system, the once relatively minor need for closer cooperation among the many moving parts of the international humanitarian system has become of paramount importance.

DIFFERENCES IN TACTICAL ENGAGEMENTS

A second and interrelated illustration of the impact of the diffuse agendas and actions of "atomized agencies" is in the selection and application of tactics for engaging NSAs—that is, agencies must find the proper ones to use with each local actor. NSAs, for their part, seek to extract whatever resources they can (i.e., aid and legitimacy) and will strike the most lucrative bargains possible with available sources. Competition among NSAs leads to individual negotiations with individual aid agencies. A symbiosis forms between two types of competition: first, that among agencies to exclusively engage local NSAs that can facilitate humanitarian action; and, second, that among local NSAs to monopolize access and resources that will then enrich themselves at the expense of others. Thus, a market exists for the services of NSAs among agencies whose capacity to work closely with a local counterpart is a necessity for donors.

In instances in which particular NSAs spoil humanitarian action consistently and give no indication of changing their ways, aid agencies may confront them and perhaps withdraw from an area of operations. Selective suspension or withdrawal by a single or a few agencies, however, has more symbolic than practical effect. Competitors, eager to give concrete expression to the humanitarian impulse and pursuing institutional interests in increasing market share, can rapidly fill gaps created by a departing agency. Consequently, diversity among agencies in the selection of tactics coupled with respect for individual agency autonomy may drive a wedge between outsiders and prevent them from developing common approaches to confronting particular mettlesome local actors. Prototypical of the disconnects among agencies is the contrasting approaches to engagement of the ICRC and the UN. The former holds open the possibility of engagement regardless of violence or other aspects that give most other agencies grounds to suspend contact. In contrast, the latter tends to place greater conditions upon those that they engage.[29] Furthermore, other agencies have their own criteria; for example, Oxfam does not participate in the *Code of Conduct for International Red Cross and Red Crescent Movement and Non-governmental Organizations in Disaster Relief*.[30]

As a result of the diversity in engagement tactics, locals can "shop around" to get the best deal, which may mean partnering with the agency that makes the fewest demands. Being able to appeal to the highest or least exigent bidder potentially benefits belligerents and undercuts collective humanitarian performance. Again, greater not lesser cohesion is required in the new wars than in natural disasters or more traditional interstate wars. The consequences of respecting the dominant culture of autonomy in the industry ensure that NSAs, unless their conduct is notorious, have guaranteed alternative sources of supply. As Cooley and Ron note, "the presence of multiple contractors also increases recipients' ability to play contractors and donors off against each other."[31] NSAs in contemporary war zones benefit from a buyer's market.

Integration raises additional tactical questions, which are examined in the following section. However, here we note that agencies view integration as being useful in some crises, or perhaps even with respect to particular NSAs in specific crises, and then at other times see such attempts as being distasteful and negating the independence that is so dear to individual organizations. Humanitarian agencies face a difficult decision between the principles and practicalities of independent operations and the potential promise of integration—that is, does integration produce problems that undermine emergency relief, or does it make longer-term redress of structural factors fomenting the crisis possible?

THE VALUE OF INDEPENDENT AND DIVERSE OPERATIONS

Why do agencies view joint planning and action as constraints on their immediate, effective, and focused action? Some humanitarians believe that autonomous responses create the flexibility necessary to successfully perform tasks and fulfill missions. For example, no group guards its autonomy more intensely than the ICRC. As such, inconsistency is not seen as a fatal flaw but a necessary cost to guarantee strength in diversity.

A notable illustration of placing value on independent action, and one that has facilitated a passionate debate among practitioners, is that of MSF's opting out of attempts to integrate its operations into the work of what it sees as ostensibly political activities.[32] MSF has two primary objections to the integration paradigm, according to the head of its New York office, Nicolas de Torrenté.[33] First, aid should not be used as a reward because it is the right of war victims. Second, the calculation of giving assistance only to those who are ethically palatable to humanitarians as a method for promoting a particular type of political change is dubious because the cost is borne by war victims themselves. As such, instrumental calculations are viewed as being morally reprehensible. MSF recognizes that there is a potential for abuse, but it is adamant that every victim be considered an individual human life and not part of any larger plan. This approach is intended to send a political message to governments about the sanctity of humanitarian work, but it makes a unified front impossible.

At one time or another, humanitarian agencies have all stressed the necessity of independence. The moral and operational quandary is that tying aid to other institutions and their priorities could impair the ability of agencies to fulfill their own missions. NGOs, for instance, were established as an alternative to government priorities and political partisanship. The worry remains that meaningful integration becomes a euphemism for submission to the agendas of politicians.

THE BLOWBACK FROM INSECURITY

An additional practical worry that complicates decisions about collective efforts arises over the safety of staff members. In tying or even associating the actions of an agency to the work of other aid organizations or especially to a political entity or its military forces (of a government, coalition, or IGO), an agency could be perched on a tenuous branch. Should the actions of partners or even perceived partners stoke resentments or, worse yet, cause casualties, the branch snaps and an agency can find itself in a security free fall.

As highlighted in chapter 4, such blowback on the work of humanitarians is prevalent, even where they have gone to great lengths to maintain their neutrality. Often, it is not so much that humanitarians have intentionally engaged in actions to achieve particular political ends that leads to their targeting but rather that the polarized contexts in which agencies operate tend to promote a "with us or against us" mentality among belligerents. To be fair, the history of international humanitarian action is filled with examples that show how associations can be mutually reinforcing and beneficial. However, it is the cases where such associations are problematic that are becoming a concern for the enterprise; when the work of others imperils a humanitarian agency, personnel begin to question the utility of partnerships, as their own lives or those of colleagues are put on the line. In this case in particular, the thread of integration implies politicization, which in turn entails severe security threats. In the 1990s two vivid illustrations include that of Somalia, where UNITAF's pursuit of warlord Mohammed Aideed led to security problems for UN humanitarian agencies, and that of Bosnia, where UNPROFOR's actions put UNHCR's staff in danger.[34] As we shall see in chapter 6, the increase in coordination resulting in greater threats to humanitarian workers is especially apparent in such crises as Afghanistan and Iraq.[35] As such, the decision to defect from collective international efforts is a matter of principle (as detailed earlier) as well as practice. Collective action is intended to bring together humanitarians and others who respond to war, but in some cases the blowback from insecurity drives defection.

INSTITUTIONAL RIVALRIES

We now turn to perhaps the most powerful and rampant material factor driving agency behavior—institutional rivalries grounded in a struggle for funding and market share. Like all ventures and organizations, humanitarian agencies require resources to carry out activities in a particular area of operations, as well as to maintain their overall structural foundations (salaries, equipment, transportation, and overhead).

Humanitarianism as an "industry" raises a host of issues that can characterize any business, ranging from the mechanics of branding and retailing to the consequences of competition. Cooley and Ron have pointed to "the NGO scramble," but, essentially, all intergovernmental and private institutions (nonprofits as well as for-private contractors) face comparable pressures and imperatives in the marketplace.

What seems "normal" business sense and practice for soybean farmers and steel companies, however, somehow seems unbecoming for aid agencies, which nonetheless require the donor resources to survive and thrive. As Cooley and Ron note, "dysfunctional organizational behavior is likely to be a rational response to systematic and predictable institutional pressures."[36] To point to material incentives and rent seeking is not to criticize individuals or impugn their moral values but rather to demonstrate the power of the market. An OCHA-commissioned study has documented the extent to which the growing number of actors vying for contracts has undermined coordination efforts of all types.[37]

Overseas development assistance has been shrinking steadily over the last quarter of a century, as shown by virtually any report on the topic.[38] Although the Millennium Project led by Jeffrey Sachs argues for a doubling of overseas development assistance by 2015, it also points out that in addition to donors' having established conditions for grants, their funds have shifted from development toward emergencies.[39] While the rise in acute disasters makes such a shift sensible, it enhances competition and trade-offs. Ian Smillie and Larry Minear have described it as "a larger piece of a smaller pie," which has led to their judgment that "competition in the aid marketplace has increased by leaps and bounds."[40] Such competition may in fact lead to more waste and overlap among aid agencies, although the basic tenets of economics supposedly argue the contrary.

Many humanitarians like to think of themselves as being above the fray. Presumably, the self-evident value of their work should suffice. Too few humanitarians seem to appreciate the extent to which self-righteousness is a poor excuse for a defensible rationale and that it is imperative to analyze the international humanitarian system as a business that has developed over time. Otherwise, to paraphrase Fiona Terry, we are "condemned to repeat" errors of the past.[41]

The conditions surrounding the availability of material resources can influence the decision to participate in or defect from collective action. On the one hand, donors may allocate funds only to those who participate in a common undertaking.[42] On the other hand, other funding sources may be attracted by unique or alternative approaches and provide an incentive to those agencies that differentiate themselves from the common front; as such, dissidents can monopolize a particular sector of emergency response, a particular crisis, or even a particular NSA partner.

Lonely defectors may or may not temporarily occupy high or low moral ground, but they also exert pressure on other agencies to become conscious of the underlying rationale behind allocations. For example, if an agency purchases access to victims through bribes—usually in the form of a "tax" on goods transported to affected populations—this behavior may not only have an impact on war victims but may also establish a precedent whereby all agencies are expected to buy access in the same way. We must keep in mind that some exploitative interlocutors may be "shopping" for agencies that can give them the best deal (i.e., allow for the greatest amount of extortion). For example, in the case of the Revolutionary United Front in Sierra Leone, the Security Council castigated agencies for deviating from a coherent framework for engagement and later concluded from the experience that "common ground rules would help to make access negotiations more predictable and effective, and reduce the risk of mistakes or of agencies being played off against each other by warring parties."[43] In short, individual agencies' cutting their own deals with those who are gatekeepers to victims ups the ante. For agencies the fear of being marginalized from humanitarian crises can drive them to deviate from joining collective efforts. Withdrawal, in turn, may lower the media profile of those who leave, which can in turn hurt fund-raising and programming for other activities in a particular war zone and in other parts of the world. Oftentimes an agency's profile is tied to its being present in the toughest of times. Thus, institutional agendas and economic incentives necessarily lead to atomistic actions by individual aid agencies. What is rational and productive for one agency may be quite irrational and counterproductive for the humanitarian enterprise as a whole.

Donors are prime movers in the humanitarian field and affect agency decision making at every level. Preferences from funders structure how operational agencies cast their programs to qualify for as large a share of the humanitarian resource pie as possible; or in business parlance, agencies engage in niche marketing. Since donors' interests fluctuate with electoral results and fads, aid agencies are obliged to dedicate their energies as much to currying favor with donors as to analyzing the new terrain and designing appropriate projects and programs. Donors often seek "glamorous" or high-profile actions while resources are lacking for other nagging but neglected humanitarian issues. Donors, be they public (bilateral or multilateral) or private (foundations and individuals but also operational NGOs that are conduits for public funds), all contribute resources when disaster strikes, but they are almost always earmarked for particular activities, in a specific crisis, and for a limited duration.

Following the generous initial outpouring of help for the tsunami victims of December 2004, a chorus of familiar worries arose about sustained funding.[44] The likely results of the attention deficit disorder of donors had a familiar ring for those seeking resources for war-torn societies. "Loud" emergencies, as long as they remain in the media spotlight, attract resources. But once they become "silent" and out of the limelight—even former "loud" crises such as those of Haiti and Somalia do not endlessly echo on—resources evaporate or are in short supply.

Despite sharing many values, NGOs and UN agencies are often obliged to define themselves in contrast to what other agencies offer—in the language of other industries, such agencies are engaging in "product differentiation." Attempts to become identified as being uniquely capable in a sector or task are a form of "branding." A key asset of agencies is their ability to gain access to war-torn regions, even in the midst of active combat. An agency that is seen as a credible interlocutor is a valuable commodity to donors—indeed, this was the traditional strength of the ICRC, even if it was always among the costliest of contractors.

As some NGOs are almost always willing to compete and deliver what a donor desires, aid agencies are limited by collective action dilemmas in decision making. To abstain from a particular area of operations or to avoid funds from a particular donor, for example, pose such problems. A threat to abstain is fairly hollow in a marketplace brimming with competitors.

Without collective bargaining or some manner of orchestrating coherent positions among participating agencies with a degree of enforcement capacity, even collectively agreed outcomes are far from certain. Confrontational messages, even from powerful agencies, can be ignored by local populations and negotiators, as well as other agencies. Ensuring unity is hard because humanitarian agencies in the field often have mixed feelings for one another as well as genuine ideological differences over agendas, priorities, and the importance of particular donor incentives.

Again, decentralization and incentives to defect are not unique in the new wars, but their impact is dramatic because of the magnitude of funds available and the possibilities for manipulation and disruption in a context in which humanitarians face enormous pressure to act—from one's conscience as well as from donors. The overall ramifications of institutional rivalries raises the cost of doing business economically (bidding wars for access from gatekeeping NSAs) and politically (undermining the effectiveness of operations erode support and respect for the enterprise and its workers). This terrain is remarkably uncertain, if not totally new.

COLLECTIVE PURSUITS AND "ATOMIZED" ACTION

What then are the likely results of attempts to meaningfully coordinate aid agencies in the context of contemporary wartime confusion? What is the impact on collective pursuits? The shortest answer is "improvisation," which continues to be the hallmark of the international humanitarian system. General Roméo Dallaire, who commanded the paltry UN peacekeeping force that was powerless to halt the Rwandan genocide in 1994, looks back over the 1990s as "a decade of adhocracy."[45] Rival interests between agencies explain how this scenario came to be, and the shortcomings in operations document the costs. The rapidity with which calls for meaningful coordination are dismissed underlines the entrenched status quo in what can only be called the "atomized" action of the international humanitarian system. The fusion of efforts across individual agencies is theoretically possible and occurs on occasion, but the energy required to do so is substantial.

The power of resources is such that few agencies can cavalierly overlook the dictates of donors because of support from members (notable exceptions include the smaller faith-based groups such as the Quakers and the Mennonites and the larger ones such as Catholic Relief Services and Lutheran World Relief). UN agencies are constitutionally unable to ignore the wishes of powerful governments. When combined with a handful of private agencies responsible for the bulk of NGO delivery, this situation means that the humanitarian enterprise represents what an economist might characterize as an "aid oligopoly." Cooley and Ron have written convincingly that the reality of the contract culture is "deeply corrosive" for the humanitarian soul.[46]

The net effect of a crowded marketplace, with multiple agencies overlapping in the same crisis and vying to protect their shares, has been to exacerbate long-standing collective action problems within the international humanitarian system. The effectiveness and respect for the enterprise as a whole are undercut with defections from a common stance, but such defections become standard in an atomized system. A notable illustration is a particular agency's engaging a militarized gatekeeping NSA to establish a presence among victims but in the process essentially undermining collective negotiations. In other words, organizations may prefer to develop exclusive room to operate ("agency space") over shared access ("humanitarian space").[47] The notion that somehow the dynamism and decentralization of the humanitarian family outweigh the disadvantages of centralization and integration has been open to question for some time. In the context of the new wars, such atomization is exposed as an unacceptably and unnecessarily weak and costly link in the chain of international responses to suffering.

While the successes of the enterprise in saving lives have been numerous and notable, so have the important failures in how agencies responded to wars in the 1990s. We contend that the persistence of these problems indicates deep structural flaws. For example, during the disaster of the early 1990s in Somalia, the work of both the ICRC and the UNHCR saved many lives. However, the latter's territorial attitude toward other humanitarian agencies made its own efforts less efficient than they could have been and undermined those of others. Oxfam's operations in Cambodia have raised similar criticisms.

The dysfunctional humanitarian family has been struggling for some time. In confronting the new wars of the 1990s, the family has papered over differences and ignored critical problems. The therapy sessions organized by UN and NGO consortiums have helped agencies to cope, but their progress is little consolation for war victims who are victimized a second time by the confusion and waste of informal associations, the fracture in formal structures, and the role of humanitarian action within larger political projects.

The wars in Afghanistan and Iraq suggest how close the enterprise is to breaking down. We now turn to these contemporary configurations—where virtually all of the challenges of the new wars and the shortcomings of new humanitarianisms rendering atomized actions come together.

6

Making Sense of
Afghanistan and Iraq

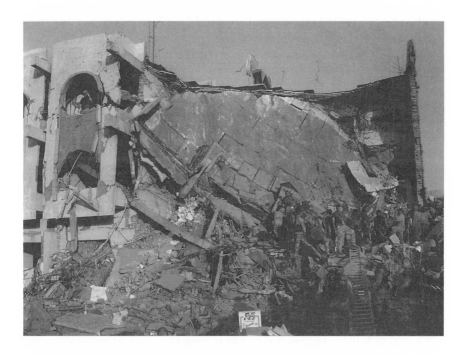

Humanitarian action has never been easy; the preceding chapters detail the peculiar challenges associated with the dynamics of the new wars and new humanitarianisms. In both Afghanistan and Iraq, interstate wars unleashed and magnified elements of the new wars. They present even greater, more convoluted challenges to humanitarian agencies. We do not argue that Afghanistan and Iraq fully follow the patterns of the new wars; rather, we illustrate how current armed conflicts embody long-term historical trends and contain elements from both interstate war and new wars. Furthermore, elements of these wars complicate the worst aspects of earlier civil wars while other elements actually suggest a dramatic alteration in the nature of the humanitarian enterprise. Never have the narratives of sword and salve been more intertwined.

The use of hijacked commercial jets by al Qaeda to attack U.S. territory on September 11, 2001, opened the most recent phase of war and humanitarianism. The next month the United States began a war in Afghanistan (see map 6.1) to dislodge and destroy the Taliban regime that harbored al Qaeda. The period of interstate war was brief. As state institutions in Afghanistan have always been feeble at best—long before September 11, Michael Ignatieff portrayed it as the kind of "bad neighborhood" where terrorism could flourish—it is unsurprising even after the elections of October 2004 that central authority is still very much a fiction in large swaths of territory.[1] Although Hamid Karzai was elected president, the small area over which his government exercised absolute authority led observers to refer to him as the "mayor of Kabul."

Violent conflict remains commonplace, as does the murder of aid workers and election officials. The much-vaunted International Security and Assistance Force, intended to prevent a return of violence, has been plagued by insufficient numbers of troops and a restricted mandate. With ISAF flawed and a new national military a far-off dream, security is elusive. The routing of the Taliban was quick, but the aftermath of strife among rival NSAs, especially warlords, persists and will for some time. Proclamations by Mullah Omar to continue the war, as well as the ease with which Taliban militants are able to regroup in tribal areas along the border with Pakistan, are ominous harbingers. The release of three UN hostages in November 2004 was a temporary breakthrough in negotiations, but it underlines the extreme vulnerability of expatriate personnel in such contemporary armed conflicts.

In Iraq, U.S.-led forces were able to rapidly dispatch an entrenched regime (see map 6.2). Saddam Hussein had wedded the Ba'ath party to state institutions, making his circle of henchmen the pillars of all facets of government. The removal of this cadre, however, did not mean either a military resolution to or a political settlement of hostilities. On May 1, 2003, barely a month after the bombing began, under a banner reading "mission accomplished" on the deck of the USS *Abraham Lincoln*, George

Map 6.1.   Afghanistan

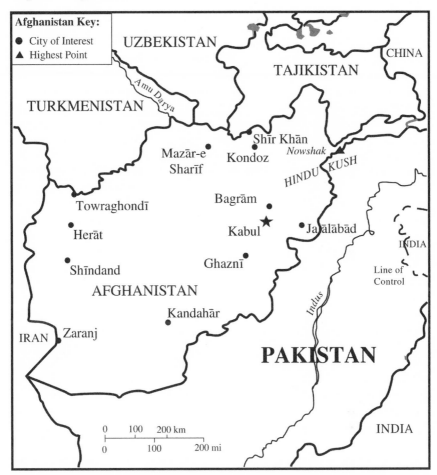

Afghanistan has a population of 27,755,775 (2002), and its capital is Kabul. It is located in southern Asia, north and west of Pakistan, and east of Iran. Its total land area is 402,338 square miles (slightly smaller than Texas), with no coastline and 12 percent arable land. Main exports are opium, fruits and nuts, hand-woven carpets, wool, cotton, hides and pelts, and precious and semi-precious gems.

W. Bush declared an end to major combat operations. This optimistic pronouncement was premature, especially as planning for postwar occupation seems to have been totally absent. Looting and insurgent violence began immediately. While the march to Baghdad was lightning fast, Washington, London, and their remaining allies continue to be mired in a political and military morass. The reelection of President Bush in November 2004 after campaigning on a policy of U.S. intervention in perceived

Map 6.2.   Iraq

Iraq has a population of 22,219,289 (1997), and its capital is Baghdad. It is located in western Asia, with a narrow outlet to the Persian (Arabian) Gulf. It is bordered by Turkey (N), Iran (E), Saudi Arabia and Kuwait (S), and Syria and Jordan (W). Its total land area is 168,754 square miles (slightly larger than California), with 36 miles of coastline and only 12 percent arable land. Main exports are crude oil and refined products and dates.

terrorist hot spots or against states working to acquire WMD suggests that the United States will be maintaining troops in Iraq for some time.

In both Afghanistan and Iraq, the fleeting moment of interstate war gave way to a prolonged period of what seem like new wars and with components that make humanitarian action more problematic than ever.[2] The difficulties that aid agencies face are not based on a lack of IHL—for example, the fourth Geneva Convention of 1949 specifically stipulates humanitarian responsibilities for occupying military powers—rather, the hostility of belligerents on both sides toward observing norms has impeded operations. This chapter surveys the present uncomfortable moment of war and humanitarianism; it discusses important elements that have been added to the already volatile mix; and it identifies key trends and threats to the humanitarian enterprise that have never been more acute or obvious.

SO, WHAT'S REALLY NEW?

Following September 11, it was quite common to hear about paradigm shifts. Afghanistan and Iraq blend elements from classic interstate war, the new wars, and the new humanitarianisms, but they also present distinctive twists on the battlefield and turns for humanitarian action. In other words, they differ in degree and dimension even more than those wars that at least partially merited the title "new" in the 1990s.

So, despite the honest debate about whether wars of the 1990s were truly "new" and whether traditional humanitarianism was adequate, Afghanistan and Iraq should definitely tip the balance. What Kal Holsti calls "change as transformation" requires new strategies and new tactics by humanitarians: "Transformation can result from quantitative changes which, when accumulated over a period of time, bring new forms to life. But, logically, the new forms must derive from old patterns. They can partly replace old forms, but by definition they must include residues or legacies of the old."[3]

In previous chapters we present historical information and then tease out perennial themes to show the evolution of the international humanitarian system; but here we do not have the luxury of retrospection. We cannot draw definitive conclusions about the course or outcome of themes. Nevertheless, the trends within each theme are indicative of the direction in which we are headed. Thus, to understand humanitarian action in Afghanistan and Iraq and, undoubtedly, in future theaters elsewhere, we begin by revisiting a distillation of major themes drawn from earlier discussions of sword and salve: *politicization, militarization,* and *marketization* and *privatization*. We do not assert that this configuration is etched in stone or that all forms of humanitarianism move and evolve together or even at the same time. But we do argue that the prominence of challenges to the core of humanitarianism—saving lives—is qualitatively transforming the enterprise. Following the analysis of theme-based trends, we turn to details of Afghanistan and Iraq before spelling out seven distinctive elements of the contemporary conundrum for humanitarians.

Politicization

Politicization has always been a part of humanitarianism—that the expression of its values constitutes a political act. Humanitarians are political because they are not indifferent about outcomes; they work to change them through advocacy and witness as well as, more concretely, their operations. We are not suggesting that politicization is unusual for the enterprise—indeed, David Forsythe's classic treatment of the ICRC in 1977 was titled *Humanitarian Politics*.[4] Moreover and as discussed earlier, humanitarian action in the late nineteenth and early twentieth centuries was not only about bringing relief to populations devastated by war but also about supporting sovereignty through interstate organizations.

For the contemporary international humanitarian system, however, politicization is more deeply ingrained via the predominant political cleavage: the war on terrorism. Not only does it divide the terrorists from the West and their allies, but it also has split governments and populations. The humanitarian impulse remains vibrant against this backdrop, but it has been susceptible to manipulation and exploitation—to such an extent that Antonio Donini worries that humanitarians "play second fiddle."[5]

The level and intensity of today's political overlay are greater and certainly more overt than at any time since the founding of the international humanitarian system. The argument here is that this transformation is so quantitatively significant as to constitute a qualitative change. Brian Urquhart, for instance, speculates that UN involvement in Iraq, including its humanitarian component, promises to be "the mother of all poisoned chalices."[6]

Iraq is currently the focus, if not the outright obsession, of many humanitarians, either as the crisis that currently commands the most attention and resources or as a barometer of the enterprise. As a result, other crises, regardless of their magnitude, exist in the political backwater. But this too is politics, which consists of drawing lines about what counts as a priority and what does not. For example, as mentioned in chapter 4, the persistent strife in the DRC has been somewhere on the radar screen, with an estimated four million deaths since 1998.[7] Yet, neither headlines nor aid match levels of anxiety. Similarly, in 2004–2005 the slow-motion genocide in the Darfur region of the Sudan killed an estimated two hundred thousand to three hundred thousand and displaced over two million, and it unfolded as powerful states displayed no political will to address the emergency. Again, this too is politics.

The explicit politicization of humanitarian action by the United States runs the risk of collapsing humanitarian responses into the same category as American political and military objectives. Where political, military, and humanitarian personnel share vague goals and operate in shared theaters, conceptual confusion and security challenges abound. How can independence, impartiality, and neutrality—or being relevant as a humanitarian but politically and militarily irrelevant—be possible? Can humanitarians be partially pregnant?

Politicization has not just seeped into humanitarianism; it has flooded it. Politicization for humanitarians resides especially in their association with the U.S. war against terrorism, although many critics, particularly in the Third World, have criticized U.S. power and its agenda as a new form of imperialism. While the United States is perhaps the most palpable source of the politicization of humanitarian action, it is not alone. Other powers are also engaged in their own wars—China in Xinjiang, Russia in Chechnya and Ossetia—and the precedents and politics of humanitarianism will necessarily filter into future crises. Moreover, humanitarianism is often portrayed as an extension of Western thought, and agencies are primarily based in Western states—but there are also Islamic charities as well. While Samuel Huntington's "clash of civilizations" is fraught with contradictions, the religious antagonisms to which he refers are nonetheless an important aspect of the armed conflicts in Afghanistan and Iraq.[8] Even following natural disasters, concerns have emerged regarding the political agendas of those who provide humanitarian assistance, as the case of Islamic charities' responding to the December 2004 tsunami demonstrate.[9] As humanitarian assistance is almost always perceived as having political connotations, Islamic NGOs have become a focal point for accusations of politicization.[10]

It is not useful to demonize Muslim agencies, because many are authentically humanitarian. At the same time, some Islamic NGOs are engaged in political acts, with four types standing out.[11] NGOs subscribing to *jihad* (holy war) tend to be subversive to humanitarianism, as they prioritize assisting Muslims, even and often especially at the expense of non-Muslim populations. Also, *dawatist* organizations emphasize proselytizing to and converting nonbelievers, a policy largely set aside by some but not all Western religious organizations. The political postures and implications of these two strategies are apparent, but other Islamic NGOs may follow a third and more subtle course. They are more like *chameleons*—intentionally using the image of NGOs to hide true aspirations and manipulate perceptions. In other cases, politicization occurs, but it is in opposition to violence or other destabilizing behavior. This fourth variant of strategies by Islamic NGOs, *conciliation*, is inclusive and seeks to build partnerships between Muslims and members of other religions. Although Western humanitarians may be sympathetic to this kind of Islamic NGO, it still amounts to foisting political agendas on humanitarian activities.

Whether implicitly upholding the state system or explicitly espousing a particular agenda, the humanitarian enterprise is vulnerable if its values and operations are nested within organizations and systems that reflect and prioritize other ones. The degree of politicization attributed to humanitarians, accurately or falsely, has spawned a threat not only to the credibility of the enterprise but to the security of its personnel. Politics has led to violence, and, as the second prevalent trend shines a light on it, violence has led to an increased militarization of humanitarian action.

Militarization

The use of military resources in crises and that of humanitarian action to fulfill military objectives suggest a disturbing militarization of humanitarianism. Traditionally, the means and ends of the military have been seen as being profoundly contrary to those of humanitarians, and attempts to mix the two have met with little enthusiasm. But in the post–Cold War era, humanitarians have viewed engagement with military forces more ambivalently and sometimes positively. The visible "peace dividend"— that now forgotten expected benefit from the end of East-West tensions— was the greater use of the military for human protection purposes.

[Historically, the respective cultures of humanitarians and soldiers share only a few key aspects—respect for neutrals or those neutralized in war, civilians and POWs—but are otherwise far afield.] For the most part, many view their cultures as being mutually exclusive, with the latter seeing humanitarian action as a distraction from core functions and the former dreading "relief at gunpoint." Moreover, troops are not normally seen as being well suited to humanitarian tasks. The disbursement of aid has usually been designed by agencies to stand alone and without any sort of coercive or political content.

On the other hand, despite the customary reluctance toward the culture and aims of warriors, humanitarians have increasingly come to respect two capacities of the armed forces—robust security and a logistics cornucopia. Although the latter has had a dramatic positive short-term impact in natural catastrophes, the use of war-fighting capacities for humanitarian intervention has had far more mixed reviews. Nonetheless, the successful deployment of military force with UN approval in several crises of the 1990s was accompanied by the support from UN secretary-general Kofi Annan in several speeches in 1999 and the normative plea by the ICISS for the "responsibility to protect," which meant, in a euphemism used throughout its report, a new level of support for the "use of military force for human protection purposes."[12]

Furthermore, some pleas to deploy military assets originated within agencies, and it is logical that the military provide solutions in such cases. As discussed in chapter 4, some of the loudest voices to halt suffering in Somalia, Rwanda, and the Balkans came directly from impatient humanitarians.

Indeed, as they tread on more dangerous terrains, the power to protect operations, victims, and aid workers becomes paramount for humanitarians. Furthermore, physically transporting assistance, manpower, and supplies requires special skills and capacities. Militaries command these resources in abundance relative to other sectors of society. To gain access to them, humanitarians have signaled that crises are almost indistinguishable from security problems in many instances; in turn, security providers see the need of humanitarians as an opportunity to grow their own operations and institutions.

Merging security and humanitarian agendas began in earnest in the late 1990s but was piecemeal. However, following the September 2001 attacks and the challenges presented by the war on terrorism, the push to integrate the two was more intense and widespread. The long-stewing humanitarian disaster in Afghanistan was interpreted as being symptomatic of a failed state that had permitted al Qaeda to be nurtured by its Taliban allies. Consequently, the view of humanitarian crises as security problems—or what Kenneth Menkhaus has called the "securitisation of complex emergencies"—has spurred calls for more military resources to be brought to bear for humanitarian purposes without adequate scrutiny of the ramifications.[13]

Within many military establishments, but especially within that of the United States, greater emphasis is being placed on the ability to facilitate or provide humanitarian assistance. For example, starting in December 2002, U.S. and NATO military forces began deploying provincial reconstruction teams (PRTs) ostensibly to create secure conditions for aid workers; but given that their operations involve tasks well beyond humanitarian mandates, they are not intrinsically humanitarian actors.[14] However, a 2004 report for Save the Children indicates that in working with PRTs, aid agencies face a definitive danger: "When PRTs engage in activities other than in the security sector, and especially when NGHA [nongovernmental humanitarian agencies] interact or work closely with the PRTs, the very presence of a PRT can instill or reinforce a perception that aid workers are 'agents' of the military."[15] Nonetheless, the United States continues to stress its ability to undertake humanitarian operations.[16]

What began as an appeal to the military to combat insecurity in clearly identified humanitarian disasters such as those of northern Iraq in 1991 and Somalia in 1992 has become complete militarization in contemporary Afghanistan and Iraq that amounts to inserting soldiers into humanitarian operations and aid workers into military operations. The latter cases are not instances of the use of military force for human protection purposes—what many label "humanitarian intervention"—but rather of humanitarian values for military purposes. The militarization of humanitarianism in such circumstances underscores that agencies are seeking access to key military capabilities (military utilization by agencies) while militaries are adding another task to their list (military penetration of humanitarian action). Will militarization enhance the capacities of agencies and expand the possibilities for their operations, or will it intrinsically besmirch and undermine the humanitarian enterprise?

Military forces engaging in humanitarian tasks are confusing and can be dangerous for the humanitarian enterprise. The ICRC, a leader among agencies, is adamant that the security of its operations derive from their principles and the support of local populations, but in extreme situations it is willing to turn to armed forces for protection. However, in these cases the ICRC has strict criteria regarding the use of armed escorts that are intended to maintain the neutrality, impartiality, and independence of the agency.[17] Yet this arrangement can be problematic, as it may jeopardize both humanitarian work and workers. As Oxfam notes, "military involvement can compromise the effective delivery of aid and lead to unintended consequences, potentially threatening the security of civilian aid workers."[18] However, agencies may have relatively little to say about the allocation of funds. According to one group of analysts surveying the current landscape, "security has become a donor-driven concept, with budgets out of all proportion to the long-term human security problems that contributed to insecurity in the first place."[19]

A distinction should be made between the legitimate use of military force to foster humanitarian values—with specific triggers, just war precautions, and right authority along the lines of the responsibility to protect—and the illegitimate use of humanitarian values to facilitate militarism. The value of a humanitarian veneer to the military is obvious when we quote Secretary of State Colin Powell's description of NGOs as a "force multiplier." He was even clearer in the same speech when he noted that they were part of his "combat team."[20] This slippery slope constitutes one of the reasons that David Rieff unkindly suggests, even after Kosovo, that "humanist rhetoric becomes an integral part of the military campaign as it unfolds, and as the fundamental element in the moral warrant for the war effort itself."[21]

Ken Roth, the executive director of Human Rights Watch, spells out why the fraudulent claims for the war in Iraq are so problematic: "The result is that at a time of renewed interest in humanitarian intervention, the Iraq war and the effort to justify it even in part in humanitarian terms risk giving humanitarian intervention a bad name. If that breeds cynicism about the use of military force for humanitarian purposes, it could be devastating for people in need of future rescue."[22] In his discussion of the politics of ICRC's possible withdrawal from Iraq, David Forsythe points out that "for both the United States and its opponents, the ICRC presence had strategic implications." He continues, "No matter how much the UN or the ICRC might try to signal that they were separate from the US-led coalition forces, for example, by not fortifying their in-country headquarters, their work for the Iraqi people dovetailed with US objectives."[23]

Distinctions between legitimate and illegitimate humanitarian action backed by the use of force can be made and must be made. It is the reason why reflection based on in-depth assessments of specifics, not the routine application of a ready-made formula of traditional principles, should be boldface in the job descriptions for humanitarians.

Marketization and Privatization

Humanitarianism and, more specifically, the tasks that form its operational capacities are increasingly subject to pressures to marketize and privatize. Budgetary as well as ideological influences have pushed private, market-based approaches for logistics, transportation, and security. Humanitarian action is seen as a product, and agencies are viewed as producers of services for hire. In the tussle for resources, not-for-profit aid agencies have felt the pressure to adapt and become more "professional" and "businesslike" in the pursuit of contracts that could be awarded to for-profit firms.[24]

The belief that the private sector can provide services more cost-effectively than institutions that are value driven has even spurred some donors to consciously funnel aid through for-profit channels. The spread of private corporations into what has conventionally been recognized as the exclusive domain of not-for-profit humanitarians can be viewed from supply and demand perspectives. On the demand side, the overwhelming dimensions of recent humanitarian needs have been documented throughout this volume.

But what about the supply side? In seeking to penetrate the market for humanitarian services, profit-oriented actors are engaged in a vast repackaging exercise. For example, doing "humanitarian" work allows Kellogg, Brown & Root and DynCorp to emphasize their experience in rebuilding war-torn societies and economies rather than become bogged down with accounting for their ties to companies or parties sustaining or propelling conflicts. Building their humanitarian credentials and capacities helps their bottom lines. Profit motives offend deeply heartfelt charitable sentiments, and many humanitarians as well as victims object on philosophical grounds to companies that profit from misery. But the reality is that businesses are an alternative source of supply for succor.

Most private contractors that are relevant to our discussions are engaged in communications, transportation, and logistics. However, even more objectionable to many humanitarians are those private firms with significant military capabilities that are providing physical security, especially in the face of the unpredictable and widespread violence in Afghanistan and, more specifically, Iraq. As humanitarianism has come to include physical protection for victims and aid workers and as UN and state-based security resources are often unavailable or insufficient, private military companies are seen by many as a solution. Although the experience with "technicals" in Somalia was generally seen as a mistake, over the course of the 1990s several instances involved contracting PMCs for humanitarian purposes. As noted in chapter 3, the case that receives the most attention is the government of Sierra Leone's use of Executive Outcomes from 1995 to 1997 to repel insurgents who had been and were violating human rights on a massive scale. This experiment brought the possibilities for privately enhanced security to the agenda, and since then there has been mounting interest in the topic.[25]

Humanitarians have conventionally dismissed PMCs as mercenaries, despite the fact that PMCs are legally incorporated. In what is viewed as a Faustian bargain and, alternately, as a victory for the market, PMC-agency interactions have grown. Although a most unexpected development, the idea of using private military contractors to provide protection or facilitate access for humanitarian agencies has slowly taken hold since the 1990s. Initially, such a practice was seen as an extreme option. For example, when UN secretary-general Kofi Annan was head of the Department of Peacekeeping Operations, he considered hiring a firm to disarm militants in Rwandan refugee camps; however, he concluded that the contract would ignite political sensitivities, suggesting that the "world may not be ready" for private peacekeepers.[26] Subsequently, one study, funded by Canadian NGOs in the aftermath of the international paralysis on the Rwanda genocide, called for the creation of a private NGO army.[27] If governments were spineless, so the argument goes, why not privatize security so that outside humanitarians can come to the rescue? Accordingly, a few agencies made such arrangements, including World Vision in Sierra Leone and UNHCR in Afghanistan.[28]

PMC protection raises a perennial question: who ultimately gains politically and economically from the humanitarian operations that they enable? Market-based solutions for principle-driven endeavors such as humanitarianism highlight the fine line between profit and predation. Without a profit margin, few PMCs would actually sign contracts with humanitarian agencies, thereby effectively limiting the extent to which private security could be a viable option. At the same time, agencies must base their work on, and make it meaningful to, war victims. But as analysts such as Mark Duffield, Alex de Waal, and Michael Maren have shown, victims do not always receive the intended benefits of operations.[29] Utilizing actors with ulterior motives—that is, profit—can distort operations, alienate victims, and undermine the reputation of humanitarians. The kidnapping and execution of civilian contractors, drivers, and security personnel in Iraq are not unrelated to the perceived extension—and, in many cases, the actual extension—of the U.S. military presence in civilian clothing.

Moreover, from a legal perspective, contractors occupy a murky position. The most egregious cross-dressing is done by PMCs. In terms of IHL, PMCs do not conform to the prototypical idea of a mercenary, and debate continues regarding whether they fall under article 47 of Additional Protocol I; however, two interrelated questions persist: their legality as armed belligerents and protections when captured. The fourth Geneva Convention (noncombatants) may not afford protection, because these contractors are armed and active. Nor does the third Geneva Convention (prisoners of war) necessarily apply because they may operate without uniforms or not adhere to formal military chains of command. Article 2, part A (4), states that this convention applies only to noncombatants: "Persons who accompany the armed force without actually being members thereof, such as civilian members of military aircraft crews, war correspondents, supply contractors, members of labour units or of services responsible for the armed forces." The rules for personnel who cook for troops on military bases (e.g., Kellogg, Brown & Root in Baghdad) are mostly defined, but those governing personnel who operate separately from U.S. armed forces and fight in the shadows (such as those hunting for bin Laden on the Afghanistan-Pakistan border) are unclear and contested. In the end, regardless of laws and norms, they may or may not abide by IHL.

Former UN special rapporteur on mercenaries Enrique Ballestros suggests that some of the purported economic advantages to using PMCs are distressing in human rights terms: "Mercenaries base their comparative advantage and greater efficiency on the fact that they do not regard themselves as being bound to respect human rights or the rule of IHL. Greater disdain for human dignity and greater cruelty are considered efficient instruments for winning the fight."[30] Furthermore, instances have occurred in which a PMC has been contracted to perform a security task with humanitarian implications, but the contractors themselves were corrupt and had employees who were later implicated in sex trafficking.[31]

Despite the range of potential political and legal problems identified, the overall progression of the relationship between the humanitarian and private military sectors is noteworthy. The intense hostility and fear that gripped humanitarians has loosened to the point where mainstream agencies have now dropped their usual reservations and are in the process of establishing relationships with PMCs. Claude Voillat, from the ICRC's relations with the private sector unit, notes, "Up to now, contacts between the ICRC and private military and security companies have taken place on an informal basis. The ICRC now plans a more systematic approach focusing on companies operating in conflict situations or providing training and advice to armed forces." Furthermore, he states that the Red Cross accepts that private solutions to security problems are here to stay and that the focus of agencies should be on regulating armed actors and ensuring their compliance. "The ICRC does not plan to take a position on the legitimacy of these private companies, but it will insist that the trend toward privatising military functions should not open the door to a weakening of respect for IHL and for its implementation."[32]

Thus, in the search for security answers, agencies are not just exploring the private option in principle but are developing formal procedures to put it into practice.

Table 6.1 consolidates the incentive structures of humanitarian agencies and PMCs. What is the overall impact on the humanitarian enterprise? Joanna Macrae points to "bilateralization" as a substantial component of marketization and privatization, which consists of "a significant shift away from non-earmarked contributions to multilateral organizations in favor of more tightly earmarked grants, and a marked shift in favour of bilateral contracting with NGOs."[33] The result is further uncertainty and market pressure on NGOs. Rony Brauman, the former head of MSF, wonders about the increased use of profit-making companies in Iraq to do what was formerly the exclusive preserve of private aid agencies: "Many NGOs fear that they will lose out to private companies, which are already claiming larger amounts of the 'NGO market.'"[34] Smillie and Minear

Table 6.1. Trade-offs in Aid Agencies' Subcontracting to Private Military Companies

Humanitarian Actor

United Nations and Humanitarian Nongovernmental Organizations

Advantages of contracting private military companies	1. Effective security resources when no political will to respond 2. Speed of deployment
Disadvantages of contracting private military companies	1. May escalate violence, fuel conflict 2. May undermine neutrality; aid workers may become targets of violence 3. May create dependency; loss of autonomy for agencies and locals 4. May abuse power because they lack accountability 5. May threaten legitimacy of enterprise; members of system divided over use and legality: international law and international humanitarian law prohibit mercenaries

Security Actor

Private Military Companies

Advantages of aid agency contracts	1. Gain legitimacy 2. Profit and market share 3. Values; humanitarian commitment
Disadvantages of aid agency contracts	1. Nebulous missions 2. Limits on means and tactics 3. Potential international prosecution

lament that "while the military and private contractors may make specific and indispensable humanitarian contributions . . . the new breed is no substitute for the old."[35]

Earlier we discuss engagement tactics and trade-offs with belligerents operating in the same theater as aid agencies. Contracts with for-profit organizations of all kinds, including those in the private military sector, raise similar dilemmas for humanitarians and the requirement for serious reflection about whether to subcontract to for-profit firms. In regard to security issues, the line between expedient necessity and ethical booby trap has become increasingly blurred. With agencies operating in more hostile and more deadly environments, contracts for security arrangements with PMCs have proliferated—what began as a trickle is increasingly a flood. Are these aberrations or the wave of the future? In either case, what are the implications for humanitarians and their traditional operating principles of independence, impartiality, and neutrality?

Answers to these questions can be gleaned from two journalists reporting the sullied reputation of humanitarians in Afghanistan: "They cannot reach parts of the country because of security threats. They are being blamed by many Afghans for the slow pace of reconstruction. They are accused of squandering funds on expensive cars and homes, and high salaries. They are being confused with soldiers and private security contractors who carry weapons but wear civilian clothes. And they are being held accountable for the actions, or lack thereof, of numerous fly-by-night aid organizations seeking to cash in on Afghanistan's rebuilding."[36]

HUMANITARIAN CRISES IN AFGHANISTAN AND IRAQ

We have alluded to elements of war in Afghanistan and Iraq, but it would be helpful to review the dire humanitarian situations in 2005. This is not a definitive portrait of these ever-evolving crises but rather a sketch so that readers have a common background to interpret our analysis of the dramatically changed operational environment for humanitarians.

Before the U.S. invasion of Afghanistan, the country had already been torn asunder by both man-made and natural disasters, leaving much of the population displaced and vulnerable. Earlier in 2001, the UN had reported that Afghans "were becoming a forgotten and abandoned people as humanitarian crises in other parts of the world diverted international attention and humanitarian assistance."[37] A severe drought gripped the country beginning in 1999 and left some 3.8 million Afghans on the brink of starvation. Between mid-2000 and June 2001, an additional 800,000 Afghans fled their homes,[38] making a total of about 3.6 million Afghan refugees (30 percent of the total number of refugees worldwide) as well as 600,000 IDPs.[39]

UNDP ranked Afghanistan the second-worst country on the planet to live in during 2001.[40] The plight of women and children was particularly appalling. The Taliban's draconian gender policies severely curtailed women's health care, resulting in growing rates of maternal mortality and diseases such as tuberculosis. One quarter of the children died of preventable diseases before the age of five, and 250,000 children died of malnutrition alone each year.[41]

Following September 11 and U.S. threats to invade, the Taliban asserted that they could no longer guarantee the security of international staff, who promptly withdrew. The regime also confiscated food supplies and shut down aid agency communications. When the U.S. invasion began in October, "aid agencies were warning of an impending humanitarian disaster." An estimated 5 million people were already in dire need of assistance; an additional 2.5 million were projected to be so; and UNHCR reported a doubling of IDPs (to 1.2 million) by the end of the year.[42]

On November 13, 2001, Northern Alliance forces entered Kabul, and by early December the last city under Taliban control, Kandahar, succumbed to U.S. supported anti-Taliban forces on the ground. The easing of hostilities permitted large-scale emergency relief operations and a substantial influx of NGOs. In January 2002, the UN launched the Immediate and Transitional Assistance Program for the Afghan People, an unprecedented initiative encompassing relief, recovery, and reconstruction with provision for the humanitarian needs of some nine million people.[43]

In 2003, however, factional fighting and an intensified campaign of attacks by Taliban fighters and al Qaeda hindered aid efforts. By mid-September, attacks against relief workers occurred once every two days, compared with one per month in the previous year; by the end of 2003, two foreign and thirteen Afghan aid workers had died from Taliban-orchestrated attacks. In 2004, the Taliban increasingly asserted itself in southern and eastern Afghanistan and routinely kidnapped and murdered aid workers, leading agencies to withdraw, including MSF, which had operated in the country since the Soviet occupation. By the end of 2004, more than thirty aid workers were dead.[44]

The costs of humanitarian action were high, but the benefits were significant. The UNHCR noted in late 2003 that "Afghanistan has been the scene of one of the largest voluntary repatriations in recent history." Within a year of the Taliban's overthrow, some 1.8 million Afghan refugees and 400,000 IDPs had returned. Increasing insecurity slowed the rates, but by late 2004 about half of those forcibly displaced (some 3.5 million) had returned.[45] In short and despite the election of Hamid Karzai in October 2004, "Afghanistan today is less a state than a precarious balance-of-power system in which warlords with private armies rule the provinces, paying the central government scant heed."[46]

In Iraq, the dictatorship of Saddam Hussein grew more and more brutal, and after the first Gulf War, in 1991, human rights and humanitarian conditions worsened considerably. The Ba'ath regime tightened its grip on society, and economic sanctions were put in place.[47] The regime killed at least a quarter of a million Iraqis, an average of ten thousand per year for a quarter century.[48] Atrocities were systematically committed against the Kurds and the Shi'ite majority, resulting in large-scale displacement and suffering. At the start of 2003, there were some nine hundred thousand IDPs and five hundred thousand Iraqi refugees and asylum seekers.[49]

The regime's defeat in the Gulf War entailed a sharp fall in the economy and a different type of suffering. Iraq fell from 91st (of 174 countries) in 1990 to 126th in the 2000 *Human Development Report*. Despite substantial oil and agriculture, gross domestic product per capita was only $1,300, and unemployment and underemployment were at 50 percent. The majority of Iraqis were totally dependent on decaying government services for basic necessities. An estimated 60 percent, for instance, lived hand-to-mouth through the Oil-for-Food Program. Furthermore, a decade of sanctions had also taken their toll; although data were clearly poor, reports were that chronic malnutrition in children under the age of five soared (from 18.7 percent to 30 percent) and infant mortality doubled. One middle-of-the-road estimate was that from August 1991 through March 1998 the number of excess deaths among children under five was 270,000, with probably 75 percent of them resulting from economic sanctions.[50]

Shortly after combat operations began on March 19, 2003, the UN launched an emergency appeal that mobilized some $2.2 billion. A large-scale disaster was avoided, but other implications of the U.S. invasion— widespread looting, arson, and general lawlessness—threatened local populations and challenged the ability of the international humanitarian system to perform effectively. For instance, the ICRC asserted that the looting was compounding the difficulty of delivering humanitarian assistance, while the World Health Organization warned of a cholera outbreak and other infectious diseases. In mid-April, Amnesty International called upon occupying forces to fulfill their obligations under the fourth Geneva Convention.[51]

While planning for military operations to unseat Saddam Hussein had apparently been superior, those for security and governance following the regime change were quite another matter. The humanitarian situation remained precarious with the widespread breakdown of essential services, resulting from the continued sabotage of oil, gas, and water pipelines and electrical power stations. Enduring armed political and religious strife, moreover, hindered the work of aid agencies. Relief convoys carrying WFP supplies were regularly looted, and the organization temporarily withdrew. In July, the International Organization for Migration was forced to suspend its operations in Mosul after its office was attacked with a rocket-propelled grenade; UNICEF withdrew its expatriate staff; and an ICRC staff member was killed near Hilla.[52]

Hussein loyalists and Islamic militants intensified their attacks against U.S.-led forces and civilian agencies, and a "terrorist component" to the increasingly organized resistance emerged by late summer in 2003.[53] After the bombing of the UN's headquarters in Baghdad in August, only a skeleton of its staff remained. The ICRC also scaled back the presence of its expatriate staff in the capital—which meant that only local staff died when its headquarters were attacked in October, halting its operations. Large numbers of NGOs withdrew international staff from the country. The security situation worsened in 2004, and some agencies that had withdrawn in the wake of the UN and ICRC bombings and returned, withdrew again. In April, for example, the UNHCR suspended repatriation from Iran, while Oxfam again ceased operations in Iraq. Kidnappings and murders were increasingly perpetrated by militant groups targeting civilian foreign nationals. The year ended with the kidnapping of three Italian aid workers, one of whom was murdered; the kidnapping and execution of the director of CARE International; the withdrawal of MSF; and seemingly escalating violence on the eve of the January 30, 2005, elections. However, the elections have not solidified domestic political order, and as struggles over the writing and acceptance of the constitution demonstrate, Iraq is potentially hurtling toward disintegration and all out civil war.

The majority of Iraqis were undoubtedly pleased that Saddam Hussein was in jail and his regime ousted, but they were still overwhelmingly angry and distraught that the humanitarian situation had barely improved in spite of the handover of governmental authority in June 2004 and elections in January 2005. The burst of armed conflict from March to May 2003 that enabled the United States to remove the Hussein regime was a precursor to the sustained violence that led to mounting civilian

Table 6.2.   Elements of the Humanitarian Landscape in Afghanistan, 2001–2005

Locus and humanitarian space	Afghanistan, western Pakistan
	Limited window in space and time
Agents of war and engagement dilemmas	U.S.; Taliban and al Qaeda allies; Afghan warlords
	Politicized humanitarianism has led to insecurity
War economy	Drug trade
Agents of relief and aid economy	Competition for limited resources
Targets and victims	Afghan civilians, as well as aid workers and journalists
Featured military technology	Small U.S. force using hi-tech to create large combat capability
International spotlight	Defining images: bin Laden tapes, Médecins Sans Frontières withdrawal

Table 6.3. Elements of the Humanitarian Landscape in Iraq, 2003–2005

Locus and humanitarian space	Iraq is center of operations; insurgents drawing on regional resources, notably from Saudi Arabia, Syria, and Iran Limited access; limited application of international humanitarian law
Agents of war and engagement dilemmas	U.S.; new Iraqi government; former Ba'ath party and Saddam loyalists, including *fedayeen*; Shi'ite paramilitaries; al Qaeda Politicized humanitarianism has led to insecurity
War economy	Oil; rebuilding infrastructure; security
Agents of relief and aid economy	Enormous resources; turf wars; belligerent funding
Targets and victims	Iraqi civilians as well as aid workers and journalists
Featured military technology	Improvised explosive devices, bombs
International spotlight	Defining images: UN headquarters attack; Abu Ghraib photos

casualties and inhibited the ability of aid agencies to respond. The UNHCR continued to discourage large-scale refugee returns while further outbreaks of violence, particularly in the Sunni triangle, led to new waves of displacement. Such vital public services such as water, sanitation, and electricity continued to be inadequate; and in a country where one in eight children under the age of five died, UNICEF reported that acute malnutrition among children had nearly doubled since March 2003.[54]

Tables 6.2 and 6.3 provide a thumbnail sketch of a depressing set of challenges to humanitarians resulting from the wars in Afghanistan and Iraq. In processing how the three major trends of the era—militarization, politicization, and marketization and privatization—filter through these two contemporary configurations of new wars, seven intertwined elements are elaborated in the following sections. Individually in some cases and collectively for certain, such elements have a dramatic impact on the prospects for humanitarian action today and tomorrow.

HYBRID WARS ON TERRORISM AND FOR EMPIRE

The point of departure for any discussion of violence and humanitarian action in Afghanistan and Iraq is the preponderant U.S. role on the world stage. These wars are a strange hybrid of classic interstate war and the new wars.

States that are under siege, let alone derelict or absent, may hide and support terrorist groups. Failed states offer great opportunities for concealment, manipulation, and sustenance; indeed, U.S. policymakers view them as "sleeping giants" for their potential to become severe security threats.[55] At the same time, weak states that have not collapsed may offer an even better sanctuary because they provide levels of infrastructure and security that failed states lack. Since September 11 and subsequent U.S. thrusts into southwest Asia, many observers wonder whether U.S. actions taken in the name of the "war on terrorism" are in fact wars for empire. For those who come to the rescue, their actual and perceived relations to U.S. foreign policy trigger both pejorative and positive chants of "imperialism."

While the locus of war is inside such strife-torn areas, the amalgam of local and global creeps across borders and traverses oceans. The United States is not a distant proxy but an active belligerent and target. The September 11 attacks highlight that part of what is unconventional about the current era of war is not just the means but also the reach. The war on terrorism as couched by Washington under the George W. Bush administration and as spelled out in the September 2002 *National Security Strategy of the United States of America*, prescribes a global war on terror with a military capability to confront terrorism, to react rapidly to crises, and to train local allies.[56] Washington has responded to terrorism by placing an interstate overlay on the issue; it has overthrown governments that it associated with terrorism; and it continues saber rattling even when it is unclear whether the states that are the focus of U.S. pressure are key to defeating terrorist threats.

For example, much of the Bush administration's bluster on terrorism uses nationality and geographic location expediently. While Saudi Arabia is a proven major source of funding and a recruitment base for al Qaeda operatives, Washington paints the Saudis as loyal allies who have been victimized by terrorism. Iraq, by contrast, had been portrayed by senior members of the Bush administration as the center of gravity for terrorism since the start of the 1990s—and their actions in 2003–2004 may have produced a self-fulfilling prophecy. Although terrorism has clearly proven to operate without much concern for state borders, the U.S. strategy in the war against terrorism presumes coherent states that are deemed as being "with or against" the United States.

Some observers suggest that although the United States had a vital security interest in Afghanistan and a legitimate claim for self-defense in attacking al Qaeda, the invasion of Iraq is more reminiscent of *imperium*. In this latest version, however, humanitarian packaging is central. In addition to those who support U.S. actions in Afghanistan and Iraq on the basis of purely geopolitical and economic interests, others favor such projects to end tyrannical regimes, improve humanitarian conditions, and make or remake democratic institutions.

One of the more controversial arguments came from a staunch human rights advocate, Michael Ignatieff. Having served as a member of the Kosovo Commission and the ICISS, he makes a conscious attempt to emphasize *jus ad bellum* justifications and humanitarianism: "Our current debate about humanitarian intervention continues to construe intervening as an act of conscience, when in fact, since the 1990s began, intervening has also become an urgent state interest: to rebuild failed states so that they cease to be national security threats."[57] Moreover, he argues that Western powers share common beliefs in democracy, human rights, and law and thus constitute a "humanitarian empire."[58] According to Ignatieff, imperial tools and tactics should be utilized to provide security and order to lawless and threatening political wastelands.

However, those who oppose empire—humanitarian or otherwise—remain convinced that present U.S. efforts to create order are mere veils for imperial economic domination, replete with exploitation and puppet leadership. This counterhegemonic critique considers the costs of empire, and its proponents hold that U.S. interventions have never lived up to their pronounced intentions and will not do so now. Moreover, manipulations of humanitarian action and agencies to serve empires or their construction are dangerous to the humanitarian enterprise and international order more generally. David Rieff has argued that agencies have been subordinate to state interests and power in Kosovo, Afghanistan, and Iraq.[59] Washington's financial control over agencies is thus a cause at least for outright alarm—"abandoning the notion of humanitarianism-against-politics for the politics of humanitarianism."[60]

On the whole, the vocabulary of empire seems off base or at least radically incomplete in describing today's humanitarian realities—what factors drive the international system and what accounts for the nature of action. While the United States is using its power in Iraq to stamp out the insurgency and resume the flow of oil to world markets, it plans to withdraw. The unwillingness of a majority of U.S. citizens to endorse long-term occupation suggest not prototypical imperialism but a bargain-basement variety. John Ikenberry notes, "ultimately, the notion of empire is misleading—and misses the distinctive aspects of the global political order that has developed around U.S. power."[61] Furthermore, pronouncements of empire do not fit with the reality of the complex relationships that underlie U.S. foreign policy. In traditional empires the core power dictated to its peripheral proxies, but at present the United States is often beholden to allied regimes whose behavior they cannot control. Arthur Schlesinger Jr. argues that this powerful but prostrate position contrasts greatly with the trappings of empire: "In their days of imperial glory, Rome, London, Paris . . . really ruled their empires. Today . . . Washington, far from ruling an empire in the old sense, has become the virtual prisoner of its client states."[62]

Picking up the economic underpinnings of this perspective, Lenin's analysis of imperialism suggests that control of economic resources constitutes an empire, but this logic is premised on a world of interstate rivalries and capitalist competition. The contemporary political backdrop of international institutions, global norms, and a changed security environment since the heyday of early-twentieth-century international wars shows the limits of this thinking. States still have the ambition to dominate internationally, but their motives and means do not fit with the usual template of imperialism.

Whatever the proverbial jury's decision, U.S. actions in Iraq have triggered an enormous backlash among Islamic militants that resembles the fury of anti-imperialism. The net result has been to enflame the security problems associated with the war on terrorism and compound charges of a war for empire. Although Afghanistan and Iraq are the principal fronts, broadly speaking, the horizon includes all areas featuring Islamic insurgency—the Middle East, the former Soviet republics, parts of southern Asia, and a wide swath of North and East Africa.

The locus of war and the accompanying restriction of space in these paramount cases are confusing for humanitarians because they draw on both interstate and new wars logics. Despite the amount of force concentrated through a quintessential Westphalian framework of state versus state, significant violence also is wielded by NSAs among themselves, against newly constituted central political authorities, and, most surprisingly, against the premier international military power.

From the point of view of humanitarians, this peculiarly twenty-first-century terrain not only brings massive delivery and protection difficulties but also poses fundamental philosophical questions. Humanitarians who consider themselves above the fray and distinct from occupying armies may be appalled, but they are obliged to understand the nature of new wars and shape their programming accordingly.

The security crises in Afghanistan and Iraq brought a new layer of humanitarian concern for populations long suffering from international sanctions and intervention, predation, and repression; but how can business as usual (under the mantel of neutrality and impartiality) be an option in the current landscape with its restricted access? Humanitarians cannot deny that their actions may be perceived as part and parcel of the machinations of unwanted outsiders. Giving food to demobilized former soldiers meets the humanitarian goals of agencies, but at the same time it also fulfills security objectives of the United States.

U.S. actions in Afghanistan and Iraq have brought narratives of counterterrorism and empire building to the fore. The charged political environments of those wars transform humanitarian assistance and protection. As a result, it is necessary to ask fundamental questions about when and where humanitarian needs are addressed and how and to what end.

Answers based on pragmatic calculations rather than pat formulae will not threaten the viability of the traditional international humanitarian enterprise and its values.

AL QAEDA AS SPOILER AND HOSTILE AID RECIPIENTS

Dangerous spoiler NSAs are a recurring element in new wars, and current antagonists in armed conflicts in the Middle East and South Asia continue this theme. Indeed, in a seeming taunt to humanitarian agencies, as well as commentary on the presumed political agendas of humanitarians and their global reach, one terrorist group has titled itself "Mujahedeen Sans-Frontières."[63] Beyond the powerful message that such a statement sends, the actions of terrorist groups are profoundly shaping humanitarian space. In fact, the threat posed by al Qaeda is wider ranging and has greater ramifications than do the spoilers discussed earlier. Al Qaeda is a terrorist organization that invokes Islamic fundamentalist ideology in attacking Western interests and populations, although the collateral damage of its strikes have harmed non-Western societies, including wreaking havoc on numerous Muslim ones. Technically organized in the early 1990s under the leadership of Osama bin Laden and several of his top lieutenants, al Qaeda identified itself with two main political grievances: U.S. troops in Saudi Arabia were an affront to Islamic holy sites, and American support for Israel was killing Palestinians and threatening Arab states.

Al Qaeda's scope is transnational, receiving support from and operating out of a range of countries spanning southeastern parts of Asia through the Middle East and Arabian peninsula to eastern and northern Africa. However, cells have also been discovered inside Western countries—mostly in Europe but also the United States—engaged in fund-raising and recruiting as well as having supported and staged attacks. In the past decade al Qaeda's attacks have grown in size and sophistication—in June 1996 a truck bomb exploded at the Khobar Towers in Saudi Arabia, killing nineteen U.S. soldiers and wounding hundreds of others; in August 1998, near-simultaneous bombings of U.S. embassies in Kenya and Tanzania killed over two hundred; in 2000, a small boat of explosives detonated, crippling the USS *Cole* and killing seventeen sailors while in a Yemeni harbor; the devastating crashes of four hijacked jetliners on September 11, 2001, in New York, Washington, D.C., and Pennsylvania resulted in over three thousand deaths; the bombing of a nightclub in Bali killed at least two hundred; the multiple bombs set off in the Madrid train station in March 2004 produced over two hundred fatalities; and the July 2005 attacks on the London subway system killed fifty-six and injured around seven hundred. The organization remains notably active in Indonesia, Yemen, Pakistan, Afghanistan, Saudi Arabia, and Iraq.

Although the September 11 attacks triggered the U.S. war to oust the Taliban from Afghanistan, al Qaeda remains a potent force within the country, and its operatives continue to receive shelter and support from the tribes that straddle the border with Pakistan. This region has a long tradition of resisting central political authority, making it a natural haven for al Qaeda and Taliban resistance to regroup, wage war, disrupt elections, and impede humanitarian efforts. Islamabad's popularity in these tribal areas has sank even lower in recent years as the United States has pressured the Pakistani government to station the army along the border to eliminate al Qaeda and its allies. It remains to be seen whether the Afghan elections of October 2004 have made a difference in drawing support away from al Qaeda in the region.

Recent estimates indicate that al Qaeda presently fields approximately eighteen thousand potential terrorists around the world, although the war in Iraq may have increased their ranks.[64] Iraq did not initially afford al Qaeda any sort of formal opportunity to actively organize and fight within its boundaries. Indeed, the secular Ba'ath regime under Saddam Hussein was hostile to al Qaeda and the idea of permitting inroads by Islamic militants. However, in the wake of U.S. intervention, state institutions have disintegrated and NSAs are positioned to assert their authority. With a host of political, cultural, religious, economic, and historical resentments to draw on—Muslim *muhjadeen* versus Christian crusaders, poor Arabs versus rich Westerners, Iraq versus the United States—al Qaeda has established a beachhead and is becoming a potent presence.

For humanitarians, the consequences are dramatic. This transnational movement does not merely seek to derail the humanitarian enterprise; it equates Western humanitarian agencies with the "infidel" Western military presence and hence considers aid workers as viable targets for *jihad*. One militant in an al Qaeda–affiliated group cuts to the chase: "We don't make a distinction between civilians and non-civilians, innocents, and non-innocents. Only between Muslims and non-believers. And the life of non-believers has no value. There's no sanctity to it."[65] Gratuitous violence against civilians—notably, beheadings of individuals and bombings of agency facilities—provides somber testimony.

The flexibility of al Qaeda has enabled it to flourish and foment strife.[66] Furthermore, the organization continues to grow, as it has morphed into a hydra-headed movement that seems to multiply as operatives are captured or killed. Al Qaeda is much bigger than any one or group of leaders. Although bin Laden remains a key figurehead, bin Ladenism as an ideological inspiration and organizational model is more of an absolute influence on worldwide terrorist activity. While al Qaeda is the most visible spoiler NSA in Iraq, its presentation of grievances seems to have stimulated other terrorist groups with comparable agendas that similarly undermine humanitarian operations, such as the Lion of Allah Brigades and the Mujahedeen Corps in Iraq.[67] Al Tawhid (led by Abu Musab al-Zarqawi), which has a presence in Iraq but claims to be the "al Qaeda of Europe," falls into this category with respect to hindering humanitarians. It was initially unclear whether al Tawhid was an ally or a rival of al Qaeda; however, in late December 2004 a tape of bin Laden indicated contact with and support for Zarqawi, and Zarqawi changed the name of his group to "al Qaeda in Mesopotamia" (sometimes referred to as "al Qaeda in the land between the two rivers").

Of great concern to U.S. policymakers and humanitarians is that those victimized by the war may become sympathetic to al Qaeda's cause, thereby creating a new class of "belligerent-victims." Little sympathy is necessary for terrorists and for those who provide them support and are hostile toward humanitarian action. But those who have legitimate needs present a troubling problem when they share terrain with terrorists.

In addition to explicit and clearly recognizable terrorist groups are those that cannot be definitively categorized as belligerents or victims. A prime example in Iraq is that of Jamaat al-Sadr al-Thani, sometimes referred to as the Mahdi's Army, led by cleric Muqtada Baqr al-Sadr. For most of 2003 and 2004, this paramilitary organization occupied Falluja and Najaf to protect Islamic holy sites and challenge U.S. military power. A stalemate of sorts ensued as parties across Iraq struggled to determine a way to utilize the political power of Sadr to maintain order and at the same time not prompt further U.S. military action of the type that took place at the end of 2004.

Despite a brief interlude in violence on election day (January 30, 2005), attacks resumed the next day and severe doubts remained regarding the ultimate viability of democratic institutions. NSAs are still the major players in Iraq, and most continue to resist the American occupation, as daily death tolls demonstrate. Their potential to hinder relief and protection persists. However, it is important not to lump all Islamic or even specifically Shi'ite NSAs in the "hostile at best, belligerent at worst" category. Grand Ayatollah Ali al-Husseini al-Sistani, for instance, is among the most popular figures in Iraq and has been a voice for moderation and receptive to overtures from outside humanitarian agencies.

It is obvious that humanitarian agencies cannot engage al Qaeda, which is antithetical to human values; but even lesser insurgents may share tactics, aims, and aspirations. For instance, Chechen rebels fighting against the Russian government appear to have taken a page from al Qaeda's playbook with their September 2004 siege and seizure of a school in Beslan, North Ossetia—1,200 were taken hostage, 331 of whom died during the attack and subsequent efforts to free them. The key questions are thus: How many such groups are out there? What are the implications for agencies that withdraw or make security arrangements to remain in such operational theaters?

BIG BUSINESS IN OIL, WAR, AND RECONSTRUCTION

The economics of warfare have always meant that victors benefit after wars, but opportunities and profits vary. As the illicit drug trade in Afghanistan conforms to the contours of the political economy in other new wars, we need not repeat earlier analyses. As a 2003 report noted, "In Afghanistan, security and drugs are inextricably linked: war and lawlessness have pushed opium production up and this in turn has fueled the activities of warlords."[68] However, beyond the war in country and economic factors driving warlordism, aspects of this economy support al Qaeda. The political economy of terrorism further underlines how a small amount of capital can translate into large-scale destruction—the paltry monies required to finance the September 11, 2001, attacks (roughly $100,000) caused enormous damage.[69] The informal networks that raise funds for al Qaeda and its allies may be considerably larger and reach further than those most commonly associated with the new wars but are otherwise quite similar.[70] As we are interested in new features in either substance or degree, the main emphasis of this section is on occupied Iraq, which raises questions about spoils and big business on a scale not seen elsewhere.

Again, Iraq fuses traditional conceptions of interstate war (state-led allocation of resources within the war zone) and new wars (NSAs using their power to extract resources). Along the former track, the United States temporarily and tenuously secured Iraqi oil fields and assets. However, at the NSA level, the dynamics of new wars jump to the fore. Iraq in particular is a windfall for private contractors, military and security firms, and individuals and enterprises involved in reconstruction and oil services.

The political economy of Iraq is at an order of magnitude higher than that of other new wars. The country sits on the world's second-largest oil reserves. Oil revenues have historically been a source of conflict and will continue to be so. Many critics have argued that the U.S.-led war is largely to guarantee access to oil supplies. By contrast, the Bush administration has attempted to argue that its interests in Iraq revolve primarily around security—the ousting of Saddam Hussein, concerns about WMD, and worries over terrorist havens. Others hold that human rights concerns also factored into the decision to invade. No single narrative can provide the complete story. The politics of terrorism, human rights, and cultural values aside, a close examination of economic activity related to Washington's actions in Iraq indicates that access to oil is one factor, but a wider circle of American industries has also benefited from the relief and reconstruction bonanza.

The amount of money at stake for oil, war, relief, and reconstruction dwarfs that in other crises, as do the humanitarian consequences. The Oil-for-Food Program provided the Iraqi government revenue to finance humanitarian assistance under the UN-authorized sanctions regime. Although consisting of just a fraction of potential exports from 1996 to 2003, it netted $64 billion.[71] The Coalition Provisional Authority (CPA) was the U.S.-established transition office to the Iraqi government prior to the UN-blessed provisional government of Ayad Allawi. This entity assumed temporary power at the end of June 2004 to assist with the June 2005 elections and the transitional government that it would install. The CPA had, at minimum, $45 billion under its control—$22 billion appropriated by Congress and $23 billion in Iraqi oil revenues and seized assets. The appropriation is mind-boggling given that the United States is the stingiest donor among the OECD countries (i.e., providing the least aid as a percentage of gross domestic product), as the amount approved by Congress is almost double he worldwide aid budget. Furthermore, the annual costs in Iraq approach eight times official ODA.

Given the rules governing contracts and the insecurity on the ground, these monies mostly found their way into the coffers of U.S. corporations. A mid-2004 review of major contracts (those worth more than $5 million) indicates that nineteen of thirty-seven went to U.S. companies and that 85 percent of the total of these contracts ($2.26 billion) were dedicated to U.S. firms.[72]

The most visible companies are the conglomerate Halliburton, mostly an oil services company, and its engineering and construction subsidiary Kellogg, Brown & Root. In 2004, Halliburton's second-quarter earnings reports indicate that one-third of its total revenues were related to its work in Iraq, and Kellogg's revenues were up 68 percent from the same quarter a year before.[73] The U.S. military has signed numerous multi-billion dollar contracts with Halliburton, and many suspect that it is not irrelevant that its former CEO was Vice President Dick Cheney, who continues to receive a lucrative pension from the company. Earlier we point to the range of interests in the political economies of armed conflict, but the size of the figures for Iraq are staggering—in the first half year following the so-called victory, $6.3 billion was allocated for fuel from Kuwait and Turkey, over $7 billion for repairing Iraq's oil infrastructure, and $4.18 billion for feeding and housing troops. This last contract was under particular scrutiny as auditors have been unable to located $1.8 billion (or 43 percent) of the work for which Kellogg had billed the Pentagon.[74]

Oil and reconstruction may get the most headlines, but Iraq and Afghanistan also have been a veritable gold mine for private security contractors. A substantial shift has taken place over the last decade and a half, with aspects of even the most quintessential of public goods—national defense—having been privatized. Wherever the modern American armed forces go, private contractors are with them in support, training, intelligence, and even combat roles. In the first Gulf War, for example, for every fifty soldiers deployed there was one contractor to provide support. In Operation Iraqi Freedom, there is one contractor for every ten soldiers.[75]

Most corporations benefiting from the war perform mundane tasks for militaries such as building housing and feeding soldiers or providing fuel for military vehicles, as well as reconstructing Iraq's oil industry and other major infrastructure projects (e.g., water treatment and electrical grids). However, others are involved in more active roles, such as intelligence gathering and producing violence through arms manufacturing and sales, providing military training, and engaging hostile forces in combat.

Furthermore, aside from supplying support services to the U.S. military, PMCs have been contracted to provide security for businesses operating in Iraq, as well as for members of the CPA and the transitional government.[76] Military contractors can earn enormous paychecks in Iraq, with low-ranking fighters earning at least $250 per day and retired U.S. and U.K. special forces paid $1,000 per day; however, the danger associated with a particular security task also affects wages—guarding high-rank officials earns substantially more than protecting civilian convoys or facilities. Even as war raged in 2003, Erinys International agreed to protect oil pipelines and has since deployed 14,500 guards at a cost of $39.2 million. Custer Battles received $16.8 million to guard the U.S. military base in Baghdad. In 2004, Triple Canopy signed a $90 million contract to guard thirteen CPA facilities. A British firm, Aegis Defense Systems, won a $293 million, three-year deal in May of the same year to supply seventy-five "close protection teams" (bodyguards) to the CPA and Iraqi officials. Although the costs themselves raise eyebrows, what has really brought attention to this particular contract is that Aegis is directed by Tim Spicer, a former special forces officer in the United Kingdom. With an unsavory past as a soldier in the British military, Spicer and members of the unit under his command engaged in sectarian violence in Ireland, and he previously directed Sandline, a PMC that violated a UN arms embargo by selling thirty-five tons of Bulgarian arms to Sierra Leone in 1998.[77] This contract brings to the public's attention and to humanitarians as well not only the politics and economics of PMCs but also the processes by which they are vetted and hired.

To regain sovereignty, facilitate greater security, and perhaps not rely so extensively on private contractors, Iraq is seeking to train local security forces. Ironically, that process also enriches PMCs. Vinnell signed a contract to train nine battalions for a new Iraqi army for $48 million. Dyn-Corp is building a new Iraqi police force; the first year of the contract alone is worth $50 million. It also figures prominently into reconstruction plans for Afghanistan, where it is providing security to President Hamid Karzai ($52 million for 2003).

The numbers of contractors at work in Iraq is difficult to measure, as data are not readily available. A September 2004 report states that there were thirty thousand, of which two-thirds perform security tasks.[78] A July 2005 report suggests a significant increase since then—fifty thousand to seventy thousand unarmed contractors and twenty-five thousand armed security professionals drawn from somewhere between sixty and eighty companies.[79] If the twenty thousand private security providers were considered one contingent, they would be the second-largest troop contributor after that of the United States—over twice as large as the second-largest military contingent, from the United Kingdom, and far larger than the total international humanitarian presence. These are only rough estimates because the CPA, U.S. military, and interim Iraqi government provide little information. However, with the security situation still perilous and the prospect of a decrease in U.S. presence, it is unlikely that the number of contractors in Iraq will decrease over the next few years.

The premises of interests in war are perennial: economic resources often attract militarized actors, sometimes driving war while at other times merely profiting from it. Afghanistan, a heroin-based economy, is more akin to the economics of the new wars, although it has experienced some recent changes with the international private security industry, which is aggressively marketing its services there. Afghanistan also demonstrates that the drug economies behind war are remarkably resilient, particularly when international development is insufficient. Iraq, a resource-rich environment, shows how really big business becomes yet another actor with which humanitarians must contend in what otherwise would be an area abandoned by major for-profit firms.

CONSPICUOUS ECONOMIC INTERESTS
IN RELIEF AND PROTECTION

The economic interests behind the violence and long-term reconstruction in Afghanistan and Iraq are hardly business as usual—but what about the incentives and economics of emergency aid? Agencies customarily attract commercial vendors, but the attention and resources in these two cases are so significant that they take humanitarian consumption of all kinds to new extremes. To begin with, agencies operating in Afghanistan and Iraq struggle with the perception that their agendas are more economic than humanitarian. For example, Bashar Dost, a planning minister in the Karzai government, stated, "I have yet to see an NGO that has spent 80 per cent of its money for the benefit of the Afghans and 20 percent for their own benefit. International NGOs get big amounts of money from their own nations just by showing them sensitive pictures and videos of Afghan people, and there are even some individuals who give all their salaries to NGOs to spend it on charity here, but [NGOs] spend all the money on themselves."[80]

Moreover, the competition among agencies for contracts is intense. Here, we essentially need to explore the extent to which economic interests corrupt or impair the delivery of humanitarian assistance in Afghanistan and Iraq. More specifically, we need to ask, does the current administrative structure of aid create an incentive structure that undermines its purpose? Before analyzing the political economy of humanitarian action in these two theaters of armed conflict—meaning an assessment of resource flows (financial and human resources) and the power that underlies them—we find it worth recalling the overall size of resource flows and the fund-raising climate.

Disbursements of humanitarian assistance worldwide—including those of the UN, ICRC, and NGOs—reached approximately $10 billion in 2004.[81] "In 2001, UN agencies reported that . . . they spent $3.2 billion on humanitarian activities and the Red Cross family plus [International Organization for Migration] spent a further $700 million. Over two thirds of UN humanitarian assistance is spent by three agencies: WFP (37%), UNHCR (21%), and UNRWA (11%)."[82] Overall, UN agencies account for slightly more public funds than do NGOs, who manage approximately $2.5 billion to $3 billion of such expenditures.[83] At the same time, because NGOs raise funds from private resources and have subcontracts from both governmental and intergovernmental institutions (essentially, the UN and the European Union), they actually deliver about two-thirds of the worldwide total. However, these sums are dwarfed by the magnitude of resource flows in other industries, such as those noted in the previous section: oil, war, and reconstruction.

Even though the global pool of humanitarian assistance has grown to $10 billion, these flows should not be taken for granted. The portfolios of private donors (individuals and foundations) have suffered stock market declines, some of which are attributable to the terrorist attacks of September 2001. Donor governments have felt a similar impact, as subsequent tax revenues have fallen and expenditures for internal and international security measures have skyrocketed. Diminishing income and reserves, combined with the new needs stemming from September 11, have increased the demands for public resources, which have increased competition among humanitarians vying for resources in Afghanistan and Iraq or elsewhere.

Figure 6.1 graphically illustrates the "spaghetti junction" flow of financial and other resources into humanitarian operations. It presents a structural snapshot of why competition has become so ferocious in the humanitarian enterprise—multiple sources of financing for agencies and multiple suppliers for donors.[84] For agencies this scenario has meant not only their vying harder to maintain their budgets but also their facing new pressures from traditional donors. A profound change in the system can be found in the structures that define relations between donors and implementing partners. NGOs have always relied on donors to under-

Figure 6.1. Resource Flows in Humanitarian Operations

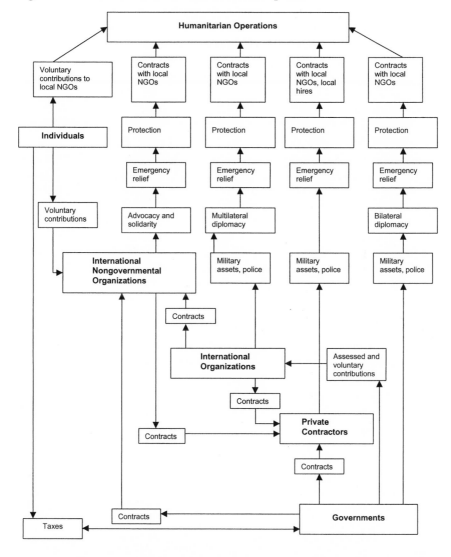

write humanitarian action, usually in the form of grants to deliver emergency aid. However, agencies have become mere implementers of donor policy to a previously unheard degree.[85]

In the past, the lifeblood of the humanitarian system involved grants to private organizations. While such NGOs raised monies from the public, much of the growth in the last two decades has resulted from "subcontracting" from governments and intergovernmental institutions, mirroring the UN's delegation of authority to coalitions of the willing for

military operations.[86] Governments transferred resources to organizations that themselves had major input into how needs were prioritized
and how resources were allocated. The "contract culture" and an accompanying need to maintain "market share" necessarily subject aid agencies to pressures from donors and their own boards of directors.

Where funding once allowed greater flexibility in the use of resources
to accomplish an agency's own mission—including, on occasion, some
risk-taking experiments—funding is increasingly earmarked for specific
activities of direct interest to a government funding source, a phenomenon that is partially captured in the term "bilateralization." The military
analogies used by former U.S. secretary of state General Colin Powell are
not aberrations—specifically, those about humanitarian action being an
essential ingredient for the success of U.S.-led occupying forces in
Afghanistan. Andrew Natsios, the administrator of USAID and himself a
former senior NGO official, followed suit with the civilian interpretation
for the humanitarian presence in occupied Iraq, proclaiming NGOs under
U.S. contracts "an arm of the US government."[87]

While channeling substantial resources to aid agencies has decided
advantages from the perspective of donors, it constrains the discretion of
aid agencies that think of themselves as being attuned to the needs of victims.[88] Hugo Slim noted that there is an overlap in the essentially liberal
goals and values between the coalition and humanitarians: "UN agencies,
NGOs and other humanitarian commentators may be in an interesting
form of denial about the morality they have in common with Coalition
authorities."[89]

Among other implications of subcontracting is that humanitarians are
obliged to make even tougher decisions about establishing priorities for
unrestricted monies that are becoming tighter and tighter. Indeed, NGO
decision makers and managers have always placed a high priority on rais-
ing such funds because they are essential for discretionary spending.
Although they help to provide succor in an emergency, they also are useful for institutional growth: to pay for administrative costs that most public donors are loath to offset, to build up a donor base for future appeals,
and to help leverage funds from public sources.

Not only does the political economy of humanitarian action in Iraq and
Afghanistan merit our consideration, but so does protection, another area
that has been substantially privatized. For instance, our discussion of
security in the new wars began with the unfortunate experience of local
"technicals" being hired in Somalia—mainly unemployed hoodlums. It
continued in Afghanistan, with members of the Northern Alliance being
trained, but has reached new heights with the hiring of PMCs in Iraq, supplemented by local security personnel.

When UN personnel returned to Iraq as part of the transition, Security
Council resolution 1526 specified that they would have their own pro-

tection force, separate from the coalition's occupying soldiers. The UN's use of PMCs to do this task is not so different from its resorting to the use of soldiers of a small and poor country such as Fiji—the first country to contribute troops to the UN protection force—whose participation in peacekeeping has been linked to reimbursements to the government for such services. Indeed, the 134-strong Fijian military contingent that arrived in Baghdad in October 2004 to provide security for a reopened UN headquarters—which essentially had been vacant since September 2003—was less numerous than the 924 or so former Fijians who were estimated to be working in Iraq for private contractors.[90]

At the same time, the arcane and secretive styles of PMCs raise questions about what exactly their services imply, especially for the "soul" of the humanitarian enterprise. The politics of privatizing protection raises sensitive issues—accusations of mercenarism and commodification—but the immediate focus is on accountability. As it stands now, humanitarians are trapped and will be in the future. They need security to execute relief operations, but the means selected to achieve it may arouse violent resentments and create even greater insecurity. As one study argues, "short-term gains from the use of [private security companies] need to be balanced against possible long-term losses at every instance of outsourcing. The problem in this respect is that isolated decisions are taken without a wide perspective on the cumulative effects of privatizing security."[91]

Which companies and in which countries they are based can be a point of contention for government officials, businesspeople, humanitarians, and human rights activists. Ultimately, controversies will persist until the legal and political status of PMCs becomes clear, their economic gains are not perceived as being exorbitant, greater transparency exists in the awarding of contracts and their rules of engagement, and an increase occurs in the oversight of contractors.

A review of the conspicuous economic interests in relief and protection in Afghanistan and Iraq illustrates growth and distortion. First, to return to Holsti's apt categorization, the extent of privatization is itself so significant as to constitute a qualitative change.[92] Second, while the market can foster increased efficiency and productivity, it can also foster unproductive uses of resources, for instance, in vacuous advertising as well as counterproductive competitive practices. This continuation is not "aid business as usual" but an unusual aid to business.

ACUTE SECURITY THREATS TO
AID PERSONNEL AND JOURNALISTS

An element of continuity between the new wars and Afghanistan and Iraq is the intentional targeting of civilians. In Afghanistan, estimates of civilian casualties since the United States launched its assault in October 2001 amount to almost thirty-five hundred killed and over sixty-two hundred injured.[93] In the two years following the March 2003 invasion of Iraq, civilians have endured extreme levels of violence, almost twenty-five thousand killed (a staggering thirty-four a day) and over forty-two thousand wounded out of a total population of twenty-five million.[94] This means that approximately 1 percent have suffered fatalities and another 2 percent have been injured. Moreover, trends indicate that Iraqi civilians increasingly incur the costs of violence, as the proportion of civilian casualties was twice as high in the second year of the war as in the first. The London-based medical journal *Lancet* has estimated that acute malnutrition almost doubled after the ouster of the Hussein regime (from 4.0 percent to 7.7 percent).[95] The continued targeting of civilians with suicide bombs continues the onslaught. While such civilian deaths are always horrific, they in fact number substantially fewer than do those in other crises discussed earlier—including the eight hundred thousand murdered in Rwanda in a few months in 1994 or the two million in Sudan's extended civil war since 1983 or the four million in the DRC since 1998.

On the Western side, since invading Afghanistan in October 2001, U.S. armed forces have had about two hundred military personnel killed.[96] For operations in Iraq, from March 20 to May 1, 2003, only 139 military fatalities were recorded. But since May 1, 2003, over two thousand coalition military forces have been killed, as well as over 280 private contractors. As these numbers indicate the period of armed conflict after the interstate war has been bloodier and certainly longer than that during the time it took to overthrow governments. Not surprisingly, when taken together, these figures point to a marked discrepancy in the overall proportion of civilian victims.

Accounting for some of the surge in noncombatant fatalities are the staff of aid agencies. A review of trends over the past decade is startling—some two hundred UN staff have been killed in malicious acts in almost fifty countries, and another three hundred have been taken hostage. The ICRC alone has lost over forty staff on mission. A recent study of the impact of firearms on aid workers provides a snapshot of one year: "Between July 2003 and July 2004 at least one hundred civilian UN and NGO personnel were violently killed."[97] Moreover, this study finds that this rise represents more than a quantitative increase in aid workers as victims but connotes a qualitative shift in targeting: "humanitarian and development workers are the explicit targets of criminal violence and, to a lesser extent, of intellectual violence from state and non-state actors." Beyond these alarming general numbers, even more acute and pronounced are the dangers in Afghanistan and Iraq. In Afghanistan alone, at least twenty-six died in 2004.[98] Even the intrepid MSF decided that enough was enough: even though it had operated in the country over the last quarter century through several regime changes—from Soviet occupation to Najibullah and then spanning the Taliban era up through the present Karzai administration—it withdrew from this theater after five of its staff were murdered in mid-2004. The reasoning behind MSF's departure from Afghanistan was that "the Americans are pretending that NGO's are with them fighting the war against terror, and they are not. That put them in danger. We want to be relevant medically and irrelevant militarily and politically."[99] While MSF was trying to square the circle in trying to avoid politics, its evaluation was on target. Aid agencies are or are perceived to be associated with the occupation—and for Iraqis, there is little difference.

Two assaults in Iraq in particular have shaken agencies to the core. The August 19, 2003, attack on UN headquarters killed twenty-two, including the charismatic head of the mission, Sergio Vieira de Mello. Some aid workers utter "August 19" with a mournful reverence that had been solely reserved for "September 11." And six weeks later, on October 28, a car bomb was delivered in a white ambulance with a Red Cross symbol, killing fifteen at the ICRC's headquarters. The UN and the ICRC withdrew, and other aid workers inside and outside Iraq trembled.

A year later, conditions had not improved. Not only had more agencies pulled out, but an especially traumatic episode became widely publicized. Margaret Hassan was a British and Irish national who was also an Iraqi by virtue of her marriage to one; she was the head of CARE International's activities and had worked in Iraq for over thirty years. Hassan was abducted and then murdered. Video footage made by her captors show her being treated like other detained Western soldiers and contractors, which offers perhaps the most spectacular testimony to date that the new wars include the intended targeting of aid workers. Indeed, insecurity in Iraq is such that virtually all agencies have left or are present with only skeleton staffs. The ICRC returned but remains incognito—without using the symbols recognized in IHL, for the first time in its history. As the *Economist* summarized, "It was not until the American-led wars in Afghanistan and Iraq that the UN and other aid agencies began to be deliberately hunted down."[100] While the experience of the 1990s suggests that this statement is not entirely true—as any humanitarian who has worked in Bosnia, Burundi, Somalia, or Chechnya would certainly confirm—the increase in the use of force by the United States appears to stimulate previously unseen levels of violence against aid workers.

Journalists have not fared better. According to the Committee to Protect Journalists, "the deadliest year in the last decade was 2004, when 56 journalists were killed. That was followed by 1995, when 51 were killed; and 2003, when 39 journalists were killed. The deadliest country for journalists in the last decade is Iraq, where 36 journalists have been killed, all since the beginning of hostilities in March 2003. Another 18 media support workers were killed in Iraq during that time."[101] The change is dramatic. "Part of the surprise may also lie in the presumption, now quaint, that reporters are regarded as neutrals in armed conflicts, that they are there to record the event for history," wrote *New York Times* reporter Dexter Filkins from Baghdad. "In Iraq, this has not been true for many months. For many insurgents here, and for a fevered class of Islamic zealots, Western reporters are fare game, targets in their war."[102] Moreover, the coverage of Iraq was curtailed and contoured by "no go" zones for journalists as well as troops. Furthermore, in a dangerous turn of events, journalists are both reporting on and making the news—the gruesome beheading of *Wall Street Journal* reporter Daniel Pearl was front-page news.

In responses to attacks, including ceremonial beheadings, humanitarians have continued pushing for enhanced legal protections. The Security Council adopted resolution 1502 a week after the attack on UN's Baghdad headquarters, which specifies that the killing of aid workers is a war crime. However, such international legislation offers little in terms of actual protection as acute security threats multiply.

In fact, many agencies are seeking to address the increase in dangers with greater security for operations. With UN staff facing dangers that seem to have increased exponentially in recent years but even more dramatically in Afghanistan and Iraq, Secretary-General Kofi Annan proposed a new security structure to the General Assembly in 2004 to help protect the more than one hundred thousand UN officials, along with some three hundred thousand dependants, stationed abroad in some 150 offices around the world: "The Organization cannot succumb to a bunker mentality and shrink from the work the world's people expect it to do. A degree of risk cannot be avoided; the challenge is to mitigate it."[103] To meet that challenge, he called for a strengthened and unified security management system combining three separate entities currently responsible for staff safety—the Office of the Security Coordinator, the UN Security and Safety Services, and the security component of the Department of Peacekeeping Operations—into a new Directorate of Security to be headed by an undersecretary-general reporting directly to him. While the secretary-general made staff security his "first priority," it is unclear how the new measures will be more effective than the blue flag was in August 2003. Moreover, as discussed earlier, some agencies are "hardening" targets by contracting private security forces.[104]

The nature of violence affects agencies in different ways because some primarily staff operations with expatriates while others rely extensively on local recruits. For example, the ICRC has twelve thousand workers in the field around the globe, but ten thousand of these positions are filled by locals, like all those who died in Baghdad in October 2003. Expatriate personnel present good targets, but they also have a passport that permits them to retreat or, in the worst-case scenarios, to withdraw.

Local staff do not have this luxury. If anything, they run higher risks than do outsiders in coming to the rescue of their compatriots; they literally have nowhere to run or hide. Indeed, agencies that attempt to minimize security threats (or promote indigenous capacity) by opting for a "go local" strategy may end up simply shifting the burden to locals, who are then seen as "collaborators."[105] The targeting of Iraqis working as police officers or reconstruction workers are cases in point. Again, this hazard has been present in polarized war zones in the past, but the contemporary theaters represent a quantum jump in danger and numbers. Furthermore, these violent climates hinder indigenous capacity building. Kidnapping, threatening, and assassinating local staff in unprecedented numbers deter those who would work with agencies and participate in the humanitarian enterprise.

Gil Loescher, a seasoned researcher looking into humanitarian and human rights issues in Iraq, was outside de Mello's office when the infamous August 19 explosion occurred. He survived the attack as a double amputee. Back at his desk, he described the new context in which aid agencies were distributing leaflets at mosques to try to explain why they should be distinguished from soldiers occupying Iraq. The mere fact of having to distribute such tracts exposes as meaningless the notion that traditional principles are intact—either in reality or in the eyes of Iraqi recipients. Writing a year later and pointing to the "independence, impartiality, and neutrality [that] are core principles governing their operations," Loescher laments that they were "an idea lost in the rubble."[106]

With a few exceptions, humanitarians have yet to factor this reality into their standard operating procedures. While the mantles of humanitarians or reporters have never been a guarantee against death, the contemporary contexts in Afghanistan and Iraq appear to be in a separate category. The grisly videotaped executions mentioned earlier—especially of journalist Daniel Pearl at the outset of the campaign in Afghanistan and of aid worker Margaret Hassan in late 2004—provide dramatic bookends for our argument about a distinctly new context for reporting on or coming to the rescue in new wars.

HIGH TECHNOLOGY VERSUS HIGH-ENOUGH TECHNOLOGY

The U.S.-led wars in Afghanistan and Iraq, and to a lesser extent Israel's armed conflict with Palestinians and Russia's with insurgents in the Caucasus, showcase high-technology militaries confronting those with substantially less technologically advanced weapon systems. The latter can opt for weapons and tactics that can neutralize the presumed advantages of the technologically superior former, a classic case of what we describe earlier as "asymmetric warfare." For example, close-quarter combat in urban settings creates opportunities for those with less-discernable military power to turn the strengths of their mightier foe to their advantage. When the more powerful military lays siege, the actual military advantage gained is usually offset by a political blowback that inspires the opposition and deters allies. Furthermore, technology cannot entirely compensate for thin occupation forces. Firepower creates leverage in winning wars, but forces must have "boots on the ground" to secure the victory, as the U.S. experience in occupied Iraq illustrates.

Even though technology may be used to wage war safely and handily, it may also inflict substantial civilian casualties. Attempted pacification or deterrence through violent intimidation and death has unleashed the full arsenal of high-tech weaponry, with mixed results and new challenges for humanitarians. Advanced military technology may have lowered the costs to states in fighting war (soldiers lost relative to enemy combatants killed), but its increased lethality has increased overall costs, when collateral damage and civilian casualties are included. The case of the "humanitarian bombing" of Kosovo may be the most dramatic illustration to date. The U.S.-led coalition experienced no casualties, but its victory through precision bombing led to civilian deaths approximating thirty-five hundred to ten thousand and damage worth $60 billion to $100 billion. It also led to the initial flight of some eight hundred thousand refugees.[107]

The aftermath of the high-tech war in Iraq indicates how high numbers of civilian casualties may follow after the so-called end of the war. Technology can be adapted. Popular weapons for Iraqi insurgents are improvised explosive devices, which are cobbled together from materials that were crafted for other, more conventionally designed munitions. Although decidedly lethal, these recycled arms are not to achieve tactical victory over the United States but rather to win on the political and strategic front by signaling resistance and increasing uncertainty.

Of greater concern is that a few NSAs, al Qaeda being the most obvious, have indicated their intention to procure WMD. The fashioning of "dirty bombs" (explosives packed with radioactive materials) and makeshift chemical or biological agents illustrates a different and all-too-plausible asymmetry for future attacks. In short, the arsenals of today's NSAs—mostly of small arms but also of improvised explosive devices and programs to assemble WMD—reflect the growing detritus of political order and national militaries. This terrain is totally new for states and militaries and for humanitarians as well.

THE INTERNATIONAL SPOTLIGHT

Since 2001 the manner in which the media influences war and humanitarianism has not experienced any profound change—it still motivates and mollifies, badgers and blinds. However, we find it worth considering several key moments of recent years that illustrate the power of the media and the condition of war and humanitarianism. We have already discussed some aspects, but we briefly recapitulate so that we can look at, instead of merely through, the looking glass.

Photos and footage, broadcasts and print clearly have an impact. Immediately jumping to mind is the mobilization of an estimated $6 billion in the month following the December 2004 tsunami and the vivid depiction of death and devastation. However, it is essential to recognize parallels between media coverage of war and humanitarianism and the significance of political interests. It is not just a matter of war's stealing the spotlight from humanitarianism but also that of which armed conflicts and victims are given attention and neglected.

Evidence about the need for action in Darfur was certainly not lacking, as UN emergency relief coordinator Jan Egeland labeled it "one of the world's worst humanitarian crises."[108] Secretary of State Colin Powell called it by name after the U.S. Congress condemned it unanimously, voting 422–0 that Khartoum was engaged in "genocide."[109] Meanwhile, the African Union indicated its willingness to send troops to protect its own monitors in the country if not menaced by Sudanese.[110] In mid-November when the Security Council met in a special session in Nairobi and did nothing, the government—and especially the government-equipped militias, the Janjaweed—had already killed more than seventy thousand black Africans and had chased some 1.5 million to 2 million into camps in Sudan and Chad. As one observer noted, "the energy spent fighting over whether to call the events there 'genocide' was misplaced. . . . The definitional dance may not have mattered."[111] Whatever the moral pronouncements on this disaster—not to mention Kashmir, Gaza, or northern Uganda—humanitarian issues are out of view without a strong political component that resonates with major-power states. In the end, with the gaze of politicians and journalists glued to Iraq, crises such as Darfur have too little political salience to appear on television or on the radar screens of the powerful.

Furthermore, the images that have defined U.S. intervention in Afghanistan and Iraq offer depressing commentary on the priority accorded humanitarianism by belligerents on all sides. The stories that capture attention are those that have brought the threat of violence into the living rooms of media consumers. After September 11 the idea that terrorism could strike at Western civilians in the safest of locations became a staple of nightly newscasts. This theme continues to be exploited for partisan political purposes.

But on the front lines, it is the war narrative that predominates (who were killed, how many, and in what way), not the humanitarian one (what are the needs of victims and how can assistance most effectively be rendered). Bin Laden's latest tape has much more media coverage than do casualties and fledgling relief efforts.

For humanitarians, two sets of images from the last few years have signaled pressures from within and outside of the system. First, the pictures associated with humanitarian agencies and staff under fire depict the enterprise as being literally under siege. In Afghanistan many locals have a negative perception of aid work, which in turn affects how donors and others view the enterprise.[112] In the attack on the UN compound in Baghdad, humanitarians lost more than just talented personnel; they lost an "idea." Pictures of aid workers withdrawing from their field missions due to security threats conveyed a general sense that humanitarianism was in retreat.

Second, the painful images of executions and suicide bombings showcase mounting disregard for international humanitarian law. Footage of beheadings and other terrorist attacks reflect the disparaging role that IHL plays in the tactics of al Qaeda and affiliates. But in perhaps an even more distressing sign of the times, the United States has ceased carrying the standard and disavowed portions of IHL, by its actions if not its words.

One sign was the designation of "ghost detainees"—a phrase coined by members of the 800th Military Police Brigade to describe those prisoners under the jurisdiction of the Central Intelligence Agency and accorded no legal protections.[113] A second indication was the government memo drafted in 2002 by future attorney general Alberto Gonzales that depicted some provisions of the Geneva Conventions as "obsolete" and "quaint" such that the U.S. president is not legally bound by them; as such, it showed a decline in respect for IHL by the world's foremost power and also further exposed the U.S. case for humanitarian intent in Afghanistan and Iraq.[114] While a handful of allied countries have supported the dubious international legal posture of the United States in the war on terrorism, some going so far as to assist with interrogations and intelligence gathering, most other countries appear antagonized. Ignoring the Geneva Conventions and abusing prisoners at the Guantánamo Bay detention facility in Cuba, at Abu Ghraib in Iraq, and at Bagram in Afghanistan have produced an international uproar and have stained an already discolored U.S. reputation.[115] Ominously, this impression leads to a third signal, the "rendition" program, whereby, to provide the United States with legal cover, detainees are sent to countries that may engage in torture to extract information. This practice is in direct contradiction with article 49 of the fourth Geneva Convention, which protects against "individual or mass forcible transfers, as well as deportations of protected persons from occupied territory . . . regardless of their motive." Following concerns among U.S. officials about the legality of the rendition program, in March 2004 another memorandum was issued in support of the practice.

As a result of defying IHL and other actions that have been perceived as being unjust, Pew poll data of countries around the world in the immediate aftermath of the war indicated a precipitous drop in U.S. popularity since a brief window of solidarity following September 11.[116] Since these surveys were conducted, other stories have come to light—such as a report by *Newsweek* that U.S. interrogators repeatedly had defiled the Koran—that suggest that media images and sound bites are fueling belligerence and that disregard for humanitarianism is spreading.[117] The humanitarian stakes in these media representations are related to whether they foster war or humanitarianism. It is bad enough that, historically, the sword leaves for the salve so little room in the spotlight. Ironically, in Afghanistan and Iraq, it is the shadow of the sword onto the salve that commands the spotlight.

THE COLLECTIVE AND CUMULATIVE CHALLENGES OF TURF WARS

In earlier chapters, we reflect on the collective action problems arising from the new wars with the expansion and evolution of the international humanitarian system as part of the new humanitarianisms. Afghanistan and Iraq substantiate that problems appearing in the 1990s were not aberrations but early evidence of basic structural flaws that are now glaring. "Coordination" may have been far-fetched but was at least conceivable when only the UN system, the ICRC, and a handful of NGOs were on the scene. Now, barriers to entry have fallen and the numbers of humanitarian players have risen dramatically while new and disparate ones (including outside militaries and PMCs) have entered with an accompanying clash over values and resources.

This "atomization" of the humanitarian enterprise makes efforts to enhance coherence seem like a fool's errand. As an indication of the magnitude of the problem, 335 INGOs and 2,300 indigenous NGOs were in Afghanistan in December 2004. The former minister of planning, before resigning, announced that 1,935 would be dissolved for failing to abide by the provision of the central government. The Agency Coordinating Body for Afghan Relief is an umbrella group consisting of *only* ninety-five well-established aid agencies—prima facie evidence that coordination is largely a fiction.[118]

We have used the term "turf wars" to describe the dynamics within the enterprise, but even more striking are the ways that the wars in Afghanistan and Iraq have been fought by belligerents and have thereby set back further the ability of the international humanitarian system to save lives. In short, the system faces both collective and cumulative stresses and challenges.

Arthur Helton—who was killed in Baghdad while interviewing de Mello in August 2003—asked a rhetorical question about aid in Afghanistan that has even greater salience for Iraq: "How coordinated can the effort be when donors will give money through both multilateral and bilateral channels, international organizations and NGOs will jockey for roles and money, and relief work will run up against recovery and development plans?"[119] The answer is evident, and it is one based on the collective action problems outlined in previous chapters and displayed in Afghanistan and Iraq: uncoordinated inputs in international humanitarian system result in uncoordinated and often counterproductive outputs.

In fact, some donors have intentionally sowed competition as a means of improving performance, which has become acute in Afghanistan and Iraq. What explains why aid agencies cannot "just say no"? Jean-Hervé Bradhol, in the introduction to an MSF volume about recent cases of humanitarian action, explains: "Broad access to funds from major aid donors, at least in the initial phase of military intervention, is guaranteed to aid agencies ever sensitive to the preservation and growth of their budgets."[120]

A study of "good donor-ship," commissioned as a result of the starkly confusing roles and agency identity crises in both Afghanistan and Iraq, found that all was not well for the sources of aid either. "Most donor behaviour is really rational from a donor point of view," noted then deputy emergency relief coordinator Carolyn McAskie. "However, the sum total of all donor behaviour doesn't produce a rational whole."[121]

For humanitarians U.S. conduct in Afghanistan, Iraq, and other places has chilling long-term implications. Disrespect for key humanitarian principles by the world's remaining superpower jeopardizes the ability of the enterprise to function, to save lives. Moreover, U.S. militarization of ostensibly nonmilitary responses to war (i.e., the channeling of resources through military actors as opposed to humanitarian or developmental agencies) suggests a transformation in the strategies and means of relief and reconstruction. Funds that had been allocated to addressing shortfalls in social services have been (and increasingly are) redirected toward security. "While agencies do not specifically track costs, both agency and contractor officials acknowledged that security costs had diverted a considerable amount of reconstruction resources and led to canceling or reducing the scope of certain reconstruction projects. For example, in March 2005, USAID cancelled two electrical power generation-related task orders totaling nearly $15 million to help pay for increased security costs being incurred at another power generation project in southern Baghdad."[122] Security for some projects consumes in excess of 25 percent of the intended budget.

No doubt, many humanitarians rejoiced at the possibility that force could be harnessed for noble aims, but joy has faded fast. The more time that passes since the invasions that overthrew the Taliban, that dislodged Saddam Hussein, and that supposedly began meaningful long-term reconstruction, the more that lofty rhetoric is exposed as being hollow. In many ways, the relationship of democracy and humanitarianism to imperialism are similar. Imperialism is not its basis, but imperialism may wipe away constraints that impede democracy. Imperialism is not humanitarianism, but it can make humanitarian access feasible.

However, if access and order are at the expense of humanity, then humanitarianism becomes a shadow of itself—more of a rhetorical parry than a genuine easing of war-induced suffering. Humanitarian resources deployed on behalf of imperialism are temporary assistance but not genuine humanitarianism. Having particular resonance is the contradiction of the hand that gives as the fist that strikes—Hugo Slim termed this dualism "belligerent funding."[123]

Ultimately, it is how humanitarian agencies respond to the main operational challenges across Afghanistan and Iraq that will have widest-ranging and longest-lasting impacts—that is, determining who if anyone to aid, how to aid them, and with whom to negotiate access. Perhaps Slim sums it up best when he proposes "humanitarian cunning," which clearly requires new tactics and new strategic thinking. "[I]t is the time to get decisive about where we can and cannot operate and to get innovative about how we do things. It is the time to be creative about humanitarian agency rather than to wallow in humanitarian agony."[124]

Humanitarian action in Afghanistan and Iraq represent the most visible and contentious course of operations to date. Although events move quickly and generalizations age poorly, it is safe to say that humanitarians have seen the future in Afghanistan and Iraq.

7

Humanitarian Strategic Thinking . . . and Doing

183

For generals as well as soldiers, the "fog of war" is vexing, and decision makers at all levels in aid agencies confront the "fog of humanitarianism." It is as dense and obfuscating as the military variety. The uncertainties that plague war and warriors are but one source of the fog that blankets humanitarian action. However, donor politics and collective action problems provide additional opaqueness to the cloud cover over policy and decision making. Humanitarians are unable to completely lift the fog—and the winds of international politics do not appear likely to disperse it—but its worst effects can be mitigated. Most critically, staff can be in a position to navigate through it if they better understand the nature of change in war and humanitarianism and adjust their programming accordingly. What is needed is a strategic vision for humanitarianism—a framework that illuminates the nuts and bolts of tactical means-ends relationships in achieving the primary goal of saving lives.

This chapter explores the role of strategic planning on humanitarian action: why it is needed (assessing and adapting to change), why it does not happen but could (comparing military and humanitarian organizations), how it works (suggesting how to put strategic planning into practice, including enhancing key capabilities), and where the system is headed (addressing recent characterizations of the enterprise as being in crisis or at least at a crossroads). First, we assess changes in humanitarianism itself to make the case for strategic thinking and doing. Second, we juxtapose the learning cultures and adaptive inclinations of militaries and humanitarian agencies to illustrate how laggard and exceptional the efforts by aid agencies are in comparison with the routine analytical output of the armed forces. Third, we provide the basis for a strategic review by agencies—a snapshot of humanitarian "power" and a checklist for evaluating their positions. Fourth, we offer suggestions for instituting strategic thinking within agencies and translating it into strategic doing. Finally, we conclude with a few thoughts on the current state of affairs and a plea to invest more in strategic analysis.

ASSESSING CHANGE IN HUMANITARIANISM: THE CASE FOR STRATEGIC THINKING AND DOING

This book has two intermingled themes—the evolution of war and the mechanics of humanitarian action—and in this section we fuse them to characterize today's humanitarian enterprise. Examining the aggregation and accumulation of crises, agencies, and actions, we return to a theme introduced at the outset of the volume—namely, the nature of change. We quickly recap and chart the elements of the new wars, the new humanitarianisms, and the abysses in Afghanistan and Iraq to identify what has changed for humanitarianism—in terms of identity, organization, behavior, and impacts.

"Change" in humanitarianism is hard to assess in that its sources are elusive and the ways that it manifests itself can be deceptive. Nevertheless, we have presented substantial evidence of changes either fully apparent or underway. To recall our initial discussion, we are mainly interested in registering macrohistorical change in the nature of the entire humanitarian enterprise, but illustrations come from more microhistorical cases based on the experiences of agencies that denote larger systemic changes. Later in this chapter, we address how agencies should proceed to assess their authority and capacity, their power and position, in the context of stresses from a whole series of changes at the microlevel. But here, we are more concerned with the health of the forest than the life of particular trees.

Three central influences in international politics shape the international humanitarian system—ideology, security, and economics. Each is manifest both broadly outside and narrowly within aid agencies. This acknowledgment of exogenous and endogenous factors draws on the two dominant schools of thought in international relations: the realist tradition emphasizing international conditions and neoliberal institutionalism stressing the nature of organizations. In this case, we mesh the role of humanitarian action in international politics with the structural constraints of the new wars and the organizational profile issues of individual agencies struggling with the new humanitarianisms.

However, the distinction into discrete pressures from outside and inside the international humanitarian system is more analytical than actual. Tensions interact and heighten one another. For example, security problems can lead to debates over values, and then shifts in values and policy can result in other security problems. Or, budgetary constraints can affect how agencies behave, and then agency behavior may dictate future allocations or priorities from donors. Table 7.1 gives an overview.

Having identified sources and signs of change, we deduce overall patterns of change and continuity in the enterprise, from its inception to the "new" overlays up through the contemporary conditions of war and humanitarianism. In humanitarianism the one fundamental continuity is the link to war. Notwithstanding this essential dynamic, we see change in both the conditions under which humanitarianism operates (security challenges) and the mechanics of humanitarian action (especially, donors playing a bigger role in guiding policy and programming). We find four types of change in humanitarianism: two inputs (identity and organization) and two outputs (behavior and impact).

Identity

Humanitarianism is traditionally identified with its focus on the welfare of affected populations in war zones, and to a large extent, since the birth of the international humanitarian system, this image has been unsullied. But the insertion of humanitarian agencies into some contemporary

Table 7.1. Sources and Signs of Change in Humanitarianism

	Ideological	Security	Economic
	Values and Culture	*Violence in Nonpermissive Environments*	*Resource Arrangements*
Resulting external pressure on humanitarianism	End of Cold War Disorder from globalization "Clash of civilizations" narrative	"Failed states" agenda crosses security and humanitarian interests Military forces performing humanitarian tasks	Other priorities besides humanitarianism for donors Many crises compete for aid
Resulting internal pressure on humanitarianism	Debates over political use of aid and force	Attacks on aid workers Integration impulses	Marketization pressures
Evident change	Diverse interpretations of values and diverse agencies Some work with military	Private military companies as humanitarian actors Donors compel integration	Agency struggles for resources Growth of privatization

armed conflicts has polarized perspectives. The majority of victims who benefit from relief and protection undoubtedly hold positive views about the enterprise and most operations. However, instances of hostile reactions to the presence of agencies, as well as profound differences among humanitarians and serious criticisms of certain actions, signal an identity crisis. In fact, a 2005 mapping exercise of operational contexts for humanitarian agencies finds that recipients "are more concerned about *what* is provided than about *who* provides it."[1]

The primordial identity of humanitarianism as straightforwardly saving lives is considerably more complicated today than it was in the late nineteenth century or during the twentieth century before the 1990s. Concerns over its impact on military and political realities had surfaced routinely, but new wars and new humanitarianisms have forced the door open to further politicization. From within, some humanitarians have pushed out the envelope of what is considered humanitarian to include peacebuilding and political transformation as well as the use of force. Publicity about malfeasance by agencies and personnel has disparaged the enterprise. Indeed, the titles of recent books characterize it in a downward spiral teeming with the sins of saints. One could run several recent book titles together about humanitarianism to posit the following: Deliver us from evil and the dark sides of virtue, or we are condemned to repeat famine crimes, bear witness to genocide, offer only a bed for the night, and pay the price of indifference along the road to hell.[2] In Afghanistan and Iraq in particular, the humanitarian mantle is in tatters.

Change in the identity of humanitarianism indicates two things. First, the idea of aid to war victims has not diminished, and in some ways the expansion of the agenda represents a strengthening and broadening of the attractiveness of the undertaking among beneficiaries, donors, and others not traditionally engaged in such activities. Indeed, despite attacks on agencies, survey data suggest that the enterprise remains quite popular. The first comprehensive survey of victims in war zones in 1999 reported that two-thirds of civilians under siege who were interviewed in twelve war-torn societies by the ICRC wanted more intervention and only 10 percent wanted none.[3] Moreover, despite a marked discrepancy between the extent to which war victims and that to which populations in states on the Security Council (likely to include donors) look to humanitarian agencies to provide assistance to those in need, most consider the ICRC, the UN, and humanitarian NGOs as the top places to turn.[4] Second, however, in some theaters the ideology of humanitarianism remains more popular than agencies or staff. The identity of humanitarians is vulnerable to being shaped by other interests. Political windows allow humanitarians to define themselves, but such windows can slam shut with one powerful event, as September 11 underlined. At present the politics of the "war on terrorism" vexes humanitarian agencies—first by determining where to deploy and second by influencing how to carry out operations—and yields greater control over the enterprise to belligerents.

The main questions are thus: How is humanitarian identity defined? Who qualifies as a standard bearer? Do traditional principles remain valid?

Organization

The continued growth and evolution of the international humanitarian system represent a dramatic change. Institutionalization of intergovernmental and nongovernmental organizations for most of the twentieth century was geared to addressing the human debris of interstate war, not the civil or transnational armed conflicts of the new wars. Further, the new humanitarianisms underscore the extent to which value-based organizations are not exempt from responding to economic incentives.

Two historical changes in humanitarianism are worth noting from an organizational perspective. The first is the tremendous growth of humanitarian institutions and the expansion of partners beyond states. The second consists of market influences that raise the salience of organizational interests in the development of policy and operations.

The main questions are thus: How do agencies develop and mature? How do they make decisions? To whom are they accountable? How do they achieve objectives? How should individual agencies and the international humanitarian system be structured?

Behavior

The behavior of humanitarian actors has certainly changed from its humble beginnings as a marginal and occasional player to aid the most visible of victims. Traditionally, behavior was narrowly defined (mainly as emergency relief); action was sporadic; and agencies confined their negotiations for access and engagement to states. However, the system has grown; many agencies have mainstreamed human rights and employed military tools; and, most important, many have engaged NSAs to ensure access and implement programming. Early in the history of the international humanitarian system, behavior was mostly the result of an impulse that found small but sure traction among private citizens in the wealthy West. Widespread appreciation for the values and the overall development of global institutions has created wider possibilities.

Changes in behavior can be seen in the substance and scope of aid agencies and their activities. Behavior can be the result of a single factor, but it is usually the reflection of multiple influences.[5] Current behavior is the product of humanitarian culture and humanitarian organizations in the new wars. To plot future behavior, all three components—culture, organization, and context—should be tabulated.

The main questions are thus: What is the actual behavior resulting from operationalizing principles? What is the configuration of factors that explains the behavior of aid agencies? How has this changed over time? What can be done to avert or compensate for failings, shortcomings, and errors?

Impacts

The change in the impact of the international humanitarian system is the most palpable of transformations over the last 150 years. Large and well-supported institutional mechanisms to save the lives of political and cultural strangers are a dominant reality of our times. The potential number of lives saved by the international humanitarian system is gigantic. For 2003 alone, OCHA estimates that over forty-five million people were in need of humanitarian assistance in war zones.[6] Further, there have been normative developments regarding the responsibility of international organizations to protect civilians from states that commit massive human rights violations against their own populations.

However, not all of the impacts of humanitarian agencies have been beneficial or benign, as we have seen. The success of the humanitarian system has in some ways been its own undoing, as more resources for more agencies have led to more collective action problems. Deals with local interlocutors also have the potential to trigger competition and undermine maximizing collective efforts.

The main questions are thus: How do political pressures and military action influence which lives are saved and how many are saved? How can the system save more lives? How can collective action problems and other corrosive dynamics be overcome?

LEARNING CULTURES AND ADAPTATION: MILITARY INSTITUTIONS VERSUS HUMANITARIAN AGENCIES

Some might think that soldiers and humanitarians are wholly distinct species because, with some exceptions, their cultures emphasize such profoundly different values toward and perspectives on violence. Although approaching war from opposing philosophical positions, their respective organizations share at least one thing: they excel when they learn about local conditions and adapt operations accordingly.

The most adept institutions have strong learning cultures that promote sensitivity, curiosity, and flexibility. In this section we discuss how learning cultures have an impact on the ability of aid agencies to adjust to new influences or to alterations in existing environments. We briefly examine learning, then compare and contrast military and humanitarian institutions.

Finally, we focus on the key impediments to agency learning and conclude by identifying missing or weak orientations and capacities.

As aid agencies vary considerably in their interpretation of humanitarian values, structure, funding, and operational capacities, so do their predispositions toward learning. Generalizing about the international humanitarian system or any other topic involves simplification. Our analysis and experience lead us to attempt the following generalization: for the most part, the process of formally identifying problems, gathering data, drawing conclusions, and translating lessons into policies and actions—that is, aid agency learning—has been neglected or at least relegated to a tertiary or even symbolic status. We return to a question with which we began this volume: why are humanitarians so far behind other organized actors in adapting to change? As much of the experience of the 1990s—and, again, more recently—demonstrates, reaction to a crisis is vintage humanitarianism but serious reflection is not part of a humanitarian's job description.

However, when organizations are unable to be effective, they often feel pressure from their own staffs and boards or from outside sources of support, which may result in calls for accountability and stimulate interest in learning. For instance, the debates that surrounded new humanitarianisms—over acceptable means, political uses of assistance, credible interlocutors and partners—stirred anxieties more than it opened doors to a deep rethinking and retooling of the entire international humanitarian system. In his most recent treatment of the UNHCR, for example, Gil Loescher points to the institution's conservative culture, which is resistant to change and inhospitable to the infusion of new ideas and outside criticism.[7] How prevalent is this type of organizational pathology?

Perhaps the ICRC best illustrates an institution's willingness to fundamentally reexamine its basic premises. This self-reflection was based on the traumatic experiences of the 1990s and has implications for the system of aid agencies more generally. The process of *Avenir* ("future" in French) was designed to be published at the dawn of the new millennium to coincide with the departure of Cornelio Sommaruga, who had been president since 1987 and was retiring on January 1, 2000, to be replaced by Jakob Kellenberger. In mid-1996 the ICRC began the effort for which a press release accurately described as being aimed at "analyzing and gaining a fresh perspective on the contemporary environment for humanitarian activity. What the ICRC has observed and the operational difficulties it has encountered, in connection with both the political world and the conduct of modern conflicts since the end of the Cold War, are at the root of this project."[8] Among the more obvious difficulties were those resorting to "technicals" in Somalia and the rising number of deaths of expatriate and local staff through the decade. As David Forsythe notes, "The ICRC at the start of the twenty-first century is decidedly more professional and less amateurish than ever before."[9] The *Avenir* process was an attempt to update the mandate, strategy, and tactics of the world's premier humanitarian institution, the first such review since a study by the Henri Dunant Institute in the mid-1970s.[10]

The ICRC's highest decision-making body, the Assembly, approved the *Avenir* report and its guidelines in December 1997 and made a number of strategic decisions. By the following spring, an implementation plan was drawn up, adopted, and then gradually executed. In short, the process amounted to rethinking the ICRC's experience over the turbulent 1990s. It involved outside consultants as well as senior staff and led to a substantial report that altered the organization's approach to management in headquarters and in the field. The previously referenced press release noted that the "conclusions reached in the report aim to remind the ICRC that, because of the shifting context in which the humanitarian work of the future will take place, it will have to reinforce the overall coherence of its activity and adapt to change, without, however, losing its identity."

In another example—not far away, in Geneva—the International Federation of Red Cross and Red Crescent Societies began a worthwhile effort in 1996 to rethink the way that projects are formulated and administered. The Sphere Project put forward a widely used set of guidelines for core standards in humanitarian programming, which were an extension of an earlier effort in 1994 to establish a code of conduct for the movement.[11] The Sphere Minimum Standards were published in 1999 and reflect "the combined efforts of 641 named individuals (and countless un-named persons) drawn from some 228 organisations"; as such, they promote accountability in the provision of disaster assistance.[12] Some observers point out that, ironically, these minimum standards for disasters are higher than those for development assistance. The establishment of industry-wide standards acceptable to the major humanitarian players also meant that smaller agencies were obliged to follow suit—some called it the "fear" project because they worried that donors might use the standards to keep certain actors out of emergencies.

Still another promising effort, this time across agencies, is the Active Learning Network for Accountability and Performance in Humanitarian Action.[13] Established in 1997, this interagency effort was specifically designed to enhance accountability by sharing the results of internal evaluations. ALNAP's membership currently comprises fifty-one full members and a growing number of observers (about 450). Full members include bilateral and multilateral donor organizations; UN agencies and organizations; NGOs and NGO umbrella organizations; the IFRC; and selected consultants, academics, and research institutes. To ensure a context that encourages self-criticism and learning within the international humanitarian sector, ALNAP is structured so that no single type of organization among the full members is able to dominate discussion or set the agenda. Representatives are drawn from a mix of policy, operations, evaluation, and monitoring sections of organizations involved in humanitarian action. Consequently, it represents an unusual structure with considerable potential for developing and introducing new thinking and approaches within the sector.

The logic is highly laudable: learning about best practices along with poor ones should be shared across institutions confronting similar challenges. Several years into the experiment and some five thousand evaluations later, ALNAP suggests more the obvious thirst for knowledge and the felt need to avoid the mistakes of the 1990s than a real demonstration of learning. Consolidating lessons that are common among participants is an essential next step that has begun with an annual *Review of Humanitarian Action*. The next step in genuine learning, however, requires that the common lessons identified be considered by policymakers and then acted on by decision makers. An even more fundamental task is to engage in the basic research that would precede any evaluation or assessment, asking such questions as What is provided? and How do we measure it?

Perhaps the period following the Rwandan genocide best illustrates the heartfelt need to spend time and energy on avoiding past mistakes, replicating success stories, and moving away from the dominant thinking of the past. With generous funding from Denmark of over $2 million, the Joint Evaluation of Emergency Assistance to Rwanda brought together over fifty specialists, whose findings were published in five volumes in March 1996.[14] To its credit DANIDA (Danish International Development Agency) hired the two main consultants who had orchestrated the original massive evaluation, John Borton and John Eriksson, to take a subsequent look at the impact of the original effort on the tenth anniversary of the genocide.

Their depressing political conclusion is as follows: "The international community had in effect used humanitarian aid as a form of substitute for effective political and military action." At the same time and perhaps as pertinent for our purposes, the authors also note the joint evaluation's most clear-cut and positive impact: "Many observers agree that the NGO sector has made significant improvements in the areas of professionalism, standards and accountability mechanisms."[15] In fact in light of ICRC's adaptations, David Forsythe argues that the so-called crisis of humanitarianism "can be overstated."[16]

But is it? For example, the UNHCR's Evaluation and Policy Analysis Unit has engaged consultants to help assess the gap between aspirations and achievements. One particularly hard-hitting analysis criticizes the "culture" of the institution that worked against reflection and planning.[17] Another took the agency to task for its efforts to assist and protect IDPs because "operational decision making is uncertain, inconsistent and unpredictable."[18] While the openness to self-criticism is a healthy sign, the lack of meaningful follow-up is part of a predictable organizational pathology.

Without more substantial and thorough-going changes in practices, our views are closer to Michael Barnett's description of the current moment as "a twilight of hopelessness."[19] In spite of several efforts within and among agencies, actual learning and consequent shifts in practice are considerably less dramatic than what might meet the eye—forward looking but sparsely practiced and short-lived. The assumption that aid agencies have changed for the better, even if the world situation has not, is debatable. "Confronted with all this hard work, thought and scruple, it might be reasonable to assume that the most egregious errors of the recent humanitarian past . . . would have become a thing of the past," writes David Rieff. In looking at the December 2004 tsunami, he notes in his trenchant prose how the crisis of humanitarianism growing from the 1990s experience in war zones was replicated: "What the tsunami has demonstrated is that, for all the conferences, internal reviews, pledges of accountability and transparency, codes of conduct and the like, the humanitarian circus is alive and well."[20]

For us, aid agency learning is shorthand for the total effort of those who gather and process information and make it accessible to others within an organization and throughout the system so that other humanitarians can act on its lessons. Yet the value of many so-called learning activities is not always apparent because the extent to which they cause alterations in policy and program is absent. "Adaptation" occurs when an organization finds short-term ways to solve problems and operate effectively. But "change" refers to substantial and profound reflections about the premises of humanitarian action and the most desirable ways to alter policies, adopt principles, and, ultimately, conduct the next generation of operations.

While the international humanitarian system has adapted over the years, the challenges of the new wars and new humanitarianisms, as exemplified in Afghanistan and Iraq, are so momentous as to necessitate bold changes in strategic thinking. However, aid agencies are far more likely to adapt than they are to change. Why? A comparison of military institutions and humanitarian agencies is instructive.

There is nothing elegant about war—it is invariably dehumanizing and has tragic consequences. But the planning, preparation, synchronization, and execution of operations by sophisticated military institutions can be a remarkable combination of creativity, command, maneuver, and finesse. In war, the military's primary function is to determine how best to use available resources (both technology and human) to overwhelm an enemy. Although most resources are devoted directly to the purchase of human resources, equipment, munitions, logistics, and communications, substantial expenditures are nonetheless dedicated to making the use of force more effective. Beyond evaluating war-fighting capacities, military organizations take into account varying political and economic pressures, ways of minimizing casualties to soldiers and civilians, and cost savings. In addition to specialized training for soldiers and military academies for officers, considerable effort is devoted to amassing historical data and to assessing performance of ongoing and previous operations in order to adapt field tactics and grand strategies for future efforts.

An extensive literature documents change within military organizations and, specifically, how it correlates with output in doctrine and behavior. In general, two schools of thought predominate: influences of international systems and those of organizational cultures.[21] For our purposes, however, it is not worth dissecting this vast literature but rather examining possible parallels that may help describe why aid agencies change or do not.

The radically different values of military and humanitarian organizations are critical in explaining differences in their respective learning cultures and curves. While critics often castigate a hierarchical and overfunded military, the pursuit of order and discipline by soldiers is the by-product of intensive training that not only instructs but bonds. The creation of standard operating procedures is a reflection of a scientific approach to managing and executing tasks under centralized authority. One might expect such a culture to be rigid and unreceptive to learning, but the opposite is in fact the norm. Success and promotion are contingent on flexibility and openness to change in strategy and tactics, as well as extreme discipline in carrying out new procedures.

At the end of wars or even in the middle of a battle, if existing techniques and technology prove inadequate, militaries are obliged to innovate and change or suffer the consequences, defeat. The military acknowledges that dated, misconceived strategies and rigid, unquestioning soldiers can be a dangerous mix. The military expression "Frederick the Great lost the Battle of Jena" is historically inaccurate as well as impossible—Frederick had died in 1786 and Napoleon did not trounce the Prussians at Jena until 1806.[22] But the statement is a commentary on the Prussian military's overly strict adherence to Frederick's outmoded strategic doctrine.

Furthermore, recognizing a need to innovate and adapt has meant that significant budgetary resources are routinely dedicated to evaluation and analysis. National defense clearly occupies a privileged position in governmental battles for resources. The potential costs of falling behind—defeat—are high enough to ensure monies for research. The material incentives for the military to succeed on the battlefield typically guarantee parliamentary largesse toward budgetary requests. There is no question of going out of business next year.

The contrast with the majority of humanitarian culture and organizations could hardly be greater. They normally beg for what may be inadequate resources to react after the fact and provide relief and protection in war's wake. At the core of humanitarianism are two basic tasks: to muster resources for emergency aid and to deliver them to those in need. It is rarely possible to go it alone in contemporary crises, and to carry out basic functions, aid agencies almost always work with other actors. In mobilizing resources, agencies rely on donors. In providing relief and protection, their work hinges on access facilitated by a host of other agencies in the same arena, including soldiers. In short, the challenges of mobilizing resources and securing access may make humanitarian action contingent on an alignment of donor wishes and the whims of interlocutors before agencies can act. Individual aid agencies are increasingly becoming cogs in a much larger international machine, handicapped or even unable to accomplish their tasks without inputs from others. This case is especially evident in the nonpermissive operational environments of the new wars.

Yet humanitarians have no boot camps for instruction about overcoming bureaucratic and operational minefields. They have no specialized academies—other than an occasional master's program. And virtually no resources, at least as a percentage of overall budgets, are allocated to their understanding current and previous operations with a view toward changing tactics or strategies. Indeed, a virtue has often been made from what in other organizational philosophies would be seen as a grave shortcoming—namely, moving as quickly as possible to the next crisis without having gathered data and evidence, evaluated it, and attempted to reformulate policies before the next effort.

Illustrative of this point is how the military conducts, disseminates, and processes research and analysis with reference to "friendly fire" casualties. In contrast, when agencies provide aid that ends up stoking war (a common charge since the well-fed dead in Bosnia), analysts may develop new conceptual frameworks and operational guidelines—for example, Mary Anderson's "do no harm" school—but they are neither uniformly promulgated nor embraced by various moving parts of the enterprise. Moreover, many evaluations of humanitarian operations establish their own measurements of success, which underlines cultural as well as knowledge-based collective action problems throughout the system. Looking at amounts of aid delivered or numbers of recipients serviced, but not contextualizing the long-term impacts, renders such metrics of humanitarianism irrelevant.

Why is it so difficult, in the words of a subtitle to a chapter in a recent IFRC annual report, to exercise "humanitarian judgment to analyze context"?[23] "When data are uncertain, humanitarians are guided by hunches, inferences, past experiences, and conceptions of best practice," David

Kennedy tells us. In the rush to respond, humanitarians understandably repeat "pat answers" that worked in the past. But instead of visceral reactions, hard-headed reflections should guide agencies: "A pragmatism of consequences runs into difficulty when expertise of this type substitutes for careful analysis of long- and short-term consequences." The humanitarian culture must change because humanitarians "tend to be uncomfortable thinking of themselves making the kind of distributional choices among winners and losers which seem required by a pragmatism of consequences."[24] Another commentator whose focus is on negotiations with nonstate actors, often armed, proposes a pragmatic orientation that is "not so much principle-driven, but rather a dynamic bartering process."[25]

The title of Fiona Terry's book *Condemned to Repeat?* poses an obvious rhetorical question in that she and others have detailed missed opportunities for learning about the nature of the highly politicized wars of the 1990s and about fund-raising imperatives. She would undoubtedly agree with Ian Smillie and Larry Minear's call for "a more holistic approach . . . that puts learning at center stage."[26]

Unfortunately, slowing down to reflect is doubly problematic. Not only are too few resources devoted to reflection, but the incentive structure is also deleterious because material rewards await those at the head of the humanitarian response queue. Reactions, not reflections, are valued. The focus on the emergency phase makes good copy, and the limited duration for spending resources compels agencies into a myopic sprint that ignores long-term consequences. If clinical psychological diagnoses were permitted, "attention deficit disorder" would accurately capture the condition of the humanitarian enterprise, whereas the organizational philosophy of the top militaries could be considered "obsessive compulsive." In terms of new threats and opportunities, the latter neurosis is preferable.

Before some final thoughts about the relative capacities of humanitarian agencies as adaptive organizations, it would be helpful to examine six impediments to learning: old orientations, poor information management, triage mentality, image considerations, limited economic resources, and a loss of human resources.[27]

It is baffling that the sea changes in world politics beginning in the late 1980s and the proliferation of new wars in the 1990s have not yet led to a next generation of humanitarian institutions. Indeed, they have not even a mechanism for transforming the existing institutional machinery. Although historical disjunctures should stimulate a retooling of the international humanitarian system, as new kinds of horrors and famine shock consciences and expose the inadequacies of existing organizations and their standard operating procedures, to date they have not. And such adaptations as we have seen have had a relatively weak empirical grounding.

The evolution of war and humanitarianism, as well as their relationship, is understood and appreciated at significantly different levels among militaries and aid agencies. The truism about generals and the last war has a humanitarian corollary: aid agencies continue to provide relief and protection as if they were responding to interstate wars. Even David Rieff, long a harsh critic of the enterprise who had called for an interventionist and political system, has now taken shelter in the original formula of neutrality and impartiality, apologizing to readers for his shift in perspective.[28] A return to this entrenched and straightforward ideological position recalls the politics of an earlier era when wars were principally fought between states and argues for the strict application of traditional principles to every humanitarian disaster. As noted, however, such knee-jerk reactions often play into the hands of malevolent actors in contemporary wars.

One of the great weaknesses in the international humanitarian system is its inability to manage effectively the information that is available to its field staff. Outdated and oftentimes incompatible technologies make communication and information exchange difficult. But the more important administrative issue is that aid agencies do not place a high-enough value on compiling their own experiences and sharing them with other institutions. This step is the first in learning.

The UNHCR is a case in point. A recent report on cultural bottlenecks within the organization describes a tendency to avoid looking ahead; as one staff member asserts, "We're CNNish. We respond; we don't do long-term strategic planning."[29] The consequences are undeniable: "Lack of planning and reflection have an impact on outcomes and ability to learn from experience."[30]

Fundamentally, humanitarians behave more with the single-mindedness and problem-solving orientation of a firefighter than with the cunning calculations of an experienced military strategist or master tactician. Consequently, their responses to the myriad changes in war zones over the last two decades stand in sharp contrast with the standard approach of militaries that oftentimes devote as many resources for preparations and training as they do operations.

Learning from mistakes requires that humanitarian agencies revisit embarrassing moments. Not only can this painful prospect be demoralizing to staff—although some find such candor, insight, and reflection refreshing—but it can also stir fears that any impression of failure will repel donors and individual contributors. To some humanitarians, reexamining their practices in Srebrencia or Goma is potentially bad advertising and bad public relations.

Humanitarians are not allergic to analyses, but such an orientation has not become ingrained and is rarely rewarded. In the course of the turbulent 1990s, small research and evaluation units were established in many larger agencies, but their cultures and budget imperatives continually push them to move on to the next crisis. Moreover, they are always scrambling to meet the budgetary requirements of crises after the fact because the duration of the emergency phase is so short and few donors or agencies are willing to dedicate resources to learning and adapting. As Koenraad Van Brabant states, "The short funding cycles of humanitarian action, even in chronic crises, are, however, a serious disincentive to more strategic thinking."[31]

Research is simply not a priority in activist institutions. It is illustrative, for instance, that the UNHCR, with a budget of some $1 billion in the late 1990s, had one half of a statistician devoted to gathering and processing data about refugee flows. Sadako Ogata, an academic herself before becoming UN high commissioner for refugees, established a small research unit, the Centre for Documentation and Research, which published four biannual reports, *The State of the World's Refugees*.[32] The unit and the reports were among the first things dismantled by her successor.

Research and evaluation are viewed as luxuries, not necessities. They are the last items to be funded and the first to be jettisoned in a financial downturn. The rhetorical question posed by colleagues and board members sounds something like the following: How is it possible to think of funding a mission historian or a project evaluator or a statistician when such costs are directly deducted from an underfunded budget to save lives? The premise of such a question suggests a profound ignorance of the nature of organizational learning.

The loss of experienced staff has also impeded learning. Human resources are vital because their experiences, even if not compiled, constitute institutional memory that can occasionally be called on. But burnout leads people to leave, and field assignments to countries can often be short. It is puzzling that when personnel retire or otherwise move, a tremendous loss is permitted to occur—the informed reflections of departing staff are precious assets and represent an investment that, if not documented, is basically wasted. But too few efforts are made to document experiences and observations for contemporaries and successors. There is simply little tradition or value placed on such work.

Humanitarians may cite "lessons learned," but they are more likely to be "lessons spurned." Even when analysis occurs, acting on it does not necessarily follow. Because historical analysis and evaluation are less developed, and training and planning less formal, than in military circles, humanitarians have a culture that does not push for implementation. Moreover, even if some institutions adapt, the rest of an essentially decentralized system may not. On principle, institutions may even refuse to change long-standing policies. For instance, Alex de Waal rues an international humanitarian system with an "extraordinary capacity to absorb criticism, not reform itself, and yet emerge strengthened."[33] The adage of "know thy enemy" has infused military strategy; to keep pace with soldiers, humanitarians need to borrow this page from the military playbook.

Agencies are seldom inclined or equipped to appreciate the effects of their actions in war zones. Without the recognition that something must change or a ready manner for processing and addressing significantly changed operational environments, agencies have relied on previously established norms and standard operating procedures. When coupled with the centrifugal forces of atomization, the humanitarian enterprise as a whole is incoherent. In other words, the lack of institutional change has led at best to agencies "muddling through."

In response to the crises of the 1990s, independent research and discussion about the humanitarian industry have grown noticeably.[34] However, it is striking how little has changed in humanitarian infrastructure in spite of such experiments as the Strategic Framework in Afghanistan or the thousands of evaluations compiled by ALNAP. Despite substantial analyses of the ills, one is tempted to posit an inverse relationship between analysis and introspection by humanitarians on the one hand and real change in policies and the standard operating procedures of agencies on the other.

As aid agencies agonize about what to do next, Marc Lindenberg and Coralie Bryant speculate that perhaps transformation is in the offing.[35] More research and comparative looks across cases are certainly in order, but as Larry Minear notes, "humanitarian organizations' adaptation to the new realities has been for the most part lethargic and phlegmatic. Institutional reform among humanitarian actors has not kept pace with the changing political-military landscape."[36] To remain true to their own values, humanitarians should critically reflect on new dynamics and develop more appropriate strategies and tactics for alleviating war's worst consequences.

Without intentionally being provocative or leveling undue praise to the armed forces, two bottom lines stand out. The first is that military science requires a counterpart, humanitarian science. An essential part of this exercise would involve the development of "doctrine," which would prescribe guidelines for engagement. Aid agencies require "humanitarian doctrine" to guide programming in an immense variety of environments, especially those of the new wars. The second bottom line is that the strategies of the new humanitarianisms must be considered in any emergency; options should not be restricted to previous operating principles. Field agencies with greater flexibility, complemented by enhanced information resources, would facilitate learning and adaptation by aid agencies.

STRATEGIC REVIEW: HUMANITARIAN POWER AND POSITION

For agencies to take the next step in addressing structural problems in the international humanitarian system and to conduct more effective relief and protection operations, an essential prerequisite involves assessing their actual power (defined as the ability to affect outcomes) and actual position (relative to other actors). We have emphasized that agencies should take stock of where they have been historically. Here we suggest a corollary, an inventory of current conditions—in military parlance, a "strategic review"—of which two components should be building blocks: humanitarian power and the position of agencies in both policymaking and operational environments.

Humanitarian agencies have power. At a rudimentary level, the resources of humanitarian aid directly affect outcomes—and they often mean the difference between life and death. When an agency decides whether to provide lifesaving aid or not, where to deliver it, what exactly to provide, and for what period and according to what standards of eligibility, it clearly exercises leverage over individuals, groups, societies, and governments. Moreover, a second form of power, the idea of valuing human life in war, can catalyze other resources to ease the plight of victims. In examining humanitarian agencies, we see both types of power on display: a capacity to influence dramatically war-torn areas through humanitarian action and the authority to command resources from public and private sources.

This analysis of authority-capacity dynamics in some ways mirrors our earlier discussion of states. Just as states can "fail"—that is, be structurally flawed to the point of seriously skewing functions or benefits or collapsing outright—aid agencies can also "fail." The power of agencies resides not only in their material capabilities but also in their moral force. A successful agency has the power to access war victims, guarantee their own personnel and facilities, and shape humanitarian outcomes.

By and large, the current generation of aid agencies has failed to confront the reality of bad consequences flowing from good intentions, preferring to retreat into denial, intensify efforts to do good, or point the finger at others, especially the military. The growing influence and power of humanitarian actors result from having entered the realm of policy. Their vocabulary has been appropriated by governments and other power brokers, and in exchange humanitarians receive necessary resources. However, while enhancing material capabilities, this economic transaction can ultimately undermine the moral power of agencies, and the ledger of economic and political capital may not balance. The bounty offered by donor states may pale in comparison to the costs engendered when agencies seemingly pursue humanitarian action at the behest of governments in the pursuit of their national interests.

In light of the heavy dose of politicization in today's war zones, it is imperative for agencies to appreciate the relationship between their authority and actual capacities. When an individual agency's or the wider system's authority is suspect, capacities are enfeebled. The identity of humanitarians as value-driven agents is intimately linked to their ability to carry out their work. As discussed earlier—broadly in chapter 4 and with particular reference to Afghanistan and Iraq in chapter 6— toiling with those who wrap themselves inappropriately in the humanitarian mantle can lead to a perilous "gray humanitarianism" that threatens the enterprise as a whole. At the same time, weak capacities and poor performance can curtail respect for the enterprise. Humanitarian power therefore reflects the collective reputation and resources of the system.

In this context, it is imperative to distinguish the legitimate use of military power for human protection purposes—for example, that in northern Iraq in 1991, Somalia in 1992, or Kosovo in 1999—from the illegitimate use in Iraq beginning in March 2003. In being associated with the latter, humanitarians may do more harm than good to their enterprise. In essence, agencies must remember that in any operation intended to serve war victims, legitimacy is a force multiplier.

In addition to humanitarian power, the second building block for strategic review consists of humanitarian position. That is, to fully grasp how the aggregation of the humanitarian impulse, institutional imperatives, and the dynamics of new wars currently manifest themselves, it is imperative to look through the eyes of civilian aid agencies to witness intra-agency (relations within an organization), interagency (relations with other players of the same type), and transagency (relations with nonhumanitarian organizations) challenges in policymaking and operational theaters. The following list depicts the number, variety, nature, and interconnectedness of seven challenges that have appeared throughout this volume:

- *Muster and deploy resources:* Bring attention to crises and engage with donors.
- *Operationalize the impulse:* Translate principles into operational guidelines.
- *Gain access to and protect victims:* Help distressed populations, which may require dealing with those who steal or manipulate aid.
- *Secure aid workers:* Fend off threats and violence for political or economic reasons.
- *Avoid or cease skewed distribution of aid:* Deliver assistance while looking downstream to anticipate leakages for political gain.
- *Prevent dependency:* Infuse resources that do not overwhelm or undercut local capacities.
- *Acknowledge collective action problems:* Know that coordinating activities in an ever-growing and decentralized system is virtually impossible and may hurt resource mobilization, and be aware that those who defect may undermine the system as a whole.

Table 7.2.   Agency Challenges in Policymaking and Operations

	Policymaking Environment	Operational Environment
Transagency relations (outside agencies)	Donor issues States politicize humanitarian action	Access and violence issues Political manipulation of aid by belligerents
Interagency relations (among agencies)	Turf wars	Lack of coordination and incoherence
Intra-agency relations (within agencies)	Value debates	Dissonance: gap between headquarters and field missions

Table 7.2 summarizes the seven challenges within, across, and beyond agencies. Moreover, the table also suggests the extent to which problems cannot be adequately parsed within only intra-, inter-, or transagency categories. Problems spill over beyond analytical categories and magnify others. For instance, debates about values and principles can split agencies internally but also marginalize an agency from its peers and deter donors. Consent by policymakers at headquarters to the strings attached to resources by government donors can yield dissent and insecurity in the field.

SHARPENING STRATEGIES AND CRAFTING CAPACITIES

Concrete suggestions for improving the international humanitarian system are dependent on a prior step—a dramatic change in humanitarians' orientation to a culture of considered reflections rather than one of visceral reactions. Comparing the military's approach to learning with the humanitarians' approach indicates a gross disparity in the low priority that the latter assigns to understanding and adapting to the collective action dynamics impairing effective action in today's war zones. The lack of a learning orientation is structural. Strategic thinking by aid agencies, if it existed, would focus on substantially adapting or forging entirely new tools for the humanitarian toolkit.

Strategy is the science of formulating a specific plan based on data to achieve a particular goal. Strategy also involves concrete analytic tools—researching previous cases, evaluating actions, refining old approaches or developing alternatives, and applying new orientations to ongoing or future operations. Not only is strategy the product of the immediate decisions that go into conceiving a particular plan, but it also encompasses prior efforts to document, interpret, and disseminate the data on which decisions are based.

As saving lives is the principal goal for aid agencies, humanitarian strategic thinking concerns how to save the most lives with available resources while confronting the panoply of challenges, as depicted in table 7.2, many of which in isolation or in conjunction constitute distinctive new conundrums for aid agencies. Strategic thinking is not a silver bullet, but data collection and hard-headed analyses are necessary if insufficient first steps. With human and economic resources dedicated to learning, agencies can improve their overall performance. What does not constitute a viable strategy is blind faith in what worked in earlier crises.

Humanitarian strategic thinking at the agency level should foster, at a minimum, better communications among agencies. As Randolph Kent has noted, "Strategy formulation requires at a minimum the involvement of all the main components within the organization—in other words, an unusual degree of intra-organisational cooperation among those responsible for emergencies, policies, development and budgeting."[37] Thus strategizing involves two steps: first, learning and adapting behavior by individual agencies; and, second, disseminating knowledge and forging coherent behavior collectively among them.

In military affairs, specialized units are not compartmentalized. They may have separate tasks but are part of a larger machine designed to achieve common objectives. Logistics and communications units have essential and assigned tasks, for instance, but their purpose is to function well as an integral part that contributes to the success of the whole—that is, the strategic plan. Strategies may be inadequate and execution faulty, but at least the military's ideal is to articulate an overarching plan, pull together to achieve it, and have multiple contingencies should circumstances change, as they always do. Under these conditions, units often have discretion and room for individual initiative, but such tactical discretion takes place within a common strategic framework.

Humanitarian agencies, on the other hand, are essentially independent moving parts of a clumsy mechanism in which effective links are missing. Individual agencies act autonomously with latitude in determining their means as well as ends and without an overarching plan. Even related members of a federation (e.g., the various Save the Children's or Oxfam's) do not necessarily have a common strategic framework; they share a name but not a strategy. A virtue is made necessity—so-called energy and dynamism that result from extreme decentralization. Supposedly, a set of principles have been spelled out, and the essence is to adhere to them whether the context is inter- or intrastate, the society in crisis is Christian or Muslim, the climate is tropical or mountainous, the security situation is calm or tenuous, or military forces are present or absent.

We are not attempting to disparage or belittle oftentimes heroic and unselfish actions by humanitarians. Rather, we are suggesting that the efforts by militaries to adapt plans in achieving objectives geared to a specific war and in limiting and managing interservice or interunit rivalries should be seen as a model for humanitarian agencies. With humanitarians fighting on two fronts—for resources from donors and for access on the ground—it is time that they devote more energy to thinking about their goals and roles; their ends and means; and to developing tools, tactics, and strategies better suited to specific dilemmas in specific contemporary wars. One humanitarian size and fashion, particularly as they were tailored in a different historical period, simply do not fit the current set of crises.

For instance, one of the paramount questions not being asked by enough agencies is, When do conditions merit withdrawal from a war zone? In looking back at the experience in Rwanda, Larry Minear recalls, "Neither before nor after the decision, however, did the NGO in question, or NGOs as a group, follow or develop any guidelines for disengagement. As a result, the decision remained highly circumstantial, offering little institutional guidance for the future."[38] This inconsistent retreat highlights the need for a consensus about criteria to withdraw from such situations. Three possible criteria concern the actual impact of operations, a judgment about adherence by belligerents to IHL and other human rights agreements, and the receptivity of donors to such a strategy.[39]

Such strategic thinking is an elementary addition to the humanitarian toolkit. Trying to understand what works and what does not, and when costs outweigh benefits, is arduous in light of the present state of knowledge that accompanies the disinclination by aid agencies to do the math. The opening sentences of a chapter on "measuring impact" in the *World Disasters Report 2003* say it well: "Measuring both the positive and negative impacts of humanitarian aid would appear, self-evidently, to be a good idea. Knowing and being transparent about the effects of one's actions is part of being an accountable organization. Yet, surprisingly, the process of developing the right tools to carry out this job is still in its infancy."[40] It is high time to move toward adolescence.

For humanitarian strategic thinking to become strategic doing, agencies desperately require a program to develop and strengthen in-house analytical capacities. Improvements are necessary throughout the system, but individual agencies should begin to develop and nurture four analytical capabilities in order to facilitate the growth of strategic orientations and to eventually make the enterprise as a whole more effective.

The first is humanitarian intelligence. A severe obstacle for agencies operating in the field or planning future efforts is an absence of timely and accurate information.[41] Without it, agencies can blunder into aiding manipulative parties and participating in other counterproductive endeavors. Information about the intentions and conduct of actors in a theater can help in selecting tactics, negotiating access, and sequencing other aspects of operations that ultimately contribute to success.

Aid agencies often enter theaters with only the most basic knowledge about belligerents and the history and culture of the area in which violence is raging; but such knowledge is rarely adequate, and rarer still are energy and personnel devoted to continually monitoring local politics that evolve once an operation is under way. Knowledge of local cultures and language skills are obvious lacunae, and many practitioners have lamented their absence long before Islamic countries became standard bill of fare. But here we are pointing to less-obvious shortcomings, namely, how several sources of humanitarian intelligence—data and analysis on belligerents, local conditions, indigenous humanitarian resources, and the impacts of assistance—can and must be developed and utilized.

Scholars can provide access to useful research. Social science can also be helpful in tailoring activities to local sensitivities and in monitoring the efficacy of ongoing operations. Locally, other sources should be drawn on, including journalists who may have access to political leaders and politically marginal and neglected areas, or truck and taxi drivers who have unusual insights into local logistics.

This type of information and analysis should be gathered by seasoned professionals and shared widely among agencies, but at present data gathering and its scrutiny are neither institutionalized nor systematic—too few resources are allocated specifically to addressing this need. As much as the energies of frontline soldiers are not best spent conducting reconnaissance instead of waging war, aid workers on the front lines have many duties, and the most beneficial use of their time is not to track down sources, compile data, and write reports. Aid agencies should dedicate resources to forming humanitarian intelligence units.

Humanitarian intelligence is not an indulgence but an indispensable expenditure. While not knowing has rarely stopped agencies from trying to help, the effects of giving aid without giving regard to its purpose have become problematic. Assistance is vital to the welfare of populations affected by war. But without humanitarian intelligence, assistance can easily become subject to political and economic manipulations that erode humanitarianism's stature and hamper the chances for success.

The second capacity is institutional memory. Perhaps the greatest shortfall in the international humanitarian system is its inability to document its own activities and the resulting repercussions. George Santanyana's warning that "those who do not know the lessons of history are doomed to repeat them" has little resonance among humanitarians. Much of the previous discussion suggests what business or educational analysts would call a "flat learning curve" within agencies. Humanitarians often compare notes with only those who reside in the same echo chamber. The development of an institutional memory for individual institutions and the system is crucial, analytically and operationally. Understanding the scope and nature of problems and critically evaluating options are keys to avoiding previous mistakes and grappling with alternative solutions for current problems. Agencies should establish formal documentation and research units. They could draw heavily on graduate students in the social sciences for technical support in fact-finding and analysis, a process that could also help future recruitment and nourish the next generation of practitioners.

Research on many aspects of humanitarianism is plentiful, but agencies rarely have the capacity to consume and digest it. Much scholarship and policy analysis remain unknown or effectively out of reach. Even if it has made its way to the bookshelves of some decision makers, it is rarely discussed internally and with other agencies as a step toward retooling or overhauling strategies or tactics. Academics remain a seriously underutilized resource for humanitarian agencies.

Agency staff possess a considerable knowledge base not formally compiled and absorbed by management. Invaluable information and experiences are neglected or wasted when personnel change jobs without adequate debriefings or an obligation to write end-of-mission reports. Sabbaticals and other means for assembling information—for instance, an overlap between outgoing and incoming staff—should be used systematically to promote the creation of better institutional memories.

The third capacity is communications and networking, which should accompany improved intelligence and institutional memories to collect and process data for those about to enter new positions or theaters. Previously, we discuss the difficulties, both structural and cultural, in promoting coordination among agencies and coherence within the international humanitarian system. Completely eliminating these tensions is unrealistic, but open channels of communication are not, and they are essential for better coordination or even modest coherence.

Field missions and personnel of different agencies often intermingle and exchange information in informal and occasionally formal contexts, but the process is haphazard and episodic, and it depends more on individuals and personalities than on structures. The present level of communication among agencies is insufficient to meet the time-sensitive and collective action problems that hamper delivery and protection in new wars. A greater investment in information technology and human resources on this front would likely pay significant dividends by streamlining and speeding up responses and making at least some information more widely available within and among organizations.

The fourth capacity is public relations. Even when humanitarians speak the same language, figuratively or literally, messages do not always translate outside the narrow community. Moreover, the far reach of media today compels humanitarians to develop capacities to shape the image of their own actions, especially to move beyond "humanitarian pornography"— simplistic depictions of helpless victims being saved by white Christian knights arriving from overseas. In addition, media power must be harnessed to demonstrate humanitarian needs and induce donors to be generous and consistent. Furthermore, media capacities should increase transparency to diffuse concerns regarding political influences in operations. In the field, humanitarians should focus on popular support and legitimize actions by appealing directly to stakeholders. Such advocacy of humanitarian principles in general, and operations in particular, can contribute to the security of aid workers, and agencies should actively promote "acceptance strategies" among local populations.[42] As witnessed in Afghanistan, agencies and locals have a relationship—it is just as important for locals to understand agencies as it is for agencies to understand locals.[43] To more effectively bring the message of humanitarians to victims as well as donors, agencies should allocate more resources for public information units and facilitate contact with journalists.

The media is host to the political battlefield of the new wars or whatever we wish to call the current generation of armed conflicts, and agencies should wage a campaign to signal precisely how their actions are grounded in more than just good intentions. They should make the case throughout the emergency phase that assistance is available to all victims who renounce violence and that as long as there are needs, agencies will remain. Without otherwise making this media effort, agencies risk being defined by the spins spun by others.

SOOTHING TOMORROW'S WARS WITH STRONGER SALVES?

This book has identified the challenges of new wars and new humanitarianisms. Besides the founding of the ICRC and the signing of the original Geneva Convention in the 1860s, most of the system—the largest intergovernmental and nongovernmental organizations and normative innovations—was developed between World War I and the 1970s. Starting mostly in the late 1980s, after the end of the Cold War, humanitarian action took on a different shape as a result of pressures from outside (primarily, the security vacuums of the new wars) but also from within the enterprise (debates over values and the role of donors). The twenty-first century gives prominent place to human disasters in unusual and treacherous terrains featuring civil wars with multiple and undisciplined belligerents wielding deadly weaponry, altered political economies of war and aid, and globalized media. The anxiety and introspection of the last decade indicate good faith but disappointing performance. The sweat of humanitarians has been copious but insufficient to match the flood of victims' tears and blood.

The crises since the 1990s have led to much soul-searching but have not as yet led to a radical rethinking of responses, let alone a radical reconstructing of the international humanitarian system. The bloody and indeterminate aftermath of military intervention in Afghanistan and Iraq,

along with the uncertainty about where the ever-widening war on terrorism will lead, ensures only one thing: the challenges of fragmentation and
NSAs are not relics of the last century but the defining parameter circum-
scribing humanitarian action in the current one.

Furthermore, we have discerned parallels between broader trends in,
and connections between, war and humanitarianism. The use of force and
its violent consequences are not only a set of material conditions that
require assistance and protection for victims but a set of ideas that must
be understood by humanitarians. Aside from apprehending the elements
of war, a better understanding of how militaries act and adapt is potentially instructive for aid agencies. Just as military science seeks to become
more sophisticated in analyzing war and thereby furnish soldiers with
better tools and tactics within achievable strategies, so too must humanitarians develop a science of their own.

Today two schools of thought pronounce themselves on the health of the
enterprise. One argues that the changes in war zones since the system's
inception do not justify significant changes in humanitarian delivery; agencies are as free or encumbered as they ever were to conduct operations. The
other takes a darker view and sees humanitarians' worst fears realized,
emphasizing agencies adrift or hijacked. The power of these perspectives
is so deep within current humanitarian culture that most humanitarians
can be considered as being in denial or suffering from hypochondria. In
our view neither defensiveness nor alarmism addresses what really has
changed and what it means for victims, agencies, and belligerents.

In casting our gaze toward the future, it is impossible to forecast exactly
where humanitarianism is headed. However, tendencies emerge in the
international humanitarian system, and it is worth pausing to speculate
where inertia is carrying agencies. An earlier caveat is worth repeating—
the fate of humanitarianism cannot be known because international politics is simply unpredictable. September 11 and the U.S.-led "war on terrorism" have revealed how quickly and profoundly values change, resources
shift, and new realities take shape—each with consequences for the
humanitarian enterprise. The tsunami in late December 2004 and the international responses demonstrated how disasters have the power to galva-
nize humanitarian impulses and reinforce international solidarity and society. Nevertheless, the relative power of sword and salve should be kept in
mind—currently, international humanitarian spending hovers around $10
billion, whereas global military expenditures top $1 trillion.[44] Beyond ques-
tions of current priorities and capacities lay those of existing and future
needs. The total populations living in failed or failing states—two billion—
suggests the scope of humanitarian challenges, present and potential.[45]

The renewal and revitalization of the humanitarian enterprise in war
zones is less likely and far more complicated than it is in natural disasters.
Our attempt to understand contemporary humanitarianism from a range

of perspectives—ideological, historical, war related, political, economic, and bureaucratic—leads to a sober assessment and a paradox. The international system continues to create and fortify the institutions that provide relief and protection, and normative progress continues as well; at the same time, however, the humanitarian enterprise is splintering.

Two tiers of agencies vie to wear the humanitarian mantle in war zones. The first consists of the large UN agencies and international NGOs that are "full service" with a broad mandate and an array of capabilities beyond relief and protection. This tier may adhere to the integration agenda, combining humanitarian action with other aspects of conflict resolution and peacebuilding. The second tier of agencies inhabits a narrower niche, focusing on the provision of emergency aid in situations where neutrality and impartiality can be maintained—or so they hope.

The tensions between the tiers will inhibit addressing key structural problems. The virtual impossibility of belligerents' distinguishing between agencies on the ground guarantees that both tiers will be accused of politicization and will face security threats regardless of their operational philosophies. The stark realization that the mantle has lost the respect of many—both belligerents and victims—and that aid workers are targeted illustrates the dramatic limits of normative and institutional progress in the face of politicization.

Too many lives are at stake. Steps on the road ahead begin with a plea to avoid acting hastily or becoming bogged down in paralysis by analysis. The only first-order principle for humanitarians should be the sanctity of life. Operational "principles," including neutrality and impartiality, are means, not ends; they are not moral absolutes. They necessarily take a backseat to more consequentialist calculations resulting from working with particular NSAs and within specific armed conflicts.

There is little room for humanitarians who refuse tough judgments and provide succor without discrimination. The age of innocence, if there ever was one, is over.[46] Instead of responding hastily, humanitarians urgently need to slow down. Wars are not tsunamis or earthquakes—human beings are responsible for the former, and humanitarians should stop treating them as equivalents. To navigate the shoals of the troubled waters in contemporary war zones, humanitarians must reflect before acting. The "fog of humanitarianism" and "gray humanitarianism" perpetually threaten agencies, a realization that should not cut short the oftentimes heroic reactions for which humanitarians are deservedly well known.

Perhaps a fitting way toward the future comes from the conclusion in David Kennedy's convincing reassessment of international humanitarianism. Careful calculations of costs and benefits—not good intentions and time-tested principles—are in the shortest supply and the greatest demand. "The remedy is a more thoroughgoing pragmatism. By rooting out bias, disenchanting the doctrines and institutional tools which substitute for analysis, insisting on a rigorous pragmatic analysis of costs and benefits, we might achieve a humanitarianism which could throw light on its own dark sides."[47]

In short, humanitarians need to understand the darker sides of virtue— now. Thoughtful and strategic humanitarianism is more appropriate than the mindless application of traditional principles for at least four reasons: goals often conflict; good intentions can have catastrophic consequences; ends can be achieved in multiple ways; and choices are necessary even if the options are less than ideal.

Instead of automatically subscribing to principles and multilateral processes and institutions, humanitarians must set aside ideology, weigh alternatives, and project longer-term outcomes. Precisely because the darker sides of virtue can sometimes overwhelm the benefits of humanitarianism, empirical assessment and analysis are essential. Judgments cannot be derived a priori from principles. There are always winners and losers, virtuous outcomes and horrendous costs. Humanitarianism provides us with an idealistic vocabulary and institutional machinery, but it should be judged not by intentions but by consequences.

In the fervor to react to crises, agencies have often devoted too little energy and too few resources to understanding the nature of the disaster and tailoring their responses accordingly. The experiences of new humanitarianisms demonstrate that doing something or doing nothing should each be an acceptable option. What one of us wrote some time ago has assumed ever-greater salience: "Don't just do something, stand there."[48] Reflection is increasingly required as a prerequisite for action and will amortize investments better than will hasty overreaction. Blindly applying the time-tested standard operating procedures of independence, impartiality, and neutrality are unlikely to provide satisfactory guidance in contemporary armed conflicts.

For instance, a major debate has been brewing over humanitarian agencies' use of private military contractors. The visceral opposition to such practices that has long characterized aid agencies must yield to a calculation of the realities of international politics (i.e., PMCs will remain a fixture while the military resources of states will not be forthcoming) and the needs of victims (i.e., security, which is often not provided by states or international organizations). The question should not be whether humanitarian agencies can stop or prevent the use of PMCs but how best to address the phenomenon and utilize the opportunities that it presents to the greatest humanitarian advantage. As Deborah Avant points out, "Rather than arguing about its overall costs or benefits, both policy makers and their constituents would be well served by thinking about the trade-offs involved in the different strategies for participating in and managing this market."[49] In previous eras the solution to dilemmas regarding force, let alone private force, were clear—there was no place for such arrangements under a rigid and effective state system. In today's crises, however, humanitarians cannot afford to hide behind long-standing standard operating procedures and resist change.

Furthermore, strategic thinking may be essential in restoring the legitimacy accorded to humanitarianism in earlier periods. Before the new wars, the vitality of the humanitarian identity alone was sufficient to raise resources and ensure effective relief and protection—but no longer. Contemporary configurations have muffled and muddled humanitarianism. While agencies worry that strategic approaches are antithetical to the normative clarity and the popularity that it engenders, misapplied and misused assistance has made strategic considerations imperative to controlling outcomes from humanitarian action and thus critical to protecting and renewing the humanitarian mantle.

The greatest debate should be over not what principles dictate humanitarian action, but what funds are available to aid agencies and how they are programmed to save lives. Humanitarians should devote substantially more human and financial resources to understanding how to dictate action as credibly as possible, on the basis of the best intelligence and analyses available. Resources without values are empty, but values without effective resources—economic but also analytic and strategic—are mere rhetoric.

Humanitarianism endeavors not to be a continuation of power by other means, but its material underpinnings interweave with politics and power. Candid assessments of the slippery slopes of compromises are a critical prerequisite to developing more effective and widely respected operations that are better resourced. The articulation of intentions, capacities, and constraints in a strategic framework has become necessary, not just for agencies, but for victims and interlocutors.

Humanitarian strategic thinking means measuring who gains and making difficult decisions about who receives aid and protection and how. With suitable and sufficient staff and expertise to support strategic thinking, choices will be painful, but many complicating factors will be clearer and their impact diminished. Essentially, between the visceral impulse to respond and the material steps to act, humanitarians must pause to anticipate more fully how their individual and cumulative actions will have an impact on human welfare.

Whereas "humanitarian" has a handsome ring of selfless caring, "strategic" seems to have the tone of cold-hearted calculation, at least to the ears of too many humanitarians for whom even such terms as "professionalization" have a hollow ring.[50] When war breaks out and humanitarian appeals are made, conventional wisdom has it that militaries act without caring and that humanitarians act without thinking. While stereotypical, such caricatures nonetheless contain elements of truth that indicate crucial defects. No one will rightly accuse humanitarians of not caring, but the charge of not thinking is borne out by tragic episodes from Bosnia to Bunia. Militaries have made a standard practice of strategic thinking in their pursuit of security objectives. Although their application of the premise is bloody, their analytic orientations and techniques are enviable. The military is often viewed as a philosophical opponent for humanitarians, but the latter should consider the former a role model in terms of learning and adaptive culture as well as hard-headed calculations.

Humanitarians should engage in strategic thinking as an investment in strategic doing. Saving lives is not only a question of the heart but one of the mind. The ultimate merit of humanitarian action lies not in its motives but in its effects. Unfortunately, as James Darcy reminds us, "the language of effectiveness, of impact, of accountability—the language, in other words, of modern bureaucracy—sits uncomfortably with the quasi-religious terminology of humanitarianism and its associated principles."[51]

In contrast, strategic humanitarian action seeks to mitigate negative impacts and reclaim humanitarianism as a powerful idea. Victor Hugo wrote that "a stand can be made against invasion by an army, but no defense can be made against invasion by an idea."[52] While the new wars can hinder humanitarian action, they cannot halt humanitarian impulses. In many ways the new humanitarianisms are responses to these obstacles, but they often trigger collective action problems. Mindless and mechanical humanitarianism is not a legitimate idea, however, but rather an unfortunate occupational lag and organizational routine that grow from the very idealism that motivates those coming to the rescue.

Tempering that idealism with improved analytical capacities will enhance the tensile strength of the international humanitarianism system. What the late Myron Wiener once dubbed "instrumental humanitarianism" is essential for both victims and global order, for saving as many lives savaged by war as possible manifests our common humanity.[53] Making humanitarianism work saves lives in the crisis at hand, but it may also save the enterprise so that it may save even more lives when the next crisis arrives.

With reform of the UN on the agenda for its sixtieth anniversary, Secretary-General Kofi Annan often spoke of a "San Francisco moment," recalling the show of foresight and solidarity near the end of World War II to establish a world organization to solve global problems. While debates over how to modernize UN institutions are much broader than humanitarian concerns, the international humanitarian system (including the ICRC and NGOs as well as the UN) is also ripe for change. Only when victims, aid agents, and belligerents all agree on the need to institutionalize humanitarian responses to war will innovations become meaningful. It is safe to say that no such consensus exists for now and the foreseeable future—this was very much in evidence at the 2005 World Summit.[54] While all may agree on a need to change the system, the desires of various parties are pulling the enterprise in different directions.

Humanitarianism is too powerful to be neglected by the powerful, and agencies must be vigilant to stave off those who wish to shape and thus constrain its impact. The limits of reactive tinkering with humanitarianism have become apparent, and humanitarians unfortunately continue to fall prey to violence and manipulation. A strategic approach backed with the tools to inform and execute humanitarian action will enhance the ability of agencies to make a difference in crises and will provide agencies with greater control over the authority and course of the enterprise.

The salve has always been a balm to the wounds inflicted by the sword. However, humanitarian action in the context of the current dynamics of war may actually compound the very wounds that it is intended to soothe. Only through an appreciation of and commitment to strategic thinking and doing can agencies hope to bolster the effectiveness of the enterprise, mitigate possibly distorting effects of aid, and reconcile today's sword and salve. This book is a modest contribution to understanding contemporary challenges by charting the tides of continuity and change and by readying agencies to dodge both metaphorical and actual bullets that threaten humanitarian action at the outset of the millennium.

Notes

PREFACE

1. International Commission on Intervention and State Sovereignty, *The Responsibility to Protect* (Ottawa: International Development Research Centre, 2001); and Thomas G. Weiss and Don Hubert, *The Responsibility to Protect: Research, Bibliography, and Background* (Ottawa: International Development Research Centre, 2001). Both volumes and an updated bibliography are available at http://web.gc.cuny.edu/RalphBuncheInstitute/ICISS/index.htm. The Research Directorate for ICISS was based at the Ralph Bunche Institute for International Studies.

2. For a discussion, see S. Neil MacFarlane, Carolin Thielking, and Thomas G. Weiss, "The Responsibility to Protect: Is Anyone Interested in Humanitarian Intervention?" *Third World Quarterly* 25, no. 5 (2004): 977–92.

3. Anthony Lewis, "The Challenge of Global Justice Now," *Dædalus* 132, no. 1 (2003): 8.

4. Mohammed Ayoob, "Humanitarian Intervention and International Society," *International Journal of Human Rights* 6, no. 1 (2002): 84.

5. Larry Minear, *The Humanitarian Enterprise: Dilemmas and Discoveries* (West Bloomfield, Conn.: Kumarian, 2002).

6. For details, see http://web.gc.cuny.edu/ralphbuncheinstitute/IUCSHA/index.html.

7. See Stanley Foundation, *UN on the Ground* (Muscatine, Iowa: Stanley Foundation, 2003).

8. Arthur C. Helton, *The Price of Indifference: Refugees and Humanitarian Action in the New Century* (Oxford: Oxford University Press, 2002).

9. Simon Chesterman, Michael Ignatieff, and Ramesh Thakur, eds., *Making States Work: State Failure and the Crisis of Governance* (Tokyo: UN University Press, 2005), 296–317.

10. Old Testament, Book of Isaiah, 2:4.

11. Ralph Waldo Emerson, "The American Scholar," an oration delivered before the Phi Beta Kappa Society, Cambridge, August 31, 1837, in *The Collected Works of*

Ralph Waldo Emerson, vol. 1, *Nature, Addresses, and Lectures* (Cambridge, Mass.: Harvard University Press, Balknap Press, 1971), 56.

INTRODUCTION

1. See the website of the Norwegian Refugee Committee, www.idpproject.org, and the International Federation of Red Cross and Red Crescent Societies, *World Disaster Report 2004* (Bloomfield, Conn.: Kumarian, 2004).

2. An initial bibliography, for instance, compiled for the International Commission on Intervention and State Sovereignty, has listed 2,200 sources in English. Two subsequent updatings have added about 250 citations per year. See Thomas G. Weiss and Don Hubert, *The Responsibility to Protect: Research, Bibliography, and Background* (Ottawa: International Development Research Centre, 2001), 223–336. The updated bibliography, along with this volume and the ICISS's report *The Responsibility to Protect* (Ottawa: International Development Research Centre, 2001), is available at http://web.gc.cuny.edu/RalphBuncheInstitute/ICISS/index.htm (accessed May 18, 2005).

3. Office for the Coordination of Humanitarian Affairs, *The Humanitarian Decade: Challenges for Humanitarian Assistance in the Last Decade and into the Future,* 2 vols. (New York: UN, 2004).

4. Jonathan Moore, ed., *Hard Choices: Moral Dilemmas in Humanitarian Intervention* (Lanham, Md.: Rowman & Littlefield, 1998); and Fabrice Weissman, ed., *In the Shadow of "Just Wars": Violence, Politics, and Humanitarian Action* (Ithaca, N.Y.: Cornell University Press, 2004).

5. David Rieff, *A Bed for the Night: Humanitarianism in Crisis* (London: Vintage, 2002), 10, 15.

6. Didier J. Cherpiel, "Introduction," in *World Disasters Report 2003* (Bloomfield, Conn.: Kumarian, 2003), 7.

7. ALNAP—the Active Learning Network for Accountability and Performance in Humanitarian Action—is an international interagency forum working to improve learning, accountability, and quality across the humanitarian sector; see www.alnap.org. Avenir ("future" in French) is the comprehensive evaluation of the International Committee of the Red Cross that led to significant changes in its organizational structure in 2000; see www.icrc.org.

8. Ernst B. Haas, *When Knowledge Is Power: Three Models of Change in International Organizations* (Berkeley: University of California Press, 1990).

9. Hugo Slim, *A Call to Alms: Humanitarian Action and the Art of War* (Geneva: Centre for Humanitarian Dialogue 2004), 4.

10. Women as well as men are involved in wars. We use this term *man-made* because it is used virtually everywhere to indicate wars in contrast to natural disasters.

11. David Kennedy, *The Dark Sides of Virtue: Reassessing International Humanitarianism* (Princeton, N.J.: Princeton University Press, 2004), xxiii.

12. Mark Duffield, *Global Governance and the New Wars: The Merging of Development and Security* (London: Zed Books, 2001), 75. Chapter 4 describes this new phenomenon.

CHAPTER 1

1. David Kennedy, *The Dark Sides of Virtue: Reassessing International Humanitarianism* (Princeton, N.J.: Princeton University Press, 2004), xix, 327.

2. Typifying these two respective approaches are Kenneth Waltz, *Theory of International Politics* (Boston: McGraw-Hill, 1979); and Robert Gilpin, *War and Change in World Politics* (Cambridge: Cambridge University Press, 1981).

3. See Larry Minear and Thomas G. Weiss, *Humanitarian Action in Times of War* (Boulder, Colo.: Rienner, 1993), 7–10.

4. See Michael Walzer, *Arguing about War* (New Haven, Conn.: Yale University Press, 2004); and Adam Roberts and Richard Guelff, *Documents on the Laws of War*, 3rd ed. (Oxford: Oxford University Press, 2000).

5. See *The Geneva Conventions of 12 August 1949* and *Protocols Additional to the Geneva Conventions of 12 August 1949* (Geneva: International Committee of the Red Cross). The clearest commentary comes from Roberts and Guelff, *Documents on the Laws*, 195–370 and 419–512.

6. For data on ratification of the Additional Protocols, see www.icrc.org/ihl.nsf/WebNORM?OpenView&Start=30&Count=30&Expand=52.1#52.1 (accessed May 18, 2005) and www.icrc.org/ihl.nsf/WebNORM?OpenView&Start=30&Count=30&Expand=53.1#53.1 (accessed May 18, 2005).

7. John F. Hutchinson, *Champions of Charity: War and the Rise of the Red Cross* (Boulder, Colo.: Westview, 1996), 346, 351.

8. Walzer, *Arguing about War*, xiii.

9. Kalevi J. Holsti, *Taming the Sovereigns: Institutional Change in International Politics* (Cambridge: Cambridge University Press, 2004), 8.

10. Ian Smillie and Larry Minear, *The Charity of Nations: Humanitarian Action in a Calculating World* (Bloomfield, Conn.: Kumarian, 2004), 8.

11. Kennedy, *Dark Sides of Virtue*, 330.

CHAPTER 2

1. Thucydides, *The Peloponnesian War*, trans. Rex Warner (London: Cassell, 1962). This work was originally written circa 420 BC following his tenure as an Athenian general in the war against Sparta (book 5, chapter 7, 360).

2. Sun Tzu and Sun Pin, *The Complete Art of War*, trans. Ralph D. Sawyer, with the collaboration of Mei-chün Lee Sawyer (Boulder, Colo.: Westview, 1996).

3. Niccolo Machiavelli, *The Prince (Il pincipe) and the Discourses (Discorsi)* (New York: Random House, 1950), originally published in 1513 and 1531, respectively; and Machiavelli, *The Art of War (L'Arte della guerra)*, trans., ed., and commentary by Christopher Lynch (Chicago: University of Chicago, 2003), originally published 1520.

4. Thomas Hobbes, *Leviathan* (Baltimore: Penguin, 1968), originally published in 1651. "During the time men live without a common power to keep them in awe, they are in that condition which is called war; and such a war is of every man against every man" (185).

5. See, for example, Charles Tilly, ed., *The Formation of National States in Western Europe* (Princeton, N.J.: Princeton University Press, 1975); and Tilly, *Coercion, Capital, and European States—AD 990–1990* (Cambridge, Mass.: Blackwell, 1992).

6. Stephen D. Krasner, *Sovereignty: Organized Hypocrisy* (Princeton, N.J.: Princeton University Press, 1999).

7. Mary Kaldor, *New and Old Wars: Organized Violence in a Global Era* (Stanford, Calif.: Stanford University Press, 1999), 13–15.

8. Tilly, *Coercion, Capital, and European States.*

9. Kalevi J.Holsti, *The State, War, and the State of War* (Cambridge: Cambridge University Press, 1996).

10. Gianfranco Poggi discusses change and variation in political governance structures of Europe, in *The Development of the Modern State: A Sociological Introduction* (Stanford, Calif.: Stanford University Press, 1978), 60–85. For a more general description of overlapping governance in this era, see David Held and others, *Global Transformations: Politics, Economics, and Culture* (Stanford, Calif.: Stanford University Press, 1999), 32–35.

11. Carl von Clausewitz, *On War* (*Vom Kriege*), ed. Col. F. N. Maude, trans. Col. J. J. Graham (New York: Penguin, 1968), book 1, chapter 1, section 28, 121.

12. For him, only states matter, and thus the history of state conflict is the totality of global history. See Robert Gilpin, *War and Change in World Politics* (Cambridge: Cambridge University Press, 1981), 15, for his definition of "hegemonic war."

13. Marcus Tullius Cicero, *Philippics* (Chapel Hill: University of North Carolina Press, 1986), book 5, 2, 5: "Nervi belli pecunia infinita" (Endless money forms the sinews of war).

14. Quote is attributed but especially fitting since Napoleon himself died of stomach cancer.

15. William McNeill, *The Pursuit of Power: Technology, Armed Force, and Society since A.D. 1000* (Chicago: University of Chicago Press, 1982), 2.

16. Victor David Hanson, *Carnage and Culture: Landmark Battles in the Rise of Western Power* (New York: Anchor, 2002), 273.

17. Michael Mann, *The Sources of Social Power*, vol. 1, *A History of Power from the Beginning to A.D. 1760* (Cambridge: Cambridge University Press, 1986).

18. Tilly, *Coercion, Capital and European States*, 54–58; Poggi, *Development of the Modern State*, 66; and Bruce D. Porter, *War and the Rise of the State: The Military Foundations of Modern Politics* (New York: Free Press, 1994), 12–14, 31, 37–39.

19. Porter, *War and the Rise*, 14, 34–36.

20. Aristide R. Zolberg, "Strategic Interactions and the Formation of Modern States: France and England," in *The State in Global Perspective*, ed. Ali Kazancigil (Paris: UNESCO, 1986), 81.

21. Charles Tilly, "War Making and State Making as Organized Crime," in *Bringing the State Back In*, ed. Charles Tilly, Theda Skocpol, and Peter Evans (Cambridge: Cambridge University Press, 1985), 169.

22. McNeill, *Pursuit of Power*, 3, contrasts Sargon (whose rule lasted from 2334 to 2279 BC) with Xerxes (King of Persia, 485–465 BC) to show how the certainty of not being overtaxed generates local political support. He also discusses regulations developed to prevent looting (72–74). All of these case studies illustrate how the economics of war can affect the legitimacy of those who control force. David Keen, "Incentives and Disincentives for Violence," in *Greed and Grievance: Eco-*

nomic Agendas in Civil Wars, ed. Mats Berdal and David Malone (Boulder, Colo.: Rienner, 2000), 28, notes how common plunder was in medieval warfare.

23. Xenophon, *Anabasis* (*March Up Country*), trans. Carleton L. Brownson, rev. John Dillery (Cambridge, Mass.: Harvard University Press, 1998).

24. Janice E. Thomson, *Mercenaries, Pirates, and Sovereigns: State-Building and Extraterritorial Violence in Early Modern Europe* (Princeton, N.J.: Princeton University Press), 8, 22–32.

25. John Gerard Ruggie, *Constructing the World Polity* (New York: Routledge, 1998), 146, 179.

26. Thomson, *Mercenaries, Pirates, and Sovereigns*, 4, 19.

27. Tilly, *Coercion, Capital, and European States*, 68–70; Martin Van Creveld, *The Rise and Decline of the State* (Cambridge: Cambridge University Press, 1999), 155–70, 242–58; and Jeremy Black, *War and the World: Military Power and the Fate of Continents, 1450–2000* (New Haven, Conn.: Yale University Press, 1998), 203–8.

28. A full translation of this key work can be found in Julian H. Franklin, *Bodin: On Sovereignty* (Cambridge: Cambridge University Press, 1992).

29. For a fuller discussion of the institutional importance of the treaties of the Peace of Westphalia, see Stephen D. Krasner, "Westphalia and All That," in *Ideas and Foreign Policy: Beliefs, Institutions, and Political Change*, ed. Judith Goldstein and Robert O. Keohane (Ithaca, N.Y.: Cornell University Press, 1993), 235–64; Krasner, *Sovereignty*, 79–81.

30. Van Creveld, *Rise and Decline*, 159–60.

31. Tilly, *Coercion, Capital, and European States*, 83.

32. Geoffrey Best, *Humanity in Warfare* (New York: Columbia University Press, 1980), 89.

33. Deborah Avant, "From Mercenary to Citizen Armies: Explaining Change in the Practice of War," *International Organization* 54, no. 1 (2000): 41–72.

34. Clausewitz, *On War*, book 1, chapter 1, section 24, 119. A theme he revisits in book 5, chapter 6, 401–10.

35. Clausewitz, *On War*, book 1, chapter 1, section 2, 101.

36. Clausewitz, *On War*, Book 1, chapter 2, 131. The stress placed on this formulation is implicit in his later discussion of how military power should be used; see "The Use of Battle" (book 4, chapter 11, 342–48) and "Ends in War More Precisely Defined" (book 5, chapters 4 and 5, 388–99).

37. Clausewitz, *On War*, book 1, chapter 1, section 28, 121. Clausewitz analyzes three components: who pays for war, who fights war, and who determines the interests in war—the people, the military, and the state, respectively.

38. W. Joseph Campbell, "You Furnish the Legend, I'll Furnish the Quote," *American Journalism Review* (December 2001), www.ajr.org/Article.asp?id=2429 (accessed May 18, 2005).

39. For an in-depth discussion of early religious antecedents to late-1990s norms of humanitarian intervention, see Sean D. Murphy, *Humanitarian Intervention: The United Nations in an Evolving World Order* (Philadelphia: University of Pennsylvania Press, 1996), 35–42; Brian D. Lepard, *Rethinking Humanitarian Intervention* (University Park: Pennsylvania State Press, 2002), 39–99.

40. Ephraim Isaac, "Humanitarianism across Religions and Cultures," in *Humanitarianism across Borders: Sustaining Civilians in Times of War*, ed. Thomas G. Weiss and Larry Minear (Boulder, Colo.: Rienner, 1993), 13.

41. Frederick Cuny, "Dilemmas of Military Involvement in Humanitarian Relief," in *Soldiers, Peacekeepers, and Disasters*, ed. Leon Gordenker and Thomas G. Weiss (London: MacMillan, 1991), 52.

42. Van Creveld, *Rise and Decline*, 161–62.

43. Hugo Grotius, *On the Law of War and Peace (De Jure Belli ac Pacis)* (Whitefish, Mont.: Kessinger, 2004), originally published 1625.

44. Emmerich de Vattel, *The Law of Nations; or, Principles of the Law of Nature Applied to the Conduct and Affairs of Nations and Sovereigns (Droit des gens; ou, Principes de la loi naturelle appliqués à la conduite et aux affaires des nations et des souverains)*, trans. Charles G. Fenwick (New York: Oceana, 1964), originally published 1758.

45. Kalevi Holsti, *Taming the Sovereigns: Institutional Change in International Politics* (Cambridge: Cambridge University Press, 2004), 281.

46. Margaret P. Karns and Karen Mingst, *International Organizations: The Politics and Processes of Global Governance* (Boulder, Colo.: Rienner, 2004), 87.

47. Adam Roberts, "Land Warfare: From Hague to Nuremberg," in *The Laws of War: Constraints on Warfare in the Western World*, ed. Michael Howard, George J. Andreopoulos, and Mark Shulman (New Haven, Conn.: Yale University Press, 1994), 121.

48. These are available from the ICRC, but they are also cited with a useful commentary in Adam Roberts and Richard Guelff, eds., *Documents on the Laws of War*, 3rd ed. (Oxford: Oxford University Press, 2000), 195–369. For additional commentary, see Michael Howard, George J. Andreopoulos, and Mark R. Shulman, eds., *The Laws of War: Constraints on Warfare in the Western World* (New Haven, Conn.: Yale University Press, 1994); and Hilaire McCoubrey and Nigel D. While, *International Law and Armed Conflict* (Aldershot, U.K.: Dartmouth, 1992).

49. Best, *Humanity in Warfare*, 123.

50. Caroline Moorehead, *Dunant's Dream: War, Switzerland, and the History of the Red Cross* (New York: Carroll & Graf, 1998), 26.

51. Michael Ignatieff, *The Warrior's Honor: Ethnic War and the Modern Conscience* (New York: Henry Holt, 1997), 5.

52. Moorehead, *Dunant's Dream*, 60, 82–83.

53. Best, *Humanity in Warfare*, 155.

54. Moorehead, *Dunant's Dream*, 125–26.

55. McNeill, *Pursuit of Power*, 68; and Hanson, *Carnage and Culture*, 153.

56. 1868 St. Petersburg Declaration Renouncing the Use, in Time of War, of Explosive Projectiles under 400 Grammes Weight; 1899 Hague Declaration 3 Concerning Expanding Bullets; 1899 Hague Declaration 2 Concerning Asphyxiating Gases; 1925 Geneva Protocol for the Prohibition of the Use in War of Asphyxiating, Poisonous or Other Gases, and of Bacteriological Methods of Warfare.

57. See Louis Holborn, *Refugees, a Problem of Our Time: The Work of the UNHCR, 1951–1972* (Methuen, N.J.: Scarecrow, 1975), 3–20; and Gil Loescher, *Beyond Charity: International Cooperation and the Global Refugee Crisis* (Oxford: Oxford University Press, 1993), 32–54.

58. The major piece of scholarship that led to the creation of "genocide" as a special category of human rights violation was Raphael Lemkin, *Axis Rule in Occupied Europe: Laws of Occupation, Analysis of Government, Proposals for Redress* (Washington, D.C.: Carnegie Endowment for International Peace, 1944), 79–95. For a com-

plete list and access to Lemkin's research, see www.preventgenocide.org/lemkin/ (accessed May 18, 2005).

59. Available at www.preventgenocide.org/law/convention/drafts/ (accessed May 18, 2005).

60. Michael Ignatieff, "Human Rights as Politics," in *Human Rights as Politics and Idolatry*, ed. Ignatieff (Princeton, N.J.: Princeton University Press, 2001), 5.

61. Geoffrey Best, *Nuremberg and After: The Continuing History of War Crimes and Crimes against Humanity* (Reading, Eng.: University of Reading Press, 1984), 5.

62. 1864 Geneva Convention, 1907 Hague Conventions, 1925 Geneva Conventions, and so on.

63. For a full discussion of the establishment and evolution of UNHCR, see Michael Barnett and Martha Finnemore, "Defining Refugees and Voluntary Repatriation at the United Nations High Commissioner for Refugees," in *Rules for the World: International Organizations in Global Politics* (Ithaca, N.Y.: Cornell University Press, 2004), 73–120.

64. See Benjamin N. Schiff, *Refugees unto the Third Generation: UN Aid to Palestinians* (Syracuse, N.Y.: Syracuse University Press, 1995).

65. Barnett and Finnemore, *Rules for the World*, 80.

66. Barnett and Finnemore, *Rules for the World*, 21.

67. Dorothea Hilhorst, "Being Good at Doing Good? Quality and Accountability of Humanitarian NGOs," *Disasters* 26, no. 3 (2002): 195.

68. See David P. Forsythe, *The Humanitarians: The International Committee of the Red Cross* (Cambridge: Cambridge University Press, 2005), 33–50; and Mary B. Anderson, "You Save My Life Today, but for What Tomorrow? Some Moral Dilemmas of Humanitarian Aid," in *Hard Choices: Moral Dilemmas in Humanitarian Intervention*, ed. Jonathan Moore (Lanham, Md.: Rowman & Littlefield, 1998), 137–56.

69. Quoted by Elizabeth Becker, "Red Cross Man in Guantanamo. A 'Busybody,' but Not Unwelcome," *New York Times*, February 20, 2002.

70. It appears in Roberta Cohen, "The Displaced Fall through the World's Safety Net," *Christian Science Monitor*, February 6, 1997; Roberta Cohen and Francis M. Deng, *Masses in Flight: The Global Crisis of Internal Displacement* (Washington, D.C.: Brookings, 1998), 10; and Cohen and Deng, "Exodus within Borders," *Foreign Affairs* 77, no. 4 (1998): 15. Their thoughts about the necessity for protection are found in *Masses in Flight*, 162–66, 176–81, 254–84.

71. Jean Pictet, "The Fundamental Principles of the Red Cross," *International Review of the Red Cross*, no. 210 (1979): 130–40, quote at 135. The actual list comprises humanity, impartiality, neutrality, independence, universality, voluntary service, and unity.

72. Cuny, "Dilemmas of Military Involvement," 52.

73. For a useful breakdown, see ICRC, *Basic Rules of the Geneva Conventions and Their Additional Protocols* (Geneva: ICRC, 1993).

CHAPTER 3

1. U.S. Army, *Field Manual (FM) 100-20—Guide to the Study of Insurgency* (Fort Huachuca, Ariz.: Government Printing Office, 1989).

2. Mao Tse Tung, *On Guerilla Warfare*, trans. Samuel B. Griffiths II (Garden City, N.Y.: Anchor, 1978); Vo Nguyen Giap, *People's War, People's Army* (New York: Praeger, 1962); Ernesto Guevara, *Guerilla Warfare* (Lincoln: University of Nebraska Press, 1985); and Sam C. Sarkesian, *Revolutionary Guerilla Warfare* (Chicago: Precedent, 1976).

3. Leslie Gelb, "The Teacup Wars," *Foreign Affairs* 73, no. 6 (1994): 1–5.

4. Edward Rice, *Wars of the Third Kind: Conflict in Underdeveloped Countries* (Berkeley: University of California Press, 1993).

5. Kalevi Holsti, *The State, War, and the State of War* (Cambridge: Cambridge University Press, 1996), 19–40, 123–49.

6. William S. Lind and others, "The Changing Face of War: Into the Fourth Generation," *Marine Corps Gazette*, October 1989, 22–26, quotes on 24. For more on this concept, see Lt. Colonel Thomas X. Hammes, "The Evolution of War: The Fourth Generation," *Marine Corps Gazette*, September 1994, 1–13.

7. Colonel Thomas X. Hammes, *The Sling and the Stone: On War in the 21st Century* (St. Paul, Minn.: Zenith Press, 2004), 208.

8. Vincent J. Goulding Jr., "Back to the Future with Asymmetric Warfare," *Parameters* 10 (Winter 2000–2001): 21–30.

9. Thomas J. Williams, "Strategic Leaders Readiness and Competencies for Asymmetric Warfare," *Parameters* 33 (Summer 2003): 19–35.

10. John Arquilla and David Ronfeldt, "Cyberwar Is Coming," *Comparative Strategy* 12 (November 1993): 141–65. This study has since been expanded into *The Advent of Netwar* (Santa Monica, Calif.: RAND, 1996).

11. Joel Cassman and David Lai, "Football vs. Soccer: American Warfare in an Era of Unconventional Threats," *Armed Forces Journal* (November 2003): 49–54.

12. Donald M. Snow, *Uncivil Wars: International Security and the New Internal Conflicts* (Boulder, Colo.: Rienner, 1996), 2.

13. Mary Kaldor, *New and Old Wars: Organized Violence in a Global Era* (Stanford, Calif.: Stanford University Press, 1999); Mark Duffield, *Global Governance and the New Wars: The Merging of Development and Security* (London: Zed, 2001); Robert Kaplan, "The Coming Anarchy," *Atlantic Monthly*, February 1994, 44–76; and Kaplan, *The Coming Anarchy: Shattering the Dreams of the Post–Cold War* (New York: Random House, 2000).

14. Some have argued that there has been an upswing in the number, intensity, and duration of civil wars, particularly since 1989. However, data indicate that the overall quantity of conflicts throughout the 1990s decreased while negotiated settlements increased. See Swedish International Peace Research Institute, *SIPRI Yearbook 1998: Armaments, Disarmament, and International Security* (Oxford: Oxford University Press, 1998), 17. This work is shortened and updated annually by Peter Wallensteen and Margareta Sollenberg in the *Journal of Peace Research*.

15. Kalevi J. Holsti, *Taming the Sovereigns: Institutional Change in International Politics* (Cambridge: Cambridge University Press, 2004), 3, emphasis in original.

16. Carl von Clausewitz, *On War* (*Vom Kriege*), ed. Colonel F. N. Maude, trans. Colonel J. J. Graham (New York: Penguin, 1968), 121.

17. See Bertrand Badie, *The Imported State: The Westernization of the Political Order* (Stanford, Calif.: Stanford University Press, 2000).

18. John Ruggie, "Territoriality and Beyond: Problematizing Modernity in International Relations," *International Organization* 47 (1993): 165.

19. Peter Wallensteen and Margareta Sollenberg, "Armed Conflict, 1989–2000," *Journal of Peace Research* 38, no. 5 (2001): 632.

20. *Relief Web: Complex Emergencies*, available at www.ReliefWeb.int/w/rwb.nsf/WCE?OpenForm.

21. Max Weber, *Politics as Vocation* (Philadelphia: Fortress, 1965), first published 1919.

22. Amin Sakil, "Dimensions of State Disruption and International Responses," *Third World Quarterly* 21, no. 1 (2000): 39–49.

23. See William Reno, "Shadow States and the Political Economy of Civil War," in *Greed and Grievance: Economic Agendas in Civil Wars*, ed. Mats Berdal and David Malone (Boulder, Colo.: Rienner, 2000), 44–45. The idea was first explored in his *Corruption and State Politics in Sierra Leone* (Cambridge: Cambridge University Press, 1995).

24. Originally in Jean-Francois Bayart, *The State in Africa: Politics of the Belly* (London: Longman, 1993); also cited in Beatrice Hibou, "The 'Social Capital' of the State as an Agent of Deception," in *The Criminalization of the State in Africa*, ed. Jean-Francois Bayart, Stephen Ellis, and Beatrice Hibou (Bloomington: Indiana University Press, 1999), 88.

25. Robert H. Jackson, *Quasi-states: Sovereignty, International Relations, and the Third World* (Cambridge: Cambridge University Press, 1990), 21.

26. I. William Zartman, ed., *Collapsed States: The Disintegration and Restoration of Legitimate Authority* (Boulder, Colo.: Rienner, 1995).

27. Tanisha M. Fazal, "State Death in the International System," *International Organization* 58 (Spring 2004): 311–44, quote at 312.

28. Joel Migdal, *Strong States, Weak Societies: State-Society Relations and State Capabilities in the Third World* (Princeton, N.J.: Princeton University Press, 1988); and Peter Evans, *Embedded Autonomy: States and Industrial Transformation* (Princeton, N.J.: Princeton University Press, 1995).

29. Janice E. Thomson, "State Sovereignty in International Relations: Bridging the Gap between Theory and Empirical Research," *International Studies Quarterly* 39 (June 1995): 213–33; and Holsti, *State, War, and the State of War*, 82–98.

30. Examples of scholarship measuring state strength exclusively in terms of capacities include Samuel Huntington, *Political Order in Changing Societies* (New Haven, Conn.: Yale University Press, 1968), and Migdal, *Strong States, Weak Societies*.

31. William J. Reno, *Warlord Politics and African States* (Boulder, Colo.: Rienner, 1998), 226.

32. Gerald B. Helman and Steven R. Ratner, "Saving Failed States," *Foreign Policy*, no. 89 (Winter 1992–93): 3–20.

33. See Robert I. Rotberg, "Failed States in a World of Terror," *Foreign Affairs* 81, no. 4 (2002): 127–40. For a fuller discussion of Africa's problems, see Martin Meredith, *The State of Africa: A History of Fifty Years of Independence* (London: Free Press, 2005).

34. See, for example, P. H. Liotta and James F. Miskel, "Redrawing the Map of the Future," *World Policy Journal* 21, no. 1 (Spring 2004): 15–21; and Richard J. Norton, "Feral Cities," *Naval War College Review* 56, no. 4 (2003), www.nwc.navy.mil/press/Review/2003/Autumn/art6-a03.htm (accessed May 18, 2005).

35. Stephen Krasner, *Sovereignty: Organized Hypocrisy* (Princeton, N.J.: Princeton University Press, 1999).

36. Mark Duffield, "Globalization, Transborder Trade, and War Economies," in *Greed and Grievance: Economic Agendas in Civil Wars*, ed. Mats Berdal and David Malone (Boulder, Colo.: Rienner, 2000), 70–74.

37. Hedley Bull, *The Anarchical Society: A Study of Order in World Politics* (London: Macmillan, 1977).

38. Jessica Matthews, "Power Shift," *Foreign Affairs* 76 (1997): 61.

39. Mohammed Ayoob, *The Third World Security Predicament: State Making, Regional Conflict, and the International System* (Boulder, Colo.: Rienner, 1995).

40. Holsti, *Taming the Sovereigns*, 318.

41. David Kennedy, *The Dark Sides of Virtue: Reassessing International Humanitarianism* (Princeton, N.J.: Princeton University Press, 2004), 235.

42. James N. Rosenau, *Turbulence in World Politics* (Princeton, N.J.: Princeton University Press, 1990).

43. Kaldor, *New and Old Wars*, 8.

44. A vast literature refers to this topic. See, for example, Ayoob, *Third World Security Predicament*; S. Neil MacFarlane, *Superpower Rivalry and 3rd World Radicalism: The Idea of National Liberation* (Baltimore: Johns Hopkins University Press, 1985); and Thomas G. Weiss and James G. Blight, eds., *The Suffering Grass: Superpowers and Regional Conflict in Southern Africa and the Caribbean* (Boulder, Colo.: Rienner, 1992).

45. Stephen J. Stedman and Fred Tanner, eds., *Refugee Manipulation: War, Politics, and the Abuse of Human Suffering* (Washington, D.C.: Brookings, 2003), 14.

46. Hibou, "'Social Capital' of the State," 102.

47. Stephen John Stedman uses the term *spoiler* in the context of peacebuilding; here we adapt the concept to the dynamics of humanitarian action. See Stedman, "Spoiler Problems in Peace Processes," in *Nationalism and Ethnic Conflict*, ed. Michael E. Brown and others (Cambridge, Mass.: MIT Press, 2001), 366–414. See also, Fred Halliday, "The Romance of Non-state Actors," in *Non-state Actors in World Politics*, ed. Daphné Josselin and William Wallace (New York: Palgrave, 2000), 23.

48. The ICRC commissioned a study from Greenberg Research on perspectives on war. ICRC, *The People on War Report* (Geneva: ICRC, 1999). Data on new-wars belligerents' knowledge of the Geneva Conventions can be found on 18–19.

49. Reno, *Warlord Politics*, 71.

50. Kaldor, *New and Old Wars*, 92, differentiates five types of forces that inhabit new wars: "regular armed forces or remnants thereof; paramilitary groups; self-defense units; foreign mercenaries; and finally, regular foreign troops generally under international auspices."

51. John MacKinlay, "Defining Warlords," *International Peacekeeping* 7, no. 1 (2000): 49.

52. Bernard Frahi, "Organized Crime and Conflict—Interaction and Policy Implications," in *Organized Crime as an Obstacle to Successful Peacebuilding: Lessons Learned from the Balkans, Afghanistan, and West Africa—7th International Berlin Workshop*, ed. Alexander Austin, Tobias von Gienanth, and Wibke Hansen (Berlin: Zentrum Für Internationale Friedenseinsätze, 2003), 35–36.

53. For more on the development of PMCs and their distinction from mercenaries, see P. W. Singer, *Corporate Warriors: The Rise of the Privatized Military Industry* (Ithaca, N.Y.: Cornell University Press, 2003), 45–47; and Robert Mandel,

Armies without States: The Privatization of Security (Boulder, Colo.: Rienner, 2002), 9–10. For more on PMCs generally, see the aforementioned citations and Ulric Shannon, "Human Security and the Rise of Private Armies," *New Political Science* 22, no. 1 (2000): 103–15; David Shearer, "Outsourcing War," *Foreign Policy* 112 (1998): 68–80; Shearer, *Private Armies and Military Intervention*, Adelphi Paper 316 (Oxford: Oxford University Press, 1998); David Isenberg, *Soldiers of Fortune Ltd.: A Profile of Today's Private Sector Corporate Mercenary Firms* (Washington, D.C.: Center for Defense Information Monograph, November 1997).

54. Herbert Howe, "Executive Outcomes and Private Security," in *Ambiguous Order: Military Forces in African States* (Boulder, Colo.: Rienner, 2001); Khareen Pech, "Executive Outcomes—a Corporate Conquest," in *Peace, Profit, or Plunder? The Privatisation of Security in War-Torn African Societies*, ed. Jakkie Cilliers and Peggy Mason (South Africa: Institute for Security Studies, 1999); and Jeremy Harding, "The Mercenary Business: 'Executive Outcomes,'" *Review of African Political Economy* 24, no. 71 (1997): 87–97.

55. Kevin A. O'Brien, "Private Military Companies and African Security 1990–1998," in *Mercenaries: An African Security Dilemma*, ed. Abdel-Fatau Musah and J. 'Kayode Fayemi (London: Pluto Press, 2000), 51–52.

56. Deborah D. Avant, *The Market for Force: The Consequences of Privatizing Security* (Cambridge: Cambridge University Press, 2005), 86–92; and P. W. Singer, *Corporate Warriors: The Rise of the Privatized Military Industry* (Ithaca, N.Y.: Cornell University Press, 2003), 112–13.

57. Michael O'Hanlon and Peter W. Singer, "The Humanitarian Transformation: Expanding Global Intervention Capacity," *Survival* 46, no. 1 (2004): 91.

58. Bernedette Muthien and Ian Taylor, "The Return of the Dogs of War? The Privatization of Security in Africa," in *The Emergence of Private Authority in Global Governance*, ed. Rodney Bruce Hall and Thomas J. Biersteker (Cambridge: Cambridge University Press, 2002), 197.

59. Ken Menkhaus, *Somalia: State Collapse and the Threat of Terrorism*, Adelphi Paper 364 (Oxford: Oxford University Press, 2004), 39–40, uses "intrinsic" and "situational" to denote difference among spoilers.

60. Originally coined by Aristide R. Zolberg, Astri Suhrke, and Sergio Aguayo, eds., *Escape from Violence: Conflict and the Refugee Crisis in the Developing World* (New York: Oxford University Press, 1989). This formulation is revisited by Fiona Terry, *Condemned to Repeat? The Paradox of Humanitarian Action* (Ithaca, N.Y.: Cornell University Press, 2002), 5–9, 34, and, most in depth, 155–70.

61. Frédéric Grare, "The Geopolitics of Afghan Refugees in Pakistan," in *Refugee Manipulation: War, Politics, and the Abuse of Human Suffering*, ed. Stephen J. Stedman and Fred Tanner (Washington, D.C.: Brookings, 2003), 58.

62. Ilene Cohn and Guy S. Goodwin-Gill, *Child Soldiers: The Role of Children in Armed Conflict* (Oxford: Clarendon Press, 1994); and Graça Machel, *The Impact of War on Children* (New York: Palgrave, 2001). Additional useful data can be found in UNICEF, *Progress since the World Summit for Children: A Statistical Review* (New York: UNICEF, 2001). A more popular version is P. W. Singer, *Children at War* (New York: Pantheon, 2005). For recent data, see his article "Western Militaries Confront Child Soldiers Threat," *Jane's Intelligence Review*, January 1, 2005: "There are now as many as 300,000 children under 18 years old presently serving as combatants

in 40 per cent of the world's armed organizations (both non-state and state linked) and they fight in almost 75 per cent of the world's conflicts."

63. David Keen, "Incentives and Disincentives for Violence," in *Greed and Grievance: Economic Agendas in Civil Wars*, ed. Mats Berdal and David Malone (Boulder, Colo.: Rienner, 2000), 27, emphasis in original.

64. See Mats Berdal and David Malone, eds., *Greed and Grievance: Economic Agendas in Civil Wars* (Boulder, Colo.: Rienner, 2000), in particular, Keen, "Incentives and Disincentives," especially 24–27, 29–31; and Reno, "Shadow States," 44–45. Also see Halvor Mehlum, Karl Ove Moene, and Ragnar Torvik, "Plunder & Protection, Inc." *Journal of Peace Research* 39, no. 4 (2002): 447–59, for a greater discussion of the opportunities for profit making via plunder and extortion in weak states.

65. Reno, "Shadow States," 61.

66. For a more general discussion of market manipulation, see Duffield, "Globalization," 74–79; Mark Duffield, "The Political Economy of Internal War: Asset Transfer, Complex Emergencies and International Aid," in *War and Hunger: Rethinking International Responses to Complex Emergencies*, ed. Joanna Macrae and Anthony Zwi (London: Zed, 1994), 56–57; and David Keen and Ken Wilson, "Engaging with Violence: A Reassessment of Relief in Wartime," in Macrae and Zwi, *War and Hunger*, 217.

67. Hibou, "'Social Capital' of the State," 71, 96.

68. Phil Williams, "Transnational Organized Crime and the State," in *The Emergence of Private Authority in Global Governance*, ed. Rodney Bruce Hall and Thomas J. Biersteker (Cambridge: Cambridge University Press, 2002), 161–82; Louis Shelly, "Transnational Organized Crime: An Immanent Threat to the Nation-State," *Journal of International Affairs* 48, no. 2 (1995): 464–89; and Phil Williams, "Transnational Criminal Organizations and International Security," *Survival* 36, no. 1 (1994): 96–113.

69. Michael Klare, *Resource Wars: The New Landscape of Global Conflict* (New York: Henry Holt, 2002).

70. Indra de Soysa, "Resource Curse: Are Civil Wars Driven by Rapacity or Paucity?" in *Greed and Grievance: Economic Agendas in Civil Wars*, ed. Mats Berdal and David Malone (Boulder, Colo.: Rienner, 2000), 113–35. Also see Richard M. Auty, *Resource Abundance and Economic Development* (Oxford: Oxford University Press, 2001).

71. Several studies have examined the role that natural resources have played in fueling contemporary conflicts, especially in Angola, Cambodia, the Democratic Republic of the Congo, Indonesia, Liberia, and Sierra Leone. For a general overview see David Keen, *The Economic Functions of Violence in Civil Wars* (Oxford: Oxford University Press, 1998); Berdal and Malone, *Greed and Grievance*; and Duffield, *Global Governance*, 161–201.

72. Paul Collier, "Economic Causes of Conflict and Their Implications for Policy," World Bank paper dated June 15, 2000. See also Paul Collier and Nicholas Sambanis, "Understanding Civil War: A New Agenda," *Journal of Conflict Resolution* 46, no. 1 (February 2002): 3–12.

73. Mary B. Anderson, *Do No Harm: How Aid Can Support Peace—or War* (Boulder, Colo.: Rienner, 2002), 46; Matthew LeRiche, "Unintended Alliance: The Cooption of Humanitarian Aid in Conflicts," *Parameters* 36, no. 1 (2004): 104–20; and

David Keen, *The Benefits of Famine and Relief in Southwestern Sudan, 1983–1989* (Princeton, N.J.: Princeton University Press, 1994).

74. Daniel Unger, "Ain't Enough Blanket: International Humanitarian Assistance and Cambodian Political Resistance," in *Refugee Manipulation: War, Politics, and the Abuse of Human Suffering*, ed. Stephen J. Stedman and Fred Tanner (Washington, D.C.: Brookings, 2003), 17–56; Grare, "Geopolitics of Afghan Refugees," 57–94; and LeRiche, "Unintended Alliance," 107, 115.

75. Human Rights Watch, "Civilian Devastation—Abuses by All Parties in the War in Southern Sudan," 1993, www.hrw.org/reports/1993/sudan/ (accessed June 8, 2005).

76. Peter Uvin, *Aiding Violence: The Development Enterprise in Rwanda* (West Hartford, Conn.: Kumarian, 1998).

77. Sarah Collinson, ed., *Power, Livelihoods, and Conflict: Case Studies in Political Economy Analysis*, HPG Report 13 (London: Overseas Development Institute, 2003), 18.

78. Duffield, "Political Economy of Internal War," 60–61.

79. Carnegie Commission on Preventing Deadly Conflict, *Preventing Deadly Conflict: Final Report* (Washington, D.C.: Carnegie Commission on Preventing Deadly Conflict, 1998), 11.

80. Kaldor, *New and Old Wars*, 8, 100.

81. Holsti, *Taming the Sovereigns*, 284–85.

82. Virgil Hawkins, "The Price of Inaction: The Media and Humanitarian Intervention," *Journal of Humanitarian Assistance*, May 15, 2001, www.jha.ac/articles/a066.htm (accessed May 19, 2005).

83. For a fuller discussion of assessing the motives behind targeting civilians in conflict, see Jean-Paul Azam and Anke Hoeffler, "Violence against Civilians in Civil Wars: Looting or Terror?" *Journal of Peace Research* 39, no. 4 (2002): 461–85.

84. See Trenches on the Web, "Special Feature: The Great War in Numbers," www.worldwar1.com/sfnum.htm (accessed May 19, 2005).

85. See Wikipedia, "World War II Casualties," http://en.wikipedia.org/wiki/List_of_World_War_II_casualties_by_country (accessed June 8, 2005).

86. *Report of the Secretary-General to the Security Council on the Protection of Civilians in Armed Conflict*, S/2002/1300, November 26, 2002; *Report of the Secretary-General to the Security Council on the Protection of Civilians in Armed Conflict*, S/2001/331, March 30, 2001; *Report of the Secretary-General to the Security Council on the Protection of Civilians in Armed Conflict*, S/1999/957, September 8, 1999. The March 30, 2001, report is cited (para. 3).

87. Carnegie Commission, *Preventing Deadly Conflict*; and International Commission on Intervention and State Sovereignty, *The Responsibility to Protect* (Ottawa: International Development Research Centre, 2001).

88. Kaldor, *New and Old Wars*, 99–100; and Michael Bryans, Bruce D. Jones, and Janice Gross Stein, *Mean Times: Humanitarian Action in Complex Political Emergencies—Stark Choices, Cruel Dilemmas* (Toronto: Program on Conflict Management and Negotiation, 1999), 5.

89. IDPs are defined as "persons or groups of persons who have been forced or obliged to flee or leave their homes or places of habitual residence, in particular as a result of or in order to avoid the effects of armed conflict, situations of generalized violence, violations of human rights or natural or human-made disasters, and

who have not crossed an international recognized State border." See Office for the Coordination of Humanitarian Affairs, *Guiding Principles on Internal Displacement* (New York: United Nations, June 2001), para. 2.

90. Roberta Cohen and Frances M. Deng, *Masses in Flight: The Global Crisis of Internal Displacement* (Washington, D.C.: Brookings, 1998); Roberta Cohen and Frances M. Deng, eds., *The Forsaken People: Case Studies of the Internally Displaced* (Washington, D.C.: Brookings, 1998); and Francis M. Deng, *Protecting the Dispossessed: A Challenge for the International Community* (Washington, D.C.: Brookings, 1993). See also, Catherine Phuong, *The International Protection of Internally Displaced Persons* (Cambridge: Cambridge University Press, 2005).

91. UNHCR, *State of the World's Refugees 2000* (Oxford: Oxford University Press, 2001), 280.

92. See Thomas G. Weiss, *International Efforts for IDP after a Decade: What Next?* (Washington, D.C.: Brookings-SAIS Project on Internal Displacement, 2003); Weiss, "Humanitarian Shell Games: Whither UN Reform?" *Security Dialogue* 29, no. 1 (1998): 9–23; and Weiss and David A. Korn, *Internal Displacement: Conceptualization and its Consequences* (London: Routledge, forthcoming).

93. Loren B. Thompson, "Key Technological Trends since World War Two," September 20, 2001, www.lexingtoninstitute.org/defense/techtrends.htm (accessed November 7, 2002).

94. Susan Benesch, "Inciting Genocide, Pleading Free Speech," *World Policy Journal* 21, no. 2 (2004): 62–69.

95. John Orme, "The Utility of Force in a World of Scarcity," *International Security* 22, no. 3 (1997–1998): 149–55.

CHAPTER 4

1. See Adele Harmer, Lin Cotterrell, and Abby Stoddard, "From Stockholm to Ottawa: A Progress Review of the Good Humanitarian Donorship Initiative," *HPG Research Briefing*, no. 18 (October 2004): 4.

2. David Rieff, "Humanitarianism in Crisis," *Foreign Affairs* 81, no. 6 (2002): 111–21.

3. Data drawn from Monty G. Marshall, "Major Episodes of Political Violence, 1946–1999," http://members.aol.com/CSPmgm/warlist.htm (accessed May 19, 2005).

4. International Rescue Committee, "Mortality in the Democratic Republic of Congo: Results from a Nationwide Survey," conducted April–July 2004, www.theirc.org/pdf/DRC_MortalitySurvey2004_RB_8Dec04.pdf (accessed June 8, 2005).

5. Mark Duffield, "The Political Economy of Internal War: Asset Transfer, Complex Emergencies, and International Aid," in *War and Hunger: Rethinking International Responses to Complex Emergencies*, ed. Joanna Macrae and Anthony Zwi (London: Zed, 1994), 58–59.

6. See Development Assistance Committee, *Development Cooperation Report 2000* (Paris: Organisation for Economic Co-operation and Development, 2001), 180–81.

7. Dorothea Hilhorst, "Being Good at Doing Good? Quality and Accountability of Humanitarian NGOs," *Disasters* 26, no. 3 (2002): 195.

8. Abby Stoddard, "Humanitarian NGOs: Challenges and Trends," in *Humanitarian Action and the 'Global War on Terror': A Review of Trends and Issues*, ed. Joanna Macrae and Adele Harmer, HPG Report 14 (London: ODI, 2003), 1–4.

9. This discussion takes off from Thomas G. Weiss, "Principles, Politics, and Humanitarian Action," *Ethics and International Affairs* 13 (1999): 1–22 and comments.

10. The details of its founding and activities leading to the award of the 1999 Nobel Prize are documented in Anne Vallarys, *Médecins Sans Frontières: La Biographie* (Paris: Fayort, 2004).

11. Jean-Hervé Bradhol, introduction to *In the Shadow of "Just Wars": Violence, Politics, and Humanitarian Action*, ed. Fabrice Weissman (Ithaca, N.Y.: Cornell University Press, 2004), 3.

12. Mary Kaldor, *New and Old Wars: Organized Violence in a New Era* (Stanford, Calif.: Stanford University Press, 1999), 126.

13. Mark Bowden, foreword to *The Humanitarian Decade: Challenges for Humanitarian Assistance in the Last Decade and into the Future*, by OCHA (New York: UN, 2004), vii.

14. Joanna Macrae, "Defining the Boundaries: International Security and Humanitarian Engagement in the Post–Cold War World," in OCHA, *Humanitarian Decade*, 117.

15. Ian Smillie and Larry Minear, *The Charity of Nations: Humanitarian Action in a Calculating World* (Bloomfield, Conn.: Kumarian, 2004), chapter 8.

16. Boutros Boutros-Ghali, *Supplement to an Agenda for Peace*, A/50/60-S/1995/1 (January 3, 1995), para. 12.

17. Michael Bryans, Bruce D. Jones, and Janice Gross Stein, *"Mean Times": Humanitarian Action in Complex Political Emergencies—Stark Choices, Cruel Dilemmas*, *Coming to Terms* 1, no. 3 (1999): 9–10.

18. Bruce M. Oswald, "The Creation and Control of Places of Protection during United Nations Peace Operations," *International Review of the Red Cross* 83, no. 844 (2001): 1013.

19. Christine Bourloyannis, "The Security Council of the United Nations and the Implementation of International Humanitarian Law," *Denver Journal of International Law and Policy* 20, no. 3 (1993): 43.

20. See Adam Roberts and Richard Guelff, eds., *Documents on the Laws of War*, 3rd ed. (Oxford: Oxford University Press, 2001), 419–512.

21. David P. Forsythe, *The Humanitarians: The International Committee of the Red Cross* (Cambridge: Cambridge University Press, 2005), 284.

22. Th. A. van Baarda, "The Involvement of the Security Council in Maintaining International Law," *Netherlands Quarterly of Human Rights* 12, no. 1 (1994): 140.

23. John Mackinlay and Jarat Chopra, *A Draft Concept of Second Generation Multinational Operations 1993* (Providence, R.I.: Watson Institute, 1993); Michael Barnett and Martha Finnemore, "Genocide and the Peacekeeping Culture at the United Nations," in *Rules for the World: International Organizations in Global Politics* (Ithaca, N.Y.: Cornell University Press, 2004), 121–55, especially 130–35; Charles W. Hasskamp, *Operations Other Than War: Who Says Warriors Don't Do Windows?* Maxwell Paper 13 (Maxwell Air Force Base, Ala.: Air War College, 1998),

www.maxwell.af.mil/au/aul/aupress/Maxwell_Papers/Text/mp13.pdf (accessed June 8, 2005); and John B. Hunt, "OOTW: A Concept in Flux," *Military Review* 4006, no. 5 (1996): 3–9.

24. Some of the earliest looks at this possibility include Thomas G. Weiss, ed., *Humanitarian Emergencies and Military Help in Africa* (London: Macmillan, 1990); Leon Gordenker and Thomas G. Weiss, eds., *Soldiers, Peacekeepers, and Disasters* (London: Macmillan, 1991); and Thomas G. Weiss and Kurt M. Campbell, "Military Humanitarianism," *Survival* 33, no. 5 (1991): 451–65.

25. See Larry Minear and others, *Humanitarianism under Siege: A Critical Review of Operation Life-line Sudan* (Trenton, N.J.: Red Sea Press, 1991); and Francis M. Deng and Larry Minear, *The Challenges of Famine Relief: Emergency Operations in the Sudan* (Washington, D.C.: Brookings, 1992).

26. Simon Bagshaw and Diane Paul, *Protect or Neglect? Toward a More Effective United Nations Approach to the Protection of Internally Displaced Persons* (Geneva: OCHA, 2004), 13.

27. Mario Bettati and Bernard Kouchner, eds., *Le Devoir d'Ingérence: Peut-on les Laisser Mourir?* (Paris: Denoël, 1987); and Mario Bettati, *Le Droit d'Ingérence: Mutation de l'Ordre International* (Paris: Odile Jacob, 1987).

28. David Rieff, "Kosovo: The End of an Era?" in *In the Shadow of "Just Wars": Violence, Politics and Humanitarian Action*, ed. Fabrice Weissman (Ithaca, N.Y.: Cornell University Press, 2004), 293.

29. See Thomas G. Weiss, "Humanitarian Shell Games: Whither UN Reform?" *Security Dialogue* 29, no. 1 (1998): 9–23.

30. Adam Roberts, "The Role of Humanitarian Issues in International Politics in the 1990s," *International Review of the Red Cross*, no. 833 (1999): 31–32.

31. UN Security Council resolution 688 (April 5, 1991).

32. UN Security Council resolution 814 (March 26, 1993).

33. UN Security Council resolution 836 (June 4, 1993).

34. UN Security Council resolution 771 (August 13, 1992) provided authorization under Chapter VII. For an analysis of this decision, see Kofi Annan, "Peacekeeping, Military Intervention, and National Sovereignty in Internal Armed Conflict," in *Hard Choices: Moral Dilemmas in Humanitarian Action*, ed. Jonathan Moore (Lanham, Md.: Rowman & Littlefield, 1998), 66–67. More resolutions on protection include UN Security Council resolution 819 (April 16, 1993), para. 1; UN Security Council resolution 824 (May 6, 1993).

35. Netherlands Institute for War Documentation, *Srebrenica, A "Safe" Area: Reconstruction, Background, Consequences, and Analyses of the Fall of a Safe Area* (Amsterdam: Boom, 2002).

36. See Thomas G. Weiss, "Collective Spinelessness: U.N. Action in the Former Yugoslavia," in *The World and Yugoslavia's Wars*, ed. Richard H. Ullman (New York: Council on Foreign Relations, 1996), 59–96.

37. UN Security Council resolution 918 (May 17, 1994).

38. UN Security Council resolution 929 (June 22, 1994).

39. Hugo Slim, *A Call to Alms: Humanitarian Action and the Art of War* (Geneva: Centre for Humanitarian Dialogue, 2004), 10.

40. There are but a few references to NSAs in IHL: article 3 to the Geneva Conventions and article 1 of Additional Protocol II.

41. Mary B. Anderson, *Do No Harm: How Aid Can Support Peace—or War* (Boulder, Colo.: Rienner, 1999), 50–51. Matthew LeRiche, "Unintended Alliance: The Co-option of Humanitarian Aid in Conflicts," *Parameters* 34, no. 1 (2004): 111.

42. Minear and others, *Humanitarianism under Siege*, chapters 3 and 4.

43. The need to unpack the concept of NSAs and distinguish among them has been a growing theme in both policy and academic circles. See, for example, Daphne Josselin and William Wallace, *Non-state Actors in World Politics* (New York: Palgrave, 2001).

44. This discussion originally appeared in Thomas G. Weiss and Peter J. Hoffman, "Making Humanitarianism Work," in *State Failure and the Crisis of Governance: Making States Work*, ed. Simon Chesterman, Michael Ignatieff, and Ramesh Thakur (Tokyo: UNU, 2005), 296–317.

45. Deborah Mancini-Griffoli and André Picot, *Humanitarian Negotiation: A Handbook for Security Access, Assistance, and Protection for Civilians in Armed Conflict* (Geneva: Centre for Humanitarian Dialogue, 2004), 11–12.

46. Stathis Kalyvas, "The Ontology of Political Violence," *Perspectives on Politics* 1, no. 3 (2003): 475.

47. Tobias Debial and others, *Between Ignorance and Intervention—Strategies and Dilemmas of External Actors in Fragile States*, SEF Policy Paper 23 (Berlin: Development and Peace Foundation, 2005), 2, 9.

48. Fiona Terry, *Condemned to Repeat? The Paradox of Humanitarian Action* (Ithaca, N.Y.: Cornell University Press, 2002), 44.

49. Nicholas Leader and Joanna Macrae, "New Times, Old Chestnuts," in *Terms of Engagement: Conditions and Conditionality in Humanitarian Action*, HPG Report 6, ed. Nicholas Leader and Joanna Macrae (London: Overseas Development Institute, July 2000), 9.

50. Hugo Slim, "Sharing a Universal Ethic: The Principle of Humanity in War," *International Journal of Human Rights* 4, no. 2 (1998): 28–48. See also, Michael Ignatieff, *The Warrior's Honor: Ethnic War and the Modern Conscience* (New York: Henry Holt, 1997). David Rieff has come full circle and now argues for a return to traditional approaches, in *A Bed for the Night: Humanitarianism in Crisis* (New York: Simon & Schuster, 2002).

51. Marc Lindenberg and Coralie Bryant, *Going Global: Transforming Relief and Development NGOs* (Bloomfield, Conn.: Kumarian, 2001), 81.

52. Larry Minear, *The Humanitarian Enterprise: Dilemmas and Discoveries* (West Bloomfield, Conn.: Kumarian, 2002), 116.

53. *Report of the Panel on United Nations Peace Operations*, UN document A/55/305–S/2000/809, August 21, 2000, ix.

54. David Forsythe's classic book is *Humanitarian Politics: The International Committee of the Red Cross* (Baltimore: Johns Hopkins University Press, 1977), and he argues that the ICRC was engaged politically. He continues and updates this theme in *The Humanitarians: The International Committee of the Red Cross* (Cambridge: Cambridge University Press, 2005).

55. S. Neil MacFarlane and Thomas G. Weiss, "Political Interest and Humanitarian Action," *Security Studies* 10, no. 1 (2000): 142.

56. Mark Duffield, *Global Governance and the New Wars: The Merging of Development and Security* (London: Zed, 2001), especially chapter 4.

57. Sadako Ogata, *The Turbulent Decade: Confronting the Refugee Crises of the 1990s* (New York: Norton, 2005).

58. In addition, the Inter-Agency Standing Committee also notes that "private contractors can sometimes venture where UN vehicles cannot." Inter-Agency Standing Committee, *Growing the Sheltering Tree—Protecting Rights through Humanitarian Action* (Geneva: UNICEF, 2002), 40.

59. See Alexander Cooley and James Ron, "The NGO Scramble," *International Security* 27, no. 1 (2002): 5–39; and Rieff, *Bed for the Night*.

60. Smillie and Minear, *Charity of Nations*, 183.

61. Austen Davies, "Thoughts on Conditions and Conditionality," in *Terms of Engagement: Conditions and Conditionality in Humanitarian Action*, HPG Report 6, ed. Nicholas Leader and Joanna Macrae (London: Overseas Development Institute, July 2000), 29–30.

62. Danielle Coquoz, "ICRC and Conditionality: Doctrine, Dilemma, and Dialogue," in *Terms of Engagement: Conditions and Conditionality in Humanitarian Action*, HPG Report 6, ed. Nicholas Leader and Joanna Macrae (London: Overseas Development Institute, July 2000), 25.

63. Alexander Cooley points out, however, that contract renewal contributes to ineffectiveness. See Cooley, "The Marketplace of Humanitarian Action: A Political Economy Perspective" (unpublished paper, Transformations of Humanitarian Action seminar series, Social Science Research Council, New York City, November 2004). For a more extensive analysis, see Cooley, *Logics of Hierarchy: The Organization of Empires, States, and Military Occupations* (Ithaca, N.Y.: Cornell University Press, 2005).

64. See Roland Paris, *At War's End: Building Peace after Conflict* (Cambridge: Cambridge University Press, 2004).

65. Dwight D. Eisenhower, farewell address, 1961, reprinted in Richard D. Heffner, ed., *A Documentary History of the United States* (New York: Mentor, 1976), 314.

66. United Nations, *Programme of Action to Prevent, Combat, and Eradicate the Illicit Trade in Small Arms and Light Weapons in All Its Aspects*, UN document A/CONF.192/1.5, July 20, 2001. For a discussion, see Keith Krause, "Multilateral Diplomacy, Norm Building, and UN Conferences: The Case of Small Arms and Light Weapons," *Global Governance* 8, no. 2 (2002): 247–63.

67. Available at www.unhchr.ch/html/menu3/b/93.htm (accessed June 8, 2005).

68. Adopted in 1977 by the Organization of African Unity; entered into force in 1985, www.icrc.org/ihl.nsf/0/5e41dd4e2010663fc125641e0052c016?OpenDocument (accessed June 8, 2005).

69. Adopted by the General Assembly in 1989, www.un.org/documents/ga/res/44/a44r034.htm (accessed June 8, 2005).

70. See www.unhchr.ch/html/menu2/7/b/mmer.htm (accessed June 8, 2005).

71. Michael T. Klare, *Resource Wars: The New Landscape of Global Conflict* (New York: Henry Holt, 2002), especially 190–212.

72. United Nations, *The Causes of Conflict and the Promotion of Durable Peace and Sustainable Development in Africa*, report of the UN secretary-general to the Security Council, April 1998. More recently the UN has explored this connection with direct reference to the war in the DRC, *Final Report of the Panel of Experts on the Ille-*

gal Exploitation of Natural Resources and Other Forms of Wealth of the Democratic Republic of Congo, UN Document S/2002/1146, October 16, 2002. Available at http://documents-dds-ny.un.org/doc/UNDOC/GEN/N02/621/79/pdf/ N0262179.pdf?OpenElement (accessed June 8, 2005).

73. Global Witness, www.globalwitness.org/campaigns/diamonds/ (accessed June 8, 2005). The UN is also engaged in action to clean up the diamond trade, see www.un.org/peace/africa/Diamond.html (accessed June 8, 2005).

74. See "Diamond Development Initiative Begins: New Approach to Africa's Diamond Problems," August 18, 2005, www.globalwitness.org/press_releases/ display2.php?id=305 (accessed September 20, 2005).

75. Klare, *Resource Wars*, 192.

76. Mary B. Anderson and Peter J. Woodrow, *Rising from the Ashes: Development Strategies in Times of Disaster* (Boulder, Colo.: Westview, 1987); and Anderson, *Do No Harm*.

77. Andrew S. Natsios, "Humanitarian Relief Intervention in Somalia: The Economics in Chaos," *International Peacekeeping* 3, no. 1 (1996): 68–91. Also see Thomas G. Weiss, *Military-Civilian Interactions*, 2nd ed. (Lanham, Md.: Rowman & Littlefield, 2005), chapter 4.

78. See, for instance, William Shawcross, *Deliver Us from Evil: Peacekeepers, Warlords, and a World of Endless Conflict* (New York: Simon and Schuster, 2000); Alex de Waal, *Famine Crimes: Politics and the Disaster Relief Industry in Africa* (Oxford: James Currey, 1997); and Michael Maren, *The Road to Hell: The Ravaging Effects of Foreign Aid and International Charity* (New York: Free Press, 1997).

79. Weissman, introduction, 12.

80. Duffield, *Global Governance and the New Wars*; and Duffield, *Aid Policy and Post-modern Conflict: A Critical Review*, Occasional Paper 19 (Birmingham, U.K.: School of Public Policy, 1998).

81. Kaldor, *New and Old Wars*, 9.

82. Roberts, "Role of Humanitarian Issues," 19.

83. UN Security Council resolutions 1199 (September 23, 1998) and 1203 (October 24, 1998).

84. Michael Ignatieff, "Human Rights: The Midlife Crisis," *New York Review of Books* 46, May 20, 1999, 58.

85. Edward Luttwak, "Kofi's Rule: Humanitarian Intervention and Neocolonialism," *National Interest*, no. 58 (1999–2000): 60.

86. Kofi A. Annan, *The Question of Intervention* (New York: United Nations, 1999). See Raimo Väyrynen, *The Age of Humanitarian Emergencies*, Research for Action 25 (Helsinki: World Institute for Development Economics Research, 1996); and Nicholas J. Wheeler, *Saving Strangers: Humanitarian Intervention in International Society* (Oxford: Oxford University Press, 2000).

87. Roméo Dallaire, *Shake Hands with the Devil: The Failure of Humanity in Rwanda* (Toronto: Carroll and Graf, 2004).

88. See *Report of the Independent Inquiry into the Actions of the United Nations during the 1994 Genocide in Rwanda*, UN document S/1999/1257, December 16, 1999.

89. *Report of the Panel on United Nations Peace Operations*, para. 50.

90. International Commission on Intervention and State Sovereignty, *The Responsibility to Protect* (Ottawa: International Development Research Centre, 2001).

91. Independent International Commission on Kosovo, *Kosovo Report: Conflict, International Response, Lessons Learned* (Oxford: Oxford University Press, 2000).

92. Alton Frye, ed., *Humanitarian Intervention: Crafting a Workable Doctrine* (New York: Council on Foreign Relations, 2000); and *Interagency Review of U.S. Government Civilian Humanitarian & Transition Programs*, July 12, 2000.

93. Advisory Council on International Affairs and Advisory Committee on Issues of Public International Law, *Humanitarian Intervention* (The Hague: AIV and CAVV, 2000); and Danish Institute of International Affairs, *Humanitarian Intervention: Legal and Political Aspects* (Copenhagen: Danish Institute of International Affairs, 1999).

94. High-Level Panel on Threats, Challenges and Change, *A More Secure World: Our Shared Responsibility*, UN document A/59/565, December 2, 2004, paras. 199–209.

95. Kofi Annan, *In Larger Freedom: Towards Development, Security, and Human Rights for All* (New York: UN, 2005), paras. 134–35; and *2005 World Summit Outcome*, UN document A/60/L.1, September 15, 2005, paras. 138–40.

96. See Thomas G. Weiss, "Internal Exiles: What Next for Internally Displaced Persons?" *Third World Quarterly* 24, no. 3 (2003): 429–77; and Weiss and David A. Korn, *Internal Displacement: Conceptualization and its Consequences* (London: Routledge, forthcoming).

97. See Denis King, "Paying the Ultimate Price: Analysis of the Deaths of Humanitarian Aid Workers (1997–2001)," January 15, 2001, www.reliefweb.int/symposium/PayingUltimatePrice97-01.html (accessed June 8, 2005). Also see National Intelligence Council, *Global Humanitarian Emergencies: Trends and Projections, 1999–2000* (Washington, D.C.: National Intelligence Council, August 1999), 14; UN Department of Public Information, *Basic Facts about the United Nations* (New York: United Nations, 2000), 251.

98. UN Security Council resolution 814, March 26, 1993.

99. UN Convention on the Safety of United Nations and Associated Personnel, adopted December 9, 1994, entry into force January 15, 1999.

100. Adam Roberts, "Humanitarian War: Military Intervention and Human Rights," *Journal of International Affairs* 69, no. 3 (1993): 429–49.

101. Bradhol, introduction, 5.

102. Michael O'Hanlon, *Technological Change and the Future of Warfare* (Washington, D.C.: Brookings, 2000), 128–33, quotes on 129–30 and 133.

103. Andrew S. Natsios, *U.S. Foreign Policy and the Four Horsemen of the Apocalypse: Humanitarian Relief in Complex Emergencies* (Westport, Conn.: Praeger, 1997), 124–39, quote at 124.

104. International Federation of Red Cross and Red Crescent Societies, *World Disasters Report 2003: Focus on Ethics in Aid* (Bloomfield, Conn.: Kumarian, 2003), 19–22.

105. Smillie and Minear, *Charity of Nations*, 3.

106. Smillie and Minear, *Charity of Nations*, 19.

107. Bryans, Jones, and Stein, *"Mean Times,"* 13.

108. Examples of this perspective are Robert D. Kaplan, *The Coming Anarchy: Shattering the Dreams of the Post–Cold War World* (New York: Random House, 2000); Kaplan, "The Coming Anarchy," *Atlantic Monthly*, February 1994, 44–76; and Samuel Huntington, *The Clash of Civilizations and the Remaking of World Order* (New York: Simon and Schuster, 1996).

109. Michael Ignatieff, "The Stories We Tell: Television and Humanitarian Aid," in *Hard Choices: Moral Dilemmas in Humanitarian Intervention*, ed. Jonathan Moore (Lanham, Md.: Rowman & Littlefield, 1998), 298, 301.

110. Nik Gowing, "The Upside and Downside of New Media Noise in Humanitarian Emergencies," in *The Humanitarian Decade: Challenges for Humanitarian Assistance in the Last Decade and into the Future*, by OCHA (New York: UN, 2004), 216.

111. John C. Hammock and Joel C. Charny, "Emergency Responses as Morality Play," in *From Massacres to Genocide: The Media, Public Policy, and Humanitarian Crises*, ed. Robert I. Rotberg and Thomas G. Weiss (Washington, D.C.: Brookings, 1996), 115–35.

112. See Michael Barnett and Martha Finnemore, "Defining Refugees and Voluntary Repatriation at the United Nations High Commissioner for Refugees," in *Rules for the World: International Organizations in Global Politics* (Ithaca, N.Y.: Cornell University Press, 2004), 73–120, especially 75 and 95. For its views on repatriation, see UNHCR, "Asylum in the Industrialized World," in *State of the World's Refugees: Fifty Years of Humanitarian Action* (New York: Oxford University Press, 2000), 155–83.

CHAPTER 5

1. Mancur Olson, *The Logic of Collective Action: Public Goods and the Theory of Groups* (Cambridge, Mass.: Harvard University Press, 1965).

2. Judith Randel and Tony German, "Trends in Financing of Humanitarian Assistance," in *The New Humanitarianisms: A Review of Trends in Global Humanitarian Action*, HPG Report 11, ed. Joanna Macrae (London: ODI, 2002).

3. Alexander Cooley and James Ron, "The NGO Scramble: Organizational Insecurity and the Political Economy of Transnational Action," *International Security* 27, no. 1 (2002): 10.

4. Joanna Macrae, "Defining the Boundaries: International Security and Humanitarian Engagement in the Post–Cold War World," in *The Humanitarian Decade: Challenges for Humanitarian Assistance in the Last Decade*, ed. OCHA (New York: OCHA, 2004), vol. 2, 117.

5. Alex de Waal, *Famine Crimes: Politics and the Disaster Relief Industry in Africa* (Oxford: James Currey, 1997); and Michael Maren, *The Road to Hell: The Ravaging Effects of Foreign Aid and International Charity* (New York: Free Press, 1997).

6. David Rieff, "Tsunamis, Accountability and the Humanitarian Crises," *HPN Humanitarian Exchange*, no. 29 (March 2005): 50.

7. Inter-Agency Standing Committee, "Working Paper on the Definition of Complex Emergency" (December 1994), in *Humanitarian Report 1997*, by the Department of Humanitarian Affairs, United Nations (New York: United Nations, 1997), 9.

8. John Mackinlay, *Globalisation and Insurgency*, Adelphi Paper 352 (Oxford: Oxford University Press, 2002), 100.

9. United Nations, *A Study of the Capacity of the United Nations Development System* (Geneva: United Nations, 1969).

10. Antonio Donini, "The Evolving Nature of Coordination," in *The Humanitarian Decade: Challenges for Humanitarian Assistance in the Last Decade*, ed. OCHA (New York: OCHA, 2004), vol. 2, 131, which updates his work *The Policies of Mercy: UN Coordination in Afghanistan, Mozambique, and Rwanda*, Occasional Paper 22 (Providence, R.I.: Watson Institute, 1996), 14.

11. Cooley and Ron, "NGO Scramble," 9.

12. Joel R. Charny, "Upholding Humanitarian Principles in an Effective Integrated Response," *Ethics and International Affairs* 18, no. 2 (2004): 18.

13. For a greater discussion of the transition from DHA to OCHA as well as the politics that drove the process, see Thomas G. Weiss, "Humanitarian Shell Games: Whither UN Reform," *Security Dialogue* 29, no. 1 (1998): 9–23.

14. Toby Porter, *An External Review of the CAP*, commissioned by OCHA's Evaluation and Studies Unit (April 18, 2002), 9, www.reliefweb.int/library/documents/2002/ocha-cap-ECOSOC-18apr.pdf (accessed September 22, 2005).

15. Porter, *External Review of the CAP*, 2, 17, 27–28.

16. This estimate is admittedly rough, but it is one agreed on by a number of analysts: Ian Smillie and Larry Minear, *The Charity of Nations: Humanitarian Action in a Calculating World* (Bloomfield, Conn.: Kumarian, 2004), 195; Cooley and Ron, "NGO Scramble," 12; and P. J. Simmons, "Learning to Live with NGOs," *Foreign Policy*, no. 112 (1997): 92.

17. Espen Barth Eide and others, "Report on Integrated Missions: Practical Perspectives and Recommendations" (independent study for the Expanded UN ECHA Core Group, New York, May 2005), 14, www.reliefweb.int/rw/lib.nsf/db900SID/SODA-6CK7SK/$FILE/report%20on%20integrated%20missions.pdf?OpenElement (accessed September 22, 2005).

18. Joanna Macrae, "Understanding Integration from Rwanda to Iraq," *Ethics and International Affairs* 18, no. 2 (2004): 30; and Bruce D. Jones, "The Changing Role of the UN in Protracted Crises," *HPG Research Briefing*, no. 17 (2004).

19. Eide and others, "Report on Integrated Missions," 28.

20. Nicholas Stockton, "The Changing Nature of Humanitarian Crises," in *The Humanitarian Decade: Challenges for Humanitarian Assistance in the Last Decade and into the Future*, by OCHA (New York: UN, 2004), 30.

21. Antonio Donini, "An Elusive Quest: Integration in the Response to the Afghan Crisis," *Ethics and International Affairs* 18, no. 2 (2004): 22–23.

22. United Nations, *Report of the Panel on United Nations Peace Operations*, A/55/305-S/2000/809, August 21, 2000.

23. For a recent set of essays, see Fabrice Weissman, ed., *In the Shadow of "Just Wars": Violence, Politics, and Humanitarian Action* (Ithaca, N.Y.: Cornell University Press, 2004).

24. See, for example, Sue Lautze and John Hammock, *Capacity Building, Coping Mechanisms and Dependency, Linking Relief and Development* (New York: UNDHA, 1996); United Nations, *DHA-UNDP Workshop: Building Bridges between Relief and Development* (New York: UN, 1997).

25. Mary B. Anderson, *Do No Harm: How Aid Can Support War—or Peace* (Boulder, Colo.: Rienner, 1999).

26. Joanna Macrae and Adele Harmer, "Beyond the Continuum: The Changing Role of Aid Policy in Protracted Crises," *HPG Research Report*, no. 18 (2004): 4–5.

27. OECD, "Aid Ministers Note Rise in Aid Volume and Push for Aid Reform and New Approach to Security-Development Linkages," April 16, 2004, www.oecd.org/document/51/0,2340,en_2649_201185_31505523_1_1_1_1,00.html (accessed June 9, 2005).

28. Macrae, "Understanding Integration," 35.

29. Nicholas Leader and Joanna Macrae, eds., *Terms of Engagement: Conditions and Conditionality in Humanitarian Action*, HPG Report 6 (London: Overseas Development Institute, 2000), 4–5.

30. Nicholas Stockton, "The 'Code of Conduct' in Practice: A Personal View," in *Terms of Engagement: Conditions and Conditionality in Humanitarian Action*, HPG Report 6, ed. Nicholas Leader and Joanna Macrae (London: Overseas Development Institute, 2000), 17–21.

31. Cooley and Ron, "NGO Scramble," 17.

32. Austen Davies, "Thoughts on Conditions and Conditionality," in *Terms of Engagement: Conditions and Conditionality in Humanitarian Action*, HPG Report 6, ed. Nicholas Leader and Joanna Macrae (London: Overseas Development Institute, 2000), 32.

33. Nicolas de Torrenté, "Humanitarianism Sacrificed: Integration's False Promise," *Ethics and International Affairs* 18, no. 2 (2004): 3–4.

34. Susan F. Martin and others, *The Uprooted: Improving Humanitarian Responses to Forced Migration* (Lanham, Md.: Lexington Books, 2005), 198.

35. De Torrenté, "Humanitarianism Sacrificed," 6; and Charny, "Upholding Humanitarian Principles," 13.

36. Cooley and Ron, "NGO Scramble," 6.

37. Nicola Reindorp and Peter Wiles, *Humanitarian Coordination: Lessons from Recent Field Experiences* (London: Overseas Development Institute, 2001).

38. OECD, *Development Co-operation Report 2004* (Paris: OECD, 2004).

39. Millennium Project, *Investing in Development: A Practical Plan to Achieve the Millennium Development Goals* (New York: UNDP, 2005), 36–50.

40. Smillie and Minear, *Charity of Nations*, 10, 8.

41. Fiona Terry, *Condemned to Repeat? The Paradox of Humanitarian Action* (Ithaca, N.Y.: Cornell University Press, 2002).

42. Charny, "Upholding Humanitarian Principles," 14.

43. Max P. Glaser, "Humanitarian Engagement with Non-state Armed Actors," in *The Parameters of Negotiated Access*, HPN Network Paper 51 (London, 2005), 5, 17; and UN Security Council document S/2001/331/, especially paras. 14–16.

44. See "Tsunami: Learning from the Humanitarian Response," special issue of *Forced Migration Review*, July 2005.

45. Roméo Dallaire, "Keynote Address," April 24, 2001, conference organized by CARE Canada and the Humanitarianism and War Project.

46. Cooley and Ron, "NGO Scramble," 13.

47. Glaser, "Humanitarian Engagement," 1.

CHAPTER 6

1. Michael Ignatieff, "Intervention and State Failure," in *The New Killing Fields: Massacre and the Politics of Intervention*, ed. Nicolaus Mills and Kira Brunner (New York: Basic Books, 2002), 229–44.

2. As per the analysis in chapter 3 on new wars, Hammes argues that Afghanistan and Iraq are representative of the shift to fourth-generation warfare. Thomas X. Hammes, *The Sling and the Stone: On War in the 21st Century* (St. Paul,

Minn: Zenith Press, 2004), 2–3; for each case in detail, see "Afghanistan: A Tribal Network," 153–71, and "Iraq: High-Tech versus Fourth Generation," 172–89.

3. Kalevi J. Holsti, *Taming the Sovereigns: Institutional Change in International Politics* (Cambridge: Cambridge University Press, 2004), 16.

4. David P. Forsythe, *Humanitarian Politics: The International Committee of the Red Cross* (Baltimore: Johns Hopkins University Press, 1977). See also, Larry Minear and Thomas G. Weiss, *Humanitarian Politics*, Headline 304 (New York: Foreign Policy Association, 1995).

5. Antonio Donini, "The Evolving Nature of Coordination," in *The Humanitarian Decade: Challenges for Humanitarian Assistance in the Last Decade*, ed. OCHA (New York: OCHA, 2004), vol. 2, 136.

6. Brian Urquhart, "The United Nations Rediscovered?" *World Policy Journal* 21, no. 2 (2004): 1.

7. International Rescue Committee, *Mortality in Eastern DRC: Results from Eleven Mortality Surveys*, May 2001 and April 2003, www.theirc.org/index.cfm/wwwID/2129 (accessed June 6, 2005).

8. Samuel Huntington, *The Clash of Civilizations and the Remaking of World Order* (New York: Simon & Schuster, 1997). This argument was originally articulated in his 1993 *Foreign Affairs* article.

9. Chris Brummitt, "Groups Linked to al Qaeda Starts 'Relief' Work in Aceh," *Washington Times*, January 7, 2005. See also, "Tsunami: Learning from the Humanitarian Response," special issue of *Forced Migration Review*, July 2005.

10. Huntington, *The Clash of Civilizations*.

11. Abdel-Rahman Ghandour, "The Modern Missionaries of Islam," in *In the Shadow of "Just Wars": Violence, Politics, and Humanitarian Action*, ed. Fabrice Weissman (Ithaca, N.Y.: Cornell University Press, 2004), 329–31.

12. Kofi A. Annan, *The Question of Intervention* (New York: UN, 1999).

13. Kenneth Menkhaus, *Somalia: State Collapse and the Threat of Terrorism*, Adelphi Paper 364 (Oxford: Oxford University Press, 2004), 7.

14. For a quick overview, see State Department, "Facts Sheet on Provincial Reconstruction Teams," September 27, 2004, www.defenselink.mil/home/articles/2004-10/a100107b.html (accessed June 6, 2005).

15. Gerard McHugh and Lola Gostelow, *Provincial Reconstruction Teams and Humanitarian-Military Relations in Afghanistan* (London: Save the Children, 2004), 34.

16. In January 2003, U.S. Department of Defense opens the Office for Reconstruction and Humanitarian Assistance, see Stuart Gordon, "Military-Humanitarian Relationships and the Invasion of Iraq (2003): Reforging Certainties?" *Journal of Humanitarian Assistance*, July 6, 2004, www.jha.ac/articles/a137.htm (accessed June 9, 2005)—and more recently, the higher profile of the Defense Security Cooperation Agency; see Sharon Weinberger, "Pentagon Agency Emphasizing Humanitarian Work," *Defense Daily*, April 26, 2005, 2.

17. ICRC, "Report on the Use of Armed Protection for Humanitarian Assistance," December 1, 1995, www.icrc.org/web/eng/siteeng0.nsf/html/57JNEG (accessed September 22, 2005).

18. Oxfam, "Iraq: Humanitarian-Military Relations," Briefing Paper 41 (Oxford: Oxfam, 2003), www.oxfam.org.uk/what_we_do/issues/conflict_disasters/downloads/bp41_iraq.pdf (accessed June 6, 2005).

19. Antonio Donini and others, *Mapping the Security Environment: Understanding the Perceptions of Local Communities, Peace Support Operations, and Assistance Agencies* (Medford, Mass.: Feinstein International Famine Center, June 2005), 55.

20. Colin L. Powell, "Remarks to the National Foreign Policy Conference for Leaders of Non-governmental Organizations" (U.S. Department of State, Washington, D.C., October 26, 2001).

21. David Rieff, "Kosovo: The End of an Era?" in *In the Shadow of "Just Wars": Violence, Politics, and Humanitarian Action,* ed. Fabrice Weissman (Ithaca, N.Y.: Cornell University Press, 2004), 287.

22. Ken Roth, "War in Iraq: Not a Humanitarian Intervention," in *Human Rights Watch World Report 2004: Human Rights and Armed Conflict* (New York: Human Rights Watch, 2004), 14.

23. David P. Forsythe, *The Humanitarians: The International Committee of the Red Cross* (Cambridge: Cambridge University Press, 2005), 99.

24. For tensions resulting from this tendency in MSF and Amnesty International, see Anne Vallaeys, *Médecins Sans Frontières: La Biographie* (Paris: Fayort, 2004); and Stephen Hopgood, *Keepers of the Flame: Amnesty International and the Politics of Authority* (Ithaca, N.Y.: Cornell University Press, 2005).

25. See Doug Brooks, "Messiahs or Mercenaries? The Future of International Private Military Services," *International Peacekeeping* 7, no. 4 (2000): 129–44; Christopher Spearin, "Private Security Companies and Humanitarians: A Corporate Solution to Securing Humanitarian Spaces?" *International Peacekeeping* 8, no. 1 (2001): 20–43; and Tony Vaux and others, *Humanitarian Action and Private Security Companies: Opening the Debate* (London: International Alert, 2002). For a more general approach to PMCs, see P. W. Singer, *Corporate Warriors: The Rise of the Privatized Military Industry* (Ithaca, N.Y.: Cornell University Press, 2003).

26. Kofi Annan, *Thirty-fifth Annual Ditchley Foundation Lecture,* SG/SM/6613, June 26, 1998, www0.un.org/News/Press/docs/1998/19980626.sgsm6613.html (accessed June 9, 2005). Also see Kofi Annan, "Transcript of Press Conference by Secretary-General Kofi Annan at United Nations Headquarters on 12 June 1997," United Nations press release SG/SM/6255. For more on the politics of this decision, see Deborah D. Avant, *The Market for Force: The Consequences of Privatizing Security* (Cambridge: Cambridge University Press, 2005), 193–97.

27. Michael Bryans, Bruce D. Jones, and Janice Gross Stein, "'Mean Times': Humanitarian Action in Complex Political Emergencies—Stark Choices, Cruel Dilemmas," *Coming to Terms* 1, no. 3 (1999).

28. P. W. Singer, *Corporate Warriors: The Rise of the Privatized Military Industry* (Ithaca, N.Y.: Cornell University Press, 2003), 82.

29. Mark Duffield, *Global Governance and the New Wars: The Merging of Development and Security* (London: Zed, 2001); Alex de Waal, *Famine Crimes: Politics and the Disaster Relief Industry in Africa* (Oxford: James Currey, 1997); and Michael Maren, *The Road to Hell: The Ravaging Effects of Foreign Aid and International Charity* (New York: Free Press, 1997).

30. Enrique Ballestros, *Report on the Question of the Use of Mercenaries as a Means of Violating Human Rights and Impeding the Exercise of the Rights of People to Self-Determination* (report to Commission on Human Rights, Geneva, January 13, 1999).

31. Stewart Payne, "Teenagers Used for Sex in Bosnia," *Telegraph*, April 25, 2002, www.telegraph.co.uk/news/main.jhtml?xml=/news/2002/04/25/wbos25.xml (accessed June 6, 2005).

32. ICRC, "The ICRC to Expand Contracts with Private Military and Security Companies," August 4, 2004, www.icrc.org/Web/Eng/siteeng0.nsf/iwpList500/21414DE8FCAF2645C1256EE50038A631 (accessed September 22, 2005).

33. Joanna Macrae, "Defining the Boundaries: International Security and Humanitarian Engagement in the Post–Cold War World," in *The Humanitarian Decade: Challenges for Humanitarian Assistance in the Last Decade*, ed. OCHA (New York: OCHA, 2004) vol. 2, 116.

34. Rony Brauman and Pierre Salignon, "Iraq: In Search of a 'Humanitarian Crisis,'" in *In the Shadow of "Just Wars": Violence, Politics, and Humanitarian Action*, ed. Fabrice Weissman (Ithaca, N.Y.: Cornell University Press, 2004), 271.

35. Ian Smillie and Larry Minear, *The Charity of Nations: Humanitarian Action in a Calculating World* (West Bloomfield, Conn.: Kumarian, 2004), 18.

36. Carlotta Gall and Amy Waldman, "Under Siege in Afghanistan, Aid Groups Say Their Effort Is Being Criticized Unfairly," *New York Times*, December 19, 2004.

37. *Human Rights Questions: Human Rights Situations and Reports of Special Rapporteurs and Representatives, Situation of Human Rights in Afghanistan*, UN document A/56/409/Add.1, November 5, 2001.

38. Agence France Presse, "World Food Programme Steps Up Supplies to Afghan Refugees," June 28, 2001, www.unhcr.ch/cgi-bin/texis/vtx/home/+WwwBmueb2YdwwwwhwwwwwwwhFqnN0bItFqnDni5AFqnN0bIcFq0EhtrwDo5BwDaGnh1tnn5a41Dna+XXWDzmxwwwwwww1FqmRbZ/opendoc.htm (accessed January 12, 2004).

39. UNHCR, "Afghanistan," *UNHCR Mid-Year Progress Report 2001* 143 (September 1, 2001), www.un.org.pk/unhcr/mid-year-rep-2001-afg.pdf (accessed January 11, 2004).

40. UNDP, *Human Development Report 2001: Making New Technologies Work for Human Development* (New York: Oxford University Press, 2001). The human poverty index, which ranks for ninety developing countries, places Afghanistan as eighty-ninth and Niger ninetieth.

41. The description of Afghanistan draws on Thomas G. Weiss, *Military-Civilian Interactions: Humanitarian Crises and the Responsibility to Protect*, 2nd ed. (Lanham, Md.: Rowman & Littlefield, 2005), 156–69.

42. Human Rights Watch, "Backgrounder: No Safe Refuge: The Impact of the September 11 Attacks on Refugees, Asylum Seekers, and Migrants in the Afghanistan Region and World Wide," October 18, 2001, www.hrw.org/backgrounder/refugees/afghan-bck1017.htm (accessed June 6, 2005).

43. For details, see Antonio Donini, "Principles, Politics, and Pragmatism in the International Response to the Afghan Crisis," in *Nation-Building Unraveled? Aid, Peace, and Justice in Afghanistan*, ed. Antonio Donini, Norah Niland, and Karin Wermester (West Bloomfield, Conn.: Kumarian, 2004), 117–42.

44. See Carlotta Gall, "More G.I.'s to Go to Insecure Afghan Areas to Permit Aid Work," *New York Times*, December 22, 2003; and Ann-Marie Michel, "Afghanistan: Aid Work under Fire," Radio Netherlands, September 10, 2004, www2.rnw.nl/rnw/en/currentaffairs/region/centralasia/afg040910.html (accessed June 6, 2005).

45. UNHCR, *Afghanistan Appeal 2003*, www.unhcr.ch/cgi-bin/texis/vtx/home/opendoc.pdf?tbl=SUBSITES&id=3e3e4aec1 (accessed June 9, 2005).

46. Rajan Menon, "Afghanistan's Minor Miracle," *Los Angeles Times*, December 14, 2004, www.globalpolicy.org/security/issues/afghan/2004/1214miracle.htm (accessed June 6, 2005).

47. The description of Iraq draws on Weiss, *Military-Civilian Interactions*, 169–81.

48. Kenneth Roth, "The Fight against Terrorism: The Bush Administration's Dangerous Neglect of Human Rights," in *Wars on Terrorism and Iraq: Human Rights, Unilateralism, and U.S. Foreign Policy*, ed. Thomas G. Weiss, Margaret E. Crahan, and John Goering (London: Routledge, 2004), 125.

49. United Nations, *Humanitarian Appeal for Iraq, Revised Inter-agency Appeal 1 April–31 December 2003*, 39.

50. David Cortright and George A. Lopez, *The Sanctions Decade: Assessing UN Strategies in the 1990s* (Boulder, Colo.: Rienner, 2000), 46.

51. Amnesty International, "Iraq: Looting, Lawlessness and Humanitarian Consequences," http://web.amnesty.org/library/index/engmde140852003 (accessed June 9, 2005).

52. OCHA, Integrated Regional Information Network, "Chronology of Key Humanitarian Developments in Iraq in 2003," January 6, 2004.

53. Kenneth Katzman, *Iraq: U.S. Regime Change Efforts and Post-Saddam Governance* (Washington, D.C.: Congressional Research Service, updated November 18, 2003), 30.

54. IRIN, "Iraq: Humanitarian Chronology 2004," January 5, 2005, http://electroniciraq.net/news/1768.shtml (accessed June 6, 2005).

55. Center for Global Development, *On the Brink: Weak States and US National Security* (Washington, D.C.: Commission on Weak States and US National Security, 2004), www.cgdev.org/doc/books/weakstates/Full_Report.pdf (accessed September 22, 2005). For more information, see State Failure Task Force, www.cidcm.umd.edu/inscr/stfail.

56. *National Security Strategy of the United States of America*, www.whitehouse.gov/nsc/nss.html (accessed June 6, 2005).

57. Michael Ignatieff, "Intervention and State Failure," *Dissent* (Winter 2002): 115.

58. Michael Ignatieff, *Empire Lite: Nation Building in Bosnia, Kosovo, and Afghanistan* (Toronto: Penguin, 2003), 17–19.

59. Rieff, "Kosovo: End of an Era?" 296.

60. David Rieff, *A Bed for the Night: Humanitarianism in Crisis* (New York: Simon & Schuster, 2002), 26.

61. G. John Ikenberry, "Illusions of Empire: Defining the New American Order," *Foreign Affairs* 83, no. 2 (2004): 154.

62. Arthur Schlesinger, Jr., "American Empire? Not So Fast," *World Policy Journal* 22, no. 1 (2005): 45.

63. Max P. Glaser, "Humanitarian Engagement with Non-state Armed Actors," *The Parameters of Negotiated Access*, HPN Network Paper 51 (London, 2005), 7.

64. International Institute for Strategic Studies, *Strategic Survey 2003/4: An Evaluation and Forecast of World Affairs* (Oxford: Oxford University Press, 2004), 6.

65. Excerpt from April 5, 2004, interview with Omar Bakri Muhammed, head of Al Muhajiroun, conducted by Paulo Maoura and published in the April 18 issue of *Público*.

66. Jessica Stern, "Al Qaeda: The Protean Enemy," *Foreign Affairs* 82, no. 4 (2003): 27–40; and Hammes, *Sling and the Stone*, 152.

67. For an inventory of groups resisting the U.S. occupation and carrying out violence, see Samir Haddad and Mazin Ghazi, *Al Zawra* (Baghdad), September 19, 2004, www.globalpolicy.org/security/issues/iraq/resist/2004/0919overview.htm (accessed June 9, 2005).

68. Paula Walsh, "Afghanistan—Drugs, Warlords, and Regionalism," in *Organized Crime as an Obstacle to Successful Peacebuilding: Lessons Learned from the Balkans, Afghanistan, and West Africa—7th International Berlin Workshop*, ed. Alexander Austin, Tobias von Gienanth, and Wibke Hansen (Berlin: Zentrum Für Internationale Friedenseinsätze, 2003), 102.

69. Moncia Serrano, "The Political Economy of Terrorism," in *Terrorism and the UN: Before and after September 11*, ed. Jane Boulden and Thomas G. Weiss (Bloomington: Indiana University Press, 2004), 198–218, especially 203.

70. Douglas Farah, *Blood from Stones: the Secret Financial Network of Terror* (New York: Broadway Books, 2004).

71. For exhaustive details, see Paul A. Volcker, Richard J. Goldstone, and Mark Pieth, *The Management of the Oil-for-Food Programme*, vol. 4, September 7, 2005, www.iic-offp.org/documents/Sept05/Mgmt_V4.pdf (accessed September 27, 2005).

72. Ariana Enjung Cha, "$1.9 Billion of Iraq's Money Goes to U.S. Contractors," *Washington Post*, August 4, 2004.

73. "Doing Business in Dangerous Places," *Economist*, August 12, 2004.

74. "Halliburton Questioned on $1.8 Billion in Iraq Work," *Wall Street Journal*, August 11, 2004.

75. Deborah Avant, "The Privatization of Security and Change in the Control of Force," *International Studies Perspectives* 5 (2004): 153.

76. For a full list of private companies contracted to work in Iraq, see www.topsy.org/contractors.html (accessed June 6, 2005).

77. Avant, *The Market for Force*, 171–72, 227; Abdel-Fatau Musah, "A Country under Siege: State Decay and Corporate Military Intervention in Sierra Leone," in *Mercenaries: An African Security Dilemma*, ed. Abdel-Fatau Musah and J. 'Kayode Fayemi (London: Pluto Press, 2000), 98–99; and Alex Vines, "Mercenaries, Human Rights, and Legality," in *Mercenaries: An African Security Dilemma*, ed. Abdel-Fatau Musah and J. 'Kayode Fayemi (London: Pluto Press, 2000), 179–80.

78. David Isenberg, *A Fistful of Contractors: The Case for a Pragmatic Assessment of Private Military Companies in Iraq* (Washington, D.C.: British American Security Information Council, September 2004), 7. This study provides a detailed list of PMCs throughout the Iraq theater. Also see press release from representative Ike Skelton, "DOD Responds to Skelton Inquiry on Contractors in Iraq," May 4, 2004. www.house.gov/skelton/pr040504a.htm (accessed June 6, 2005).

79. United State Government Accountability Office, *Rebuilding Iraq: Actions Needed to Improve Private Security Providers*, GAO-05-737 (Washington, D.C.: 2005), 8.

80. Quote from interview taken from Abdul Baseer Saeed, "Minister Scorns NGOs' Work" (Institute for War and Peace Reporting, London, November 11, 2004), www.globalpolicy.org/ngos/state/2004/1111scorn.htm (accessed June 6, 2005).

81. Ian Smillie and Larry Minear, *The Charity of Nations: Humanitarian Action in a Calculating World* (Bloomfield, Conn.: Kumarian, 2004), 8.

82. Development Initiatives, *Global Humanitarian Assistance 2003* (Nottingham, Eng.: Russell Press, 2003), 7.

83. Development Initiatives, *Global Humanitarian Assistance 2003*, 8.

84. An earlier version of this figure notes the sprawling mess of the international humanitarian system, but this model goes further to include the greater role of private contractors. See Thomas G. Weiss and Cindy Collins, *Humanitarian Challenges and Intervention*, 2nd ed. (Boulder, Colo.: Westview, 2000), 49.

85. Mark Duffield, "The Political Economy of Internal War: Asset Transfer, Complex Emergencies, and International Aid," in *War and Hunger: Rethinking International Responses to Complex Emergencies*, ed. Joanna Macrae and Anthony Zwi (London: Zed Books, 1994), 59. In terms of UNHCR, see Evaluation and Policy Analysis Unit of United Nations High Commissioner for Refugees, *The State of UNHCR's Organization Culture* (Geneva: EPAU/UNHCR, 2005), 103, www.unhcr.ch/cgi-bin/texis/vtx/research/opendoc.pdf?tbl=RESEARCH&id=428db1d62 (accessed September 22, 2005).

86. For a discussion of the phenomena, see Thomas G. Weiss, ed., *Beyond UN Subcontracting: Task-Sharing with Regional Security Arrangements and Service-Providing NGOs* (London: Macmillan, 1998).

87. Andrew Natsios address to InterAction, "NGOs Must Show Results; Promote Ties to U.S. or 'We Will Find New Partners,'" June 9, 2003, www.interaction.org/library/detail.php?id=1762 (accessed June 6, 2005).

88. Rony Brauman and Pierre Salignon, "Iraq: In Search of a 'Humanitarian Crisis,'" in *In the Shadow of "Just Wars": Violence, Politics, and Humanitarian Action*, ed. Fabrice Weissman (Ithaca, N.Y.: Cornell University Press, 2004), 271; and Maria Lange and Mick Quinn, *Conflict, Humanitarian Assistance, and Peacebuilding: Meeting the Challenges* (London: International Alert, 2003), 15.

89. Hugo Slim, *With or Against? Humanitarian Agencies and Coalition Counterinsurgency* (Geneva: Centre for Humanitarian Dialogue, 2004), 3.

90. BBC, "Labour Minister Says 1,058 Fijians Working in Iraq, Kuwait," April 19, 2005, Fiji government website, Suva.

91. Caroline Holmqvist, *Private Security Companies: The Case for Regulation*, SIPRI Policy Paper 9 (Solna, Swed.: Stockholm International Peace Research Institute, 2005), 58.

92. Holsti, *Taming the Sovereigns.*

93. For casualty counts in Afghanistan and Iraq, see www.unknownnews.net/casualties.html (accessed June 8, 2005).

94. Iraq Body Count, *A Dossier of Civilian Casualties in Iraq, 2003–2005* (July 2005), 4, 12, and 16.

95. Les Roberts and others, "Mortality before and after the 2003 Invasion of Iraq: Cluster Sample Survey," *Lancet* 364, no. 9448 (November 20, 2004): 1857.

96. For a full listing and chronology of U.S. and coalition-forces casualties in Afghanistan and Iraq, see http://icasualties.org/oif/default.aspx (accessed November 20, 2005).

97. Cate Buchanan and Robert Muggah, *No Relief: Surveying the Effects of Gun Violence on Humanitarian and Development Personnel* (Geneva: Centre for Humanitarian Dialogue, 2005), 7, 9.

98. Gall and Waldman, "Under Siege in Afghanistan."

99. Cited in John S. Burnett, "In the Line of Fire," *New York Times*, August 4, 2004.

100. "More Dangerous to Work Than Ever," *Economist*, November 20, 2004, 49.

101. The Committee to Protect Journalists has been tracking data since 1992. See "Journalists Killed in the Line of Duty during the Last Ten Years," www.cpj.org/killed/Ten_Year_Killed/Intro.html (accessed June 6, 2005).

102. Dexter Filkins, "Get Me Rewrite. Now Bullets Are Flying," *New York Times*, October 10, 2004.

103. *Strengthening and Unified Security Management System for the United Nations*, UN document A/59/365, September 17, 2004, 11.

104. Buchanan and Muggah, *No Relief*, 28–29.

105. Antonio Donini and others, *Mapping the Security Environment: Understanding the Perceptions of Local Communities, Peace Support Operations, and Assistance Agencies* (Medford, Mass.: Feinstein International Famine Center, 2005), 60.

106. Gil Loescher, "An Idea Lost in the Ruble," *New York Times*, August 20, 2004.

107. Independent International Commission on Kosovo, *The Kosovo Report: Conflict, International Response, Lessons Learned* (Oxford: Oxford University Press, 2000), 90, 305, 308.

108. Barbara Borst, "UN Security Council Urges Progress in Cease-Fire Talks on Western Sudan," Associated Press, April 2, 2004.

109. UN OCHA, "Sudan: US Congress Unanimously Defines Darfur Violence as 'Genocide,'" July 23, 2004, www.globalsecurity.org/military/library/news/2004/07/mil-040723-irin03.htm (accessed June 6, 2005).

110. Ewen MacAskill, "African Union Undertakes to Protect Darfur Refugees: Sudanese Government Says That Intervention Goes beyond Body's Remit," *Guardian* (London), July 9, 2004.

111. Scott Straus, "Darfur and the Genocide Debate," *Foreign Affairs* 84, no. 1 (2005): 124, 132.

112. Donini and others, *Mapping the Security Environment*, 19, 55.

113. On January 19, 2004, Major General Antonio M. Taguba was appointed to investigate the conduct of the Eight Hundredth MP Brigade since November 2003. His findings were issued on May 5, 2004, "U.S. Army Report on Abuse of Iraqi Prisoners," www.globalsecurity.org/intell/library/reports/2004/800-mp-bde.htm (accessed June 6, 2005).

114. The memo from Alberto R. Gonzales on the application of the Geneva Convention on Prisoners of War, dated January 25, 2002, states that "the war against terrorism is a new kind of war" and that "this new paradigm renders obsolete Geneva's strict limitation on questioning of enemy prisoners and renders quaint some of its provisions requiring that captured enemy be afforded such things as commissary privileges, scrip (i.e., advances of monthly pay), athletic uniforms and scientific instruments." The memo, moreover, typifies the prerogatives of powerful states to craft loopholes rather than acknowledge a departure from international norms: "By concluding that [the convention] does not apply to Al Qaeda and Taliban, we avoid foreclosing options for the future, particularly against nonstate actors." See http://msnbc.msn.com/id/4999148/site/newsweek/ (accessed June 6, 2005).

115. Numerous media reports of torture have surfaced, but especially shocking has been the discovery that medical personnel at the Guantanamo Bay detention facility participated in interrogations, a violation of the principle of "clinical confidentiality" under international humanitarian law. M. Gregg Bloche and Johnathan H. Marks, "Doctors and Interrogators at Guantanamo Bay," *New England Journal of Medicine* 335, no. 1 (July 7, 2005): 6–8.

116. See Pew Research Center for the People and the Press, Global Attitudes Project. The first survey asked thirty-eight thousand people in forty-four countries about their changing opinions of the United States from 2000 to 2002. "What the World Thinks in 2002: How Global Publics View: Their Lives, Their Countries, The World, America," released December 4, 2002, http://people-press.org/reports/display.php3?ReportID=165 (accessed June 6, 2005). Two other follow-up studies reach similar conclusions: "America's Image Further Erodes, Europeans Want Weaker Ties—but Post-war Iraq Will Be Better Off, Most Say," released March 18, 2003, http://people-press.org/reports/display.php3?ReportID=175 (accessed June 6, 2005). "Views of a Changing World 2003: War with Iraq Further Divides Global Publics," released June 3, 2003, http://people-press.org/reports/display.php3?ReportID=185 (accessed June 6, 2005).

117. See issue dated May 9, 2005. Although report was retracted in the May 16 issue, major riots nevertheless erupted in Afghanistan and Pakistan.

118. Gall and Waldman, "Under Siege in Afghanistan."

119. Arthur C. Helton, "Rescuing the Refugees," *Foreign Affairs* 81, no. 2 (2002): 72. Also see his *The Price of Indifference: Refugees and Humanitarian Action in the New Century* (Oxford: Oxford University Press, 2002).

120. Jean-Hervé Bradhol, introduction to *In the Shadow of "Just Wars": Violence, Politics, and Humanitarian Action*, ed. Fabrice Weissman (Ithaca, N.Y.: Cornell University Press, 2004), 12.

121. Quoted by Larry Minear and Ian Smillie, *The Quality of Money: Donor Behaviour in Humanitarian Financing* (Somerville, Mass.: Humanitarianism and War Project, 2003), 5. See also Joanna Macrae et al., *Uneven Power: The Changing Role of Official Donors in Humanitarian Action*, HPG Report 12 (London: Overseas Development Institute, 2002).

122. United State Government Accountability Office, *Rebuilding Iraq*, 4–5, but see 30–34, esp. table on 33.

123. Hugo Slim, *A Call to Alms: Humanitarian Action and the Art of War* (Geneva: Centre for Humanitarian Dialogue, 2004), 4.

124. Slim, *Call to Alms*, 2.

CHAPTER 7

1. Antonio Donini and others, *Mapping the Security Environment: Understanding the Perceptions of Local Communities, Peace Support Operations, and Assistance Agencies* (Medford, Mass.: Feinstein International Famine Center, 2005), 53.

2. We have strung together the titles from William Shawcross, *Deliver Us from Evil: Peacekeepers, Warlords, and a World of Endless Conflict* (New York: Simon & Schuster, 2000); David Kennedy, *The Dark Sides of Virtue: Reassessing International*

Humanitarianism (Princeton, N.J.: Princeton University Press, 2004); Fiona Terry, *Condemned to Repeat? The Paradox of Humanitarian Action* (Ithaca, N.Y.: Cornell University Press, 2002); Alex de Waal, *Famine Crimes: Politics and the Disaster Relief Industry in Africa* (Oxford: James Currey, 1997); Michael Barnett, *Eyewitness to a Genocide: The United Nations and Rwanda* (Ithaca, N.Y.: Cornell University Press, 2002); David Rieff, *A Bed for the Night: Humanitarianism in Crisis* (New York: Simon & Schuster, 2002); Arthur C. Helton, *The Price of Indifference: Refugees in Humanitarian Action in the New Century* (Oxford: Oxford University Press, 2002); and Michael Maren, *The Road to Hell: The Ravaging Effects of Foreign Aid and International Charity* (New York: Free Press, 1997).

3. Greenberg Research, *The People on War Report* (Geneva: ICRC, 1999), xvi.

4. Greenberg Research, *People on War Report*, 57, 77.

5. Michael Barnett and Martha Finnemore, *Rules for the World: International Organizations in Global Politics* (Ithaca, N.Y.: Cornell University Press, 2004), 41–44.

6. See OCHA, "Humanitarian Issues," http://ochaonline.un.org/webpage .asp?Nav=_humanissues_en&Site=_humanissues (accessed June 7, 2005).

7. Gil Loescher, *The UNHCR and World Politics: A Perilous Path* (Oxford: Oxford University Press, 2001).

8. ICRC, "Initial Conclusion of the ICRC Avenir Report," press release, www.icrc.org/Web/Eng/siteeng0.nsf/htmlall/57JNW5 (accessed June 6, 2005).

9. David P. Forsythe, *The Humanitarians: The International Committee of the Red Cross* (Cambridge: Cambridge University Press, 2005), 310. For a more elaborate treatment, see chapter 6, "ICRC Structure and Management: Personnel, Policy Making, Resources," 201–41. See also Forsythe, "1949 and 1999: Making the Geneva Conventions Relevant after the Cold War," *International Review of the Red Cross*, no. 834 (1999): 265–76.

10. David D. Tansley, *Final Report: Agenda for Red Cross* (Geneva: Henri Dunant Institute, 1975).

11. See www.sphereproject.org/index.htm (accessed June 6, 2005).

12. For a description and discussion, see Lola Gostelow, "The Sphere Project: The Implications of Making Humanitarian Principles and Codes Work," *Disasters* 23, no. 4 (1999): 316–25.

13. See www.alnap.org (accessed June 6, 2005).

14. See Joint Evaluation of Emergency Assistance to Rwanda, *The International Response to Conflict and Genocide: Lessons from Rwanda*, 5 vols. (Copenhagen: Strandberg Grafisk, Odense, 1996).

15. John Borton and John Eriksson, *Lessons from Rwanda—Lessons for Today* (Copenhagen: Ministry of Foreign Affairs, 2004).

16. Forsythe, *Humanitarians*, 313.

17. Barb Wigley, *The State of UNHCR's Organization Culture*, UNHCR document EPAU/2005/08, May 2005.

18. Vanessa Mattar and Paul White, *Consistent and Predictable Responses to IDPs: A Review of UNHCR's Decision-Making Processes*, UNHCR document EPAU/2005/2, March 2005, 3.

19. Michael Barnett, "What Is the Future of Humanitarianism?" *Global Governance* 9, no. 3 (2003): 410.

20. David Rieff, "Tsunamis, Accountability, and the Humanitarian Circus," *HPN Humanitarian Exchange*, no. 29 (2005): 49–50.

21. For a study of change in military doctrine that finds greater explanatory power in international rather than organizational factors, see Barry Posen, *The Sources of Military Doctrine: France, Germany, and Britain between the World Wars* (Ithaca, N.Y.: Cornell University Press, 1984). However, other scholars emphasize the culture and dynamics within organizations. See also, Theo Farrell, "Culture and Military Power," *Review of International Studies* 24, no. 3 (1998): 407–16; Elizabeth Kier, *Imagining War: French and British Doctrine between the Wars* (Princeton, N.J.: Princeton University Press, 1997); and Peter Katzenstein, *The Culture of National Security: Norms and Identity in World Politics* (New York: Columbia University Press, 1996).

22. Walter Bagehot, "The Changes of Ministry," *The English Constitution* (1867), 6, www.bibliomania.com/2/1/328/2415/frameset.html (accessed June 6, 2005).

23. IFRC, *World Disasters Report 2003: Focus on Ethics in War* (West Bloomfield, Conn.: Kumarian, 2003), 36.

24. Kennedy, *Dark Sides of Virtue*, xxiii–xxiv.

25. Max P. Glaser, *Humanitarian Engagement with Non-state Armed Actors: The Parameters of Negotiated Access*, HPN Network Paper 51 (London, 2005), 2.

26. Ian Smillie and Larry Minear, *The Charity of Nations: Humanitarian Action in a Calculating World* (West Bloomfield, Conn.: Kumarian, 2004), 224.

27. This list is consolidated from our research conducted for the Stanley Foundation's UN on the Ground Project, held over the course of 2001 to 2003 and published in 2003 in a monograph with the same title. The discussion also draws on Koenraad van Brabant, "Organisational and Institutional Learning in the Humanitarian Sector," in *The Charitable Impulse: NGOs and Development in East and North-East Africa*, ed. Ondine Barrow and Michael Jennings (West Bloomfield, Conn.: Kumarian, 2001), 183–99.

28. David Rieff, *At the Point of a Gun: Democratic Dreams and Armed Intervention* (New York: Simon & Schuster, 2005), 7–9, 254.

29. Wigley, *State of UNHCR's Organization Culture*, 79.

30. Wigley, *State of UNHCR's Organization Culture*, 5.

31. Van Brabant, "Organisational and Institutional Learning," 193.

32. Published by Oxford University Press in 1993, 1995, 1997, and 2000.

33. De Waal, *Famine Crimes*, vi.

34. For example, see the 2,200 entries essentially in English from the 1990s in the keyworded bibliography in Thomas G. Weiss and Don Hubert, *The Responsibility to Protect: Research, Bibliography, and Background* (Ottawa: International Development Research Centre, 2001), supplementary volume of the International Commission on Intervention and State Sovereignty, also at www.iciss-ciise.gc.ca (accessed June 9, 2005). Three subsequent updates have increased the total to 2,850 through December 2004.

35. See Marc Lindenberg and Coralie Bryant, *Going Global: Transforming Relief and Devleopment NGOs* (West Bloomfield, Conn.: Kumarian, 2001), especially 65–99.

36. Larry Minear, *The Humanitarian Enterprise: Dilemmas and Discoveries* (West Bloomfield, Conn.: Kumarian, 2002), 7.

37. Randolph Kent, *Humanitarian Futures: Practical Policy Perspectives*, HPG Network Paper 46 (2004), 9.

38. Minear, *Humanitarian Enterprise*, 174.

39. Mikael Barfod, "Humanitarian Aid and Conditionality: ECHO's Experience and Prospects under the Common Foreign and Security Policy," in *Terms of*

Engagement: Conditions and Conditionality in Humanitarian Action, HPG Report 6, ed. Nicholas Leader and Joanna Macrae (London: Overseas Development Institute, 2000), 37–43.

40. IFRC, *World Disasters Report 2003*, 135.

41. Intelligence (timely information and critical policy analysis) to inform humanitarian agencies' decision making has been identified as a critical need by many practitioners. See Stanley Foundation, *UN on the Ground* (Muscatine, Iowa: Stanley Foundation, 2003); and Thomas G. Weiss and Peter J. Hoffman, "Making Humanitarianism Work," in *Making States Work: State Failure and the Crisis of Governance*, ed. Simon Chesterman, Michael Ignatieff, and Ramesh Thakur (Tokyo: UN University Press, 2005), 296–317.

42. Glaser, *Humanitarian Engagement*, 16.

43. Centre for Humanitarian Dialogue, *Humanitarian Engagement with Armed Groups: The Central Asian Islamic Opposition Movements* (Geneva: Centre for Humanitarian Dialogue, 2003), 3, 43.

44. See Smillie and Minear, *Charity of Nations*, 8; and Stockholm International Peace Research Institute, "Recent Trends in Military Expenditure," www.sipri.org/contents/milap/milex/mex_trends.html (accessed June 8, 2005).

45. The Fund for Peace and the Carnegie Endowment for International Peace, "The Failed States Index," *Foreign Policy* (July–August 2005): 58.

46. This argument was originally made in Thomas G. Weiss, "Principles, Politics, and Humanitarian Action," *Ethics and International Affairs* 13 (1999): 1–22. Rethinking the enterprise is also a theme in Adrian Wood, Raymond Apthorpe, and John Borton, eds., *Evaluating International Humanitarian Action: Reflections from Practitioners* (London: Zed, 2001).

47. Kennedy, *Dark Sides of Virtue*, 309.

48. Larry Minear and Thomas G. Weiss, *Humanitarian Action in Times of War: A Handbook for Practitioners* (Boulder, Colo.: Rienner, 1993).

49. Deborah D. Avant, *The Market for Force: The Consequences of Privatizing Security* (Cambridge: Cambridge University Press, 2005), 264.

50. For a discussion of internal clashes, including among founding and subsequent generations, see Anne Vallaeys, *Médécins Sans Frontières: La Biographie* (Paris: Fayard, 2004), 551–84; and Stephen Hopgood, *Keepers of the Flame: Amnesty International and the Politics of Authority* (Ithaca, N.Y.: Cornell University Press, 2005).

51. James Darcy, "Acts of Faith? Thoughts on the Effectiveness of Humanitarian Action" (discussion paper prepared for the Social Science Research Council, New York City, April 12, 2005), 3.

52. Victor Hugo, *Histoire d'un Crime* (written 1851–1852, published 1877). "On resiste a l'invasion des armees; on ne resiste pas a l'invasion des idees."

53. Myron Wiener, "The Clash of Norms: Dilemmas in Refugee Politics," *Journal of Refugee Studies* 11 (1998): 1–21.

54. 2005 World Summit Outcome, UN document A/60/L.1, September 15, 2005.

Index

Abu Ghraib prison (Iraq), 178
Active Learning Network for
  Accountability and Performance
  in Humanitarian Action
  (ALNAP), 191–92, 216n7
Aegis Defense Systems, 166
Afghanistan, *141*, 147, 153–54, *156*, 178;
  attacks on aid workers, 154; civilian
  vs. military casualties, 171–72; IDPs
  and refugees, 153, 154; NGO
  withdrawals from, 154, 172–73;
  state authority, 140; U.S. invasion
  of, 154, 172; war economy, 164, 167
African Union, 177
Agency Coordinating Body for Afghan
  Relief, 179
Aguayo, Sergio, 68
aid agencies: attacks on personnel, 111,
  154, 156, 172, 173, 175; criticism of,
  2, 107–8, 167; tiers of, 209; trade-
  offs in subcontracting to PMCs,
  152, 153; traditional operating
  principles, 4. *See also*
  humanitarianism; new
  humanitarianisms; *specific* aid
  agencies
aid agencies, learning culture, 190–99;
  analysis efforts, 190–93;
  impediments to, 195–99; military's
  learning culture, comparison to,
  195, 197

aid agencies, strategic review, 199–202;
  position, 201–2, *202;* power,
  200–201
aid economies, 71–72, 105; new
  humanitarianisms responses to,
  107–8
Aideed, Mohammed, 78
aid workers: attacks against, 111, 154,
  156, 172, 173, 175; local recruits,
  174–75
Alexander II (Russian czar), 41
Allawi, Ayad, 165
al Qaeda, 161–63; Afghanistan, 147,
  154; military technology, 176;
  political grievances, 161; sources
  of support, 158, 161–62; terrorist
  attacks, 140, 161
al Tawhid, 163
American Red Cross, 38
Amnesty International, 155
Anabasis (Xenophon), 30
Anderson, Mary, 94, 107, 195
Angola, 106
Annan, Kofi, 109–10, 111, 146, 150, 174,
  212
armed forces. *See* military
Arrault, Henri, 39
Artaxerxes, 30
The Art of War (Sun Tzu), 26
asymmetric warfare, 56, 175–76
Avant, Deborah, 32, 210

About the Authors

Peter J. Hoffman is Senior Mellon Research Fellow in security and humanitarian action, research associate at the Ralph Bunche Institute for International Studies, and adjunct professor of political science at Hunter College. He has written on the dynamics of war and international responses, including contributions to the International Commission on Intervention and State Sovereignty, *The Responsibility to Protect: Research, Bibliography, and Background* (2001), various resources for the Humanitarianism and War Project based at Tufts University and the Stanley Foundation's UN on the Ground Project. He is presently completing a doctoral dissertation at The Graduate Center of The City University of New York on humanitarian agencies' interactions with private military companies.

Thomas G. Weiss is Presidential Professor of political science at The Graduate Center of The City University of New York and director of the Ralph Bunche Institute for International Studies, where he is also co-director of the United Nations Intellectual History Project and editor of *Global Governance* and where he served as research director of the International Commission on Intervention and State Sovereignty. He has written extensively about international organization, peace and security, humanitarian action, and development. His recent authored books include *Ahead of the Curve? UN Ideas and Global Challenges* (2001, named Outstanding Academic Title of 2003 by *Choices*); *The Responsibility to Protect: Research, Bibliography, and Background* (2001); *The United Nations and Changing World Politics* (2004), fourth edition; *Military-Civilian Interactions: Humanitarian Crises and the Responsibility to Protect* (2005), second edition; and *UN Voices: The Struggle for Development and Social Justice* (2005). Two recent edited volumes are *Terrorism and the UN: Before and* *after September 11* (2004) and *Wars on Terrorism and Iraq: Human Rights, Unilateralism, and U.S. Foreign Policy* (2004). He is currently at work authoring *The UN and Global Governance: An Idea and Its Prospects* and *Internal Displacement: Conceptualization and its Consequences,* and editing the *Oxford Handbook on the United Nations.*